Common Wealth

Edward Mitchell
Fred Koetter
Aniket Shahane

Edward Mitchell, Daphne Binder, Jared Abraham, Ian Spencer, editors

Yale University School of Architecture

Common Wealth
Copyright © 2016 Yale School of Architecture, Yale University

ISBN 978-1-945150-23-4

PCN Library of Congress Cataloging in Publication: 2016958178

Published by
Yale School of Architecture
180 York Street
New Haven, Connecticut 06520

Distributed by Actar D
355 Lexington Avenue
New York, NY
www.actar-d.com

It is available as a print on demand book:
www.architecture.yale.edu

This book is part of the Studio Book Series published through the
Dean's office.

Dean
Deborah Berke

Director of Publications
Nina Rappaport

Editors
Edward Mitchell, Daphne Binder, Jared Abraham, Ian Spencer

Copy Editor
Ann Holcomb

Series design
mgmt.design, Brooklyn, New York

Cover photograph by Daphne Binder

Contents

Acknowledgements

We owe our gratitude to the talented group of students who worked on these studies over a three-year period, patiently entertaining our intuitive, discursive approach to education and the debates we consider critical in formulating a future for our practice and our cities. All of the students in the Post-Professional Design Studios at Yale held between 2012–2014 made important contributions in shared research and design speculation. Our thanks then first and foremost go out to the following students: Jared Abraham, Charlotte Algie, Daphne Binder, Eunil Cho, Karolina Czeczek, Raphael de la Fontaine, John Farrace, Julia Futo, Swarnhab Ghosh, Yoojin Han, Alisa Hintz, Elvira Hoxha, Shuangjing Hu, Stephanie Jazmines, Roberto Jenkins, Karl Karam, Amir Karimpour, Apoorva Khanolkar, Hochung Kim, Jason Kurzweil, Read Langworthy, Stephanie Lee, Jingwen Li, Mengran Li, Kate Lisi, Jizhou Liu, Laurence Lumley, Daniel Luster, Mansi Maheshwari, Adil Mansure, Michael McGrattan, Peter McInish, Eleanor Measham, Olen Milholland, Abdulgader Naseer, Miron Nawratil, James Petty, Alicia Pozniak, Katarzyna Pozniak, Matthew Rauch, Craig Rosman, Grant Scott, Sofia Singler, Isaac Southard, Ian Spencer, Mengshi Sun, Jie Tian, Jay Tsai, Adam Wagoner, Kin Tak Yu, Mengyao Yu, and Boyuan Zhang. Without their individual talent, energy, and enthusiasm we would never have seen this book project to completion.

We would also like to thank John Jacobson who helped organize studio travel. Richard DeFlumeri, Jean Sielaff, and Robie-Lyn Harnois were critical in hosting our jurors in New Haven and fielding our frequent requests for assistance.

There are many organizations and individuals who made significant contributions to the project. We would like to thank Kishore Varanasi of CBT, who provided background material on the Fort Point and Central Square sites, organized site visits, and made a valiant attempt to have the work shown in Central Square; Michael McKinnell, who generously shared his time and his preliminary drawings for the competition and development of Boston City Hall; and Alex Twining, who gave us an intimate perspective on the role of the developer in constructing the future of Boston. Several individuals helped with the field trips to areas and institutions affiliated with these studies. Lorna Congdon, senior curator of Library and Archives, Historic New England, arranged for us to view the original Kallman McKinnell drawings. And a very special thanks goes to the inimitable Patrick Hickox, who gave fabulous tours of Boston, Newport, and Cambridge and inspired us with his great enthusiasm for Boston.

Other individuals who lent support include Tim Love of Utile and Associate Professor of Architecture at Northeastern, who attended many of the reviews and introduced us to several town officials in the region; Ila Berman, Anya Bokov, Mark De Shong, Eva Franch I Gilabert, Doug Gauthier, Kevin Grey, Brian Healy, Mariana Ibañez, Lydia Kalipoliti, Keith Krumweide, Michael Kubo, Alfie Koetter, Michael Kubo, John McMorrough, Gregg Pasquarelli, Alan Plattus, Kim

Poliquin, Amanda Reeser-Lawrence, Elihu Rubin, Sarah Whiting, Dongwoo Yim, and Chris Yost—valuable jurors for these studios that helped direct us to future considerations and research. Nina Rappaport gets special thanks for her enthusiasm and support for seeing the book through to publication.

None of this, though, would be possible without the support of Dean Robert A.M. Stern, who saw the pedagogic value to our Post-Professional students, supported the publication of our books, and attended all of our reviews. Under his leadership our program has made huge advances, and his dedication to scholarship and the historic architecture of New England is infectious. And, finally, we would like to thank Koetter Kim Architects. Suzie Kim generously hosted our studio at her home, shared her talents and insights on several juries, and, most importantly, mentored our students and drove them to strive to be at their very best during their time at Yale. And we give our final thanks once again to Fred Koetter, who retired after five decades of teaching, and who inspired us with his leadership, provided a blueprint for thinking about the city, and entertained us with his dry humor and depth of knowledge. Fred has been a dedicated member of the Yale faculty, and gave his time because of his great dedication to the students and to architectural education. Though he is no longer a regular contributor to the Studio, his legacy, made up in equal parts by his humanity and enormous intelligence, will continue to inspire all of us.

ABOVE *Boston Common*, Christian Remick, 1768.

ABOVE Student final reviews, December 2013.

Common Wealth

A Prospective View

Edward Mitchell

It is not down in any map; true places never are.
There are times when even the most potent governor must wink at
transgression, in order to preserve the laws inviolate for the future.

Herman Melville

Common Wealth is in some respects a sequel to the Post-Professional Studio's previous study, *A Train of Cities*, which documented three years of student work along the South Coast of Massachusetts. In that earlier studio we explored the possible effects of reopening older train lines emanating from Boston into the outlying suburbs, agricultural areas, and historic maritime centers of the state. Those studies explored the idea of a larger urban network and the potential to develop these communities as vibrant independent centers which, though invigorated by the power and wealth of Boston—the Hub City—might achieve new identities and economies that capitalize on the economic engine of Boston proper.

Following the 2008 financial crisis, a mild pall fell over the architectural community. The bold proposals of the oughts dimmed in the economic crisis. And so the South Coast studios, which began during that period, had an added incentive to explore more modest scales of intervention. This idea of the network was a vehicle for Fred and me to subtly question the very premises of the boom economy and its somewhat destructive implications on the fabric, culture, and history of the lesser regions of the state. While Boston was still in a period of resurgence, that prosperity had yet to "trickle down" into the hinterlands. And, while the mild recovery during the time of these studios has again emboldened developers and architects, turning us back to Boston once again, these earlier questions about the problems of a single economic source remain relevant to these Boston-based studios. Wealth can generate architectures, but it does not necessarily clarify what we have in common.

This book is a conclusion of sorts and a moment of transition in the recent history of the Yale Post-Professional Studios. Fred Koetter, the main supporter of the program and an instructor for both the studios and seminars, announced his retirement following the 2012–2013 studio. Aniket Shahane, a Yale Post-Professional graduate began his teaching during this period too. Aniket—Fred and I recalled—had, in a related study of the Route 128 ring, come closest to capturing both the programmatic invention and the formal sophistication that we looked for in studio work; given his recent success as a practitioner, he seemed the ideal candidate to add to the mix animating the studio culture. Knowing that Fred would step down before-

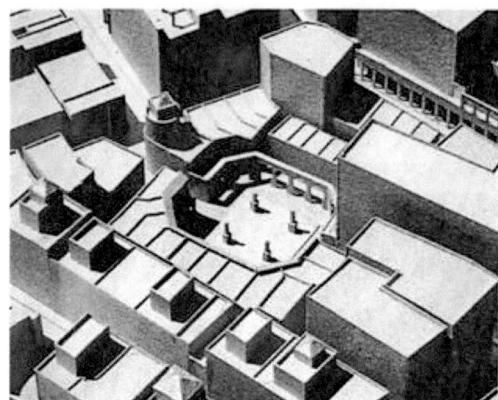

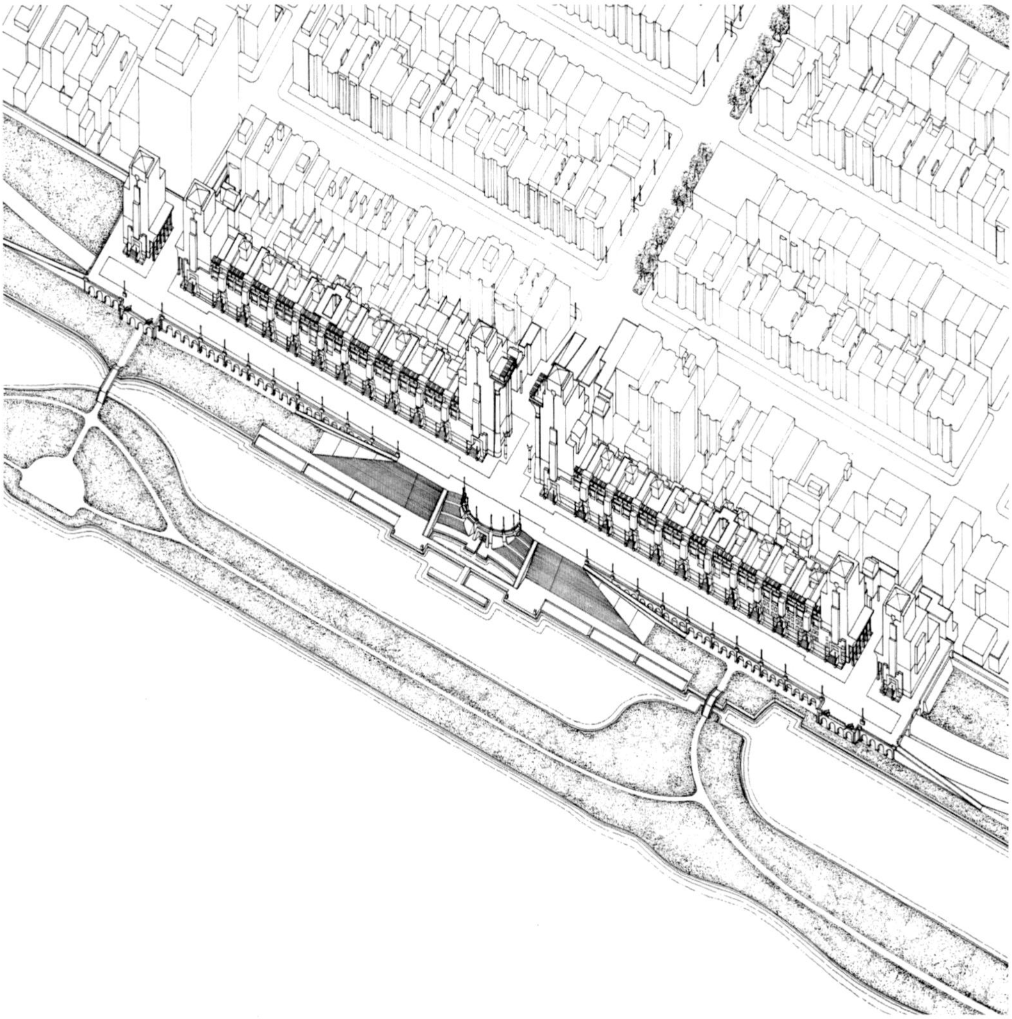

TOP LEFT Koetter Kim. The Boston Plan, University Park.
TOP RIGHT Koetter Kim. The Boston Plan, Chinatown, model studies.
BOTTOM Koetter Kim. The Boston Plan, Storrow Drive.

hand, and encouraged by many of the visitors to our reviews, we decided to return to Boston itself as a didactic and somewhat autobiographical turn on the studios and their history.

For students just beginning careers as practitioners we felt that Boston afforded certain life lessons on how to develop a personal set of goals and that it lent itself to a form of speculation necessary to sustain both a career and a set of conceptual values. Fred Koetter and Susie Kim had also used the city as a laboratory early in their careers. One recalls that their Boston studies of Chinatown, Storrow Drive, the Prudential Center, and University Park were conceived in an economic downturn during the mid-1980s. Both architects have confessed to me that at the time they had little conception of starting an actual practice. Their inventive and insightful speculations on the future of their adopted city were seen as academic exercises, extensions of their respective studies under Colin Rowe at Cornell. One can see two distinct formal aspirations in that work—Fred's tendency towards big moves that often radically reform the urban context, and Susie's more surgical collages that tactically form memorable places within ad hoc fabrics of Boston's neighborhoods. Of those studies, University Park had the most direct impact on their practice, spawning a planning study and several buildings that leveraged their office into a worldwide practice that exerted considerable influence on the profession at large, if not always on Boston itself. The second studio in the Yale

sequence represented in this book indeed returned to University Park, encouraged by Alex Twining, himself a Yale School of Architecture graduate, and a successful residential and commercial developer in the area surrounding MIT.

But at no time were we interested in repeating earlier work. Urban design is by nature a complex endeavor with immediate as well as long-term effects. Urban design involves the negotiation between public and private interests; global, regional and local forces and needs; collective and individual expression. The potentially conflicting demands faced by urban designers have been variously articulated in theory and practice in terms of constructed relationships between general codes—the law, zoning, history—and individual intervention and rights. These sometimes conflicting sources are also structured within architecture by debates between architecture's common language (typology) versus individual expression, figure versus ground, building form versus infrastructure, tradition versus progress, and even architecture versus urbanism. Any urban design proposal does more than simply solve the problem of a program; it embodies a position about, and has consequences for, urban life and urban form. The increased amount of wealth contributing to another period of Boston's renaissance has produced many architectural speculations on building forms, but we felt few carried a compelling projective picture of what the city might become. Many buildings, in other words, but not much city. What we attempted to teach was not just how to make an intelligent urban design proposal, but, more importantly, how to think about the city as part of the architect's conceptual agenda.

One could say that the locus of architectural debate in the 1960s shifted from the architectural object to the city itself. In 1973, the Italian authors of the seminal book, *The American City*—Francesco Dal Co, Manfredo Tafuri, et al—compiled case studies of the history of urban development between the Civil War and the New Deal. Their outline remains useful as both a point of departure and as a tool of critical measure of the current developer-driven climate. Their thesis acknowledged similarities and differences between European and American city development. Both grew around industry, but central to the book's thesis is a formal proposition, that the European city was still governed by its historic pre-industrial patterns and hierarchies, while the American city was based on the grid. The grid, the introduction states, is a "neutral support for capitalism's free exploitation," resulting in what the authors called the "laissez-faire city." *The American City* lays out four distinct responses to the capitalist city organized by four different concepts and urban forms from which those principles are derived. Those are: the Imperial City, the Parks or Reform Movement, the Agrarian Utopia, and the Skyscraper. The American planning history that each chapter outlines is ostensibly a response to unbridled capitalism, either as an outcome in the case of the suburb and the skyscraper or as a formal counter-response and corrective in the examples of the Imperial City and the urban park.

The American City is now forty years old and the content covered transpired 80–150 years ago, necessitating, if not revision, then at least a critical reevaluation of what has transpired since. We might speculate on what, if any, new ideas might be considered as critical architectural responses to the city.

The laissez-faire city remains the norm of American urbanism. But to simply identify the often chaotic nature of the contemporary city would be to ignore that the laissez-faire city itself is planned—perhaps not with the utopian ambitions of the master plan or the good intentions behind grand public works, but through other illusive and sometimes detrimental effects of capital and speculation. The response by contemporary architects and urban designers seems to have returned to hybrids that blur distinctions between capitulation or quasi-utopian idealization. These hybrids are not so different from the four modes outlined in *The American City*. The Imperial City strategy, predicated on a corporate top-down model of delivery and representation is the optimal mode of the corporate architectural and engineering office and is the operative mode for everything from the university to the corporate campus. Urban Reform, with its moral overtones and scale that rivals the Imperial City's cultural ambitions, is echoed by the motivations of Landscape Urbanism and the sustainable city movement. The skyscraper persists, both as a type but also—as Tafuri might have put it—an anti-urban monument, an enclave whose scale and organization rivals and replicates the city proper. And the Agrarian Utopia can be found in other forms, the horizontal sprawl of the suburbs being the most obvious and fundamental development in American urbanism after World War II.

While *The American City's* schema is useful, on a formal basis Boston is both a "European" medieval city and a Modern gridded city. It is also a hybrid of distinct historic epochs: pre-colonial settlement patterns determined by natural elements (the North End); large-scaled design of artificial landscapes and grid structures (Back Bay); massive industrialization and infrastructure support (South Boston); Urban Reform (the Emerald Necklace and the Boston Public Library); the growth of mid-century corporate culture and the urban enclave (the Prudential Center); Urban Renewal (North Station); and post-Modern, late-capitalist development, or the City of Spectacle (the Convention Center.) Moreover, Boston is not a ubiquitous grid but a collection of distinct districts and enclaves that informs both its physical fabric and its unique political organization.

In addition, the period discussed in *The American City* is prior to the major urban projects following the war. The radical restructuring of the city in the decades after the war, particularly the period of Urban Redevelopment, was spurred by federal projects gifted to the city during the Kennedy administration; those interventions, however, only exacerbated the city's decline, notoriously leveling some of Boston's most distinct neighborhoods. The intrusion of I-95 though the heart of the city—though tracing older infrastructure like the railways, and replacing a slightly dysfunctional bottleneck at the core with a modern system of transportation—remains one of the most destructive acts of modern planning that nearly erased one of America's oldest and most historic downtowns.

A number of other texts sought to interrogate and critique the dominant Modernist paradigm, namely its roots in utopian politics and quasi-scientific determinism. *Collage City* by Fred Koetter and Colin Rowe was one of the more significant books of the early '70's. It existed as both a rumor and a method well before its publication in 1977. *Collage City* proposed the idea that form itself could counter the ubiquitous presence of the grid and questioned the tendencies of both rationalism ("let the scientists design the city") and populism ("let the people design the city"), promoting instead the belief that design—the rhetorical of architecture as a discourse—could provide a counter to the mechanistic systems of city-making that threatened to undo architecture and, by implication, the city's humanist ambitions.

Decidedly counter to utopian impulses, the Koetter Kim thesis sees Boston in Popper-like fashion as a sometimes messy, democratic, and dissonant series of constructed architectural arguments. Boston, they essentially argued, is itself a "collage city," a patchwork of ideas and public invocations manifest in its formal urban structure and its architectural heritage. The Koetter Kim analysis of Boston counters the underlying thesis of *The American City*, namely that the forces of capitalism which broke down the logic of the historic city resulted in

what Tafuri would call the "naturalization" of the city as an economically driven enterprise at once ubiquitous and increasingly isolating and mute. In Koetter Kim's first monograph, Boston is described as a group of "little cities," or as districts or "cities-within-cities." This characteristic pattern of urban development is a factor of the historic geography of the city: a primary peninsula and series of islands and bays that over time filled in as the city grew. Boston, as Kevin Lynch once showed, can be understood as a patchwork of fabrics only incidentally controlled by the latter development of grids in areas like Back Bay and Central Square in Cambridge. This pattern reinforced Boston's distinct neighborhoods, and the visible typologies of these respective districts gives these areas their distinct flavor. This neighborhood fabric was also sometimes seen as a negative, making Boston more provincial than gridded cities like New York or Chicago. Those physical boundaries and distinct local differences were also seen as conservative and conventional, ghettoizing ethnic neighborhoods rather than contributing to their identity.

The third significant critical rejoinder, swerving from the other two arguments, can be found in Rem Koolhaas' *Delirious New York*. That book's thesis was that capitalism led not so much to a rational mechanism but to a hedonistic and surrealistic juxtapositions of program and space. Koolhaas noted that, when *The American City* and *Collage City* were written, the American city was under threat of disappearance. Some would argue that it has disappeared, others that it never existed. The cause of its demise would include changes in industrial practice beginning in the 1920s which began to more fully manifest themselves after World War II: the continuing rise of the automobile; the desire for social mobility; and developments in capitalism, among others. It has been said that the city was not theorized until its disappearance and that these two texts were evidence of the belated nature of critical discourse. Koolhaas charged architecture with the capacity and expressive character of what we will call "Collision City." That early work is reinforced by his research for "Project on the City" at Harvard. However, and one might note that this is latent in Koolhaas' work, the current control of urbanization seems to be not in the hands of architects or politicians—older institutional forms—but in the hands of odd hybrids of advertising, real estate development, and social media platforms.

Two studio studies in this book, Fort Point Channel and the proposal for a new Boston City Hall, follow from the historic complexities of this period of urban renewal. Fort Point, in its current state, is an unresolved remnant of renewal. Despite recent development, which includes the Convention Center and the Federal Courthouse, speculative plans by others, in our eyes, are a somewhat disappointing series of interventions. As of this writing, this new district remains awkwardly foreign to its surroundings due to both programmatic and architectural factors. It is at once designed for tourists and visitors to the city and its large scale shift lacks continuity or complementary associations with its surrounds. Despite the amount of money poured into this area, we felt that a true district had yet to emerge, that the sometimes formulaic solutions of contemporary development failed to construct a lively and memorable street fabric, producing instead isolated monuments to capital, inward-turning and conventional. The students' Fort Point proposals were tasked to reimagine the entry to the city by car, train, and ship, but also to formulate a more compelling vision of what a new mixed-use district might include, to invent a new audience for the city, and to possibly connect up the fragmented areas around South Station.

The second site represented a more immediate and newer set of conflicts brought on by Boston's recent success. Like other parts of greater Boston, this area of Cambridge suffered decline in part from rumors that a major artery was to cut through the neighborhood, and this, along with the loss of industry, was a factor in its decline. As stated earlier, the area of Central Square was presented as a follow-up to the Koetter Kim University Park plan to expand the back-of-house research facilities near MIT. That plan exemplified a practical

approach to making places in the city grid. Recent development in nearby Kendall Square also factored into the context. University Park is now built out, and Kendall Square has been virtually reinvented. Both areas revitalized moribund areas of the city, vestiges of former industrial sites that were no longer vital to the city's life and economy. University Park was intended as a mixed-use laboratory campus, but pressures by merchants along Massachusetts Avenue who feared a drain on the local businesses, and internal logistics having to do with laboratory development, tabled the active commercial ground floor envisioned in the original master plan. What did remain is a fairly successful urban park that defines the district. Kendall Square, developed a decade or so later, lacks the public space definitions that characterize University Park, but has been, to a degree, more successful in luring in commercial retail. But, in both cases, the massive nature of the lab building type and the security and program requirements tend to produce stand-alone buildings with limited street engagement. The restrictions on program can make the areas feel like enclaves, relatively quiet outside of business hours. In addition, the secretive nature of the work does not always make for good neighbors to the active residential areas now immediately adjacent to these complexes.

The increasing demand for even more lab space and the lucrative nature of this type of development, can yield almost three times the leasing rates from residential returns, even in one of the United States' most overpriced housing markets. This means that the only new sites for the expansion of the MIT campus are either going to encroach further into the Central Square area or force new research facilities to move elsewhere, either to the outer small cities or perhaps, as speculated earlier, into the areas around South Station. In conversations with the developer Alex Twining and CBT Architects who were working on the project simultaneously with the studio, we looked at how residential development, rather than laboratory development, might negotiate the current market demands against the always contentious and highly engaged interests of "the People's Republic of Cambridge." Wealth confronts the Common. While there is a history of resistance to development in these areas and a latent nostalgia for the gritty, for Boston, commerce along Mass Ave., the immediate interests of the neighborhood are in conflict with the city-wide need to densify neighborhoods along mass transit lines and to supply modest if not affordable apartments for the new denizens of the East Coast's version of Silicon Valley. It should be noted that subsequent studios are now looking north to the former mill towns as alternatives to an outpriced residential market in Boston.

Finally, our third studio reexamines 1960s Boston's greatest symbolic and architectural achievement. Boston City Hall, the most singular monument of the period of renewal, was rumored to be torn down and moved to the Fort Point area. Though this plan no longer seems operative, the incentive may have come from several directions which are revealing about the building. First, rampant speculation may have led officials to believe that the value of the land would offset the enormous costs of demolition and construction for a new facility. Though Boston is booming, it is not clear that the finances made any sense. Secondly, the building's program, which could include other municipal offices, may well have exceeded the capacity of the building. This is as much a testament to the further bureaucratization of city government as it is a problem of adding to a singular edifice. Third, the building, highly praised at its inception and even after ten years of construction, is often cited as the least-loved building in greater Boston; however, a recent resurgence in interest by the architectural community of the Brutalist period may also have played a factor in preserving the building. Anecdotally, most architects I have spoken with have never entered the building. Whether this is due to its overfamiliarity, its perception from the outside that it is an impenetrable and inhospitable fortress, or just plain lack of curiosity is regrettable. To this day, the Boston City Hall remains one of the greatest achievements in public architecture of the postwar period, a testament to the faith in good government

and a faith in architecture to embody innovative and inventive tectonics and civic symbolism. Again, the didactic lessons for students are large. Though it is nearly inconceivable today, Kallman McKinnell won an open competition for the project when Michael McKinnell, an educator at Columbia, was only twenty-five years old, the average age of a student in the Yale Post-Professional program. More will be said about the building later in the book.

The city, as it may have been defined in other periods of wealth, exemplified by the artifacts of the City Beautiful movement or Urban Renewal, is no longer operating under the same paradigms. And, yet, the city persists. Boston has rebounded from its low point in the 1960s and '70s when it was a poster child for blight, white flight, and the devastating effects of urban renewal. Beginning in the 1980s, shortly after the Bicentennial, the city began to recover, with Boston becoming a tourist destination and a center for the financial and technology industries. Today Boston struggles, as all cities do, with conflicts between its significant historic institutions and urban form and its need to develop its typological and political legacies, as well as its need to innovate and evolve.

While the overall regional and municipal issues facing the city in the coming decades are hinted at in this work, the strategy of exploring the separate issues of infrastructure, new business districts, dense housing and neighborhood development, and civic symbolism and government are all touched upon in the architectural solutions proposed by the students. We hope and have found that the provocative nature of the work is useful in amplifying debate beyond the more mundane and formulaic conventions of development and urban design. Those provocations, we hope, will stimulate greater and more inventive speculations—all within the realm of possibility—for Boston's future.

On Studios. About Cities.

Aniket Shahane

The Studio

Why did you come back? It is a question we often ask the students at the beginning of the semester.
On the one hand, the inquiry is meant to spark a discussion with the students about their goals, their
backgrounds, their experiences, and previous training. On the other, it is a means to set the table for the
semester—to let the students know that this time around, at the start of their *post*-professional academic
career, we, as critics are interested in the *questions* the students will design as much as any project
proposal. As the first studio of a two-year program, we see the course as a springboard for the second
phase of their academic career—one in which we hope students will design their own boundaries, both
for their studio project as well as within the discipline of architecture. In other words, one which will
encourage the students to generate their own position in a given context.

The City

"I don't want to be a product of my environment. I want my environment to be a product of me."
—Frank Costello on South Boston in the film *The Departed*

Cities have always been places of conflict and celebration—intricate and messy organisms that require
the negotiation of values among multiple constituencies. If the design of an individual building tends to
focus its energy within the bounds of a given site, the design of a city, in many ways, is the definition of site
itself. In that regard, the city seems an appropriate setting for this studio. Maybe it's the only setting for
this studio.

Boston then, as the common ground for these last three studio projects, is the result of neither coincidence
nor convenience. It has proven to be, in many ways, the perfect City-Site. Boston contains all the qualities
(and quantities) of urbanism ripe for speculating on the notion of City. The labyrinthine quarters of the
downtown, Beacon Hill, and North End are as intricate and messy as I-93 was rational and ruthless. It is
the site of provincial attitudes and global reach, probably best exemplified in South Boston. "Southie"
has transformed itself from being known primarily as a tough, Irish-Catholic working-class, triple-decker
neighborhood into one that is home to a slew of world-class institutions by international architects.
Boston has a history of going big and radical, as with the development of the Back Bay neighborhood in the
nineteenth century and the Big Dig project of the 2000s. It can just as easily do lackluster and conservative,
exemplified in the thin brick veneer often used to clad many recent nondescript developments. It is a site of
marathons and terrorism, of revolutions and parades, all encompassed within a dense 48 square miles and

a population of under three-quarters of a million in the "city proper."

The urban "situation" (to borrow one of Fred Koetter's terms) that is inherent in Boston forces a kind of thinking that is different from what is often taught in a first professional architecture program. In the city, context—the physical, economic, political, and cultural—is intertwined with time in ways that are complex and unpredictable. The potential for change is ever-present and demands a stance on the future that is both explicit and open-ended. This is the headspace we like our students to enter into in these studios as they wrestle with their own speculations on the city, for it privileges *position* about a project as much as the actual project itself. And it is one of the reasons, we hope, for the diversity of work presented in this book— from the level of resolution shown at the scale of a detail to that of a streetscape, from the design of a small building to that of an entire neighborhood.

The Work

"God created paper for the purpose of drawing architecture on it. Everything else is, at least for me, an abuse of paper."
— Alvar Aalto

Though each of the studios had their own set of specific issues, there were some larger themes that seemed to emerge each semester: bigness and infrastructure; symbolism and iconicity; fabric and the notion of Public, and of course, drawing

and representation, to name a few. Perhaps some of these topics are inevitable in any project that studies the city. But others are certainly reflections of the students' diverse interests and skills combined with our own predilections as critics. To see all of the drawings, models, images, and texts from the last three years of the Post-Professional Studio archived in this book, in this manner is, for me at least, an attempt to find the overlaps, contradictions, and revelations across semesters, sites, and students—to understand the work of the Post-Professional Studio as one body of work. At first glance, Matthew Rauch and Hochung Kim's project in the Fort Point studio may look like a counterpoint to Peter McInish and Laurence Lumley's project for Central Square, but in fact it is not. Both projects emerged from an attitude about context— that the city is composed of a series of set pieces that don't always coalesce. The scale of the existing built form informs the nature of the new interventions and their ability to craft a narrative. Rauch and Kim's large buildings skillfully absorb other large buildings such as the Convention Center, the Gillette Building, and South Station into a coherent urban situation. The monumental floodable new plaza around which this new city is organized reflects not only the scale of the architectural gestures, but also a position about the future of a city that reaches beyond its own physical limits. McInish and Lumley's project takes the same position on a very different site. The result is a series of micro-interventions and an intricate network of small plazas that amplify the existing characteristics of Cambridge's fabric.

McInish and Lumley are concerned less with the actual form of the buildings themselves and more with their scale, their proximities to each other and the small public spaces they may sponsor. In this project, a detail such as a paver, a street lamp, or a piece of furniture is as important to the life of the city as the plaza outside a train station.

The notion of symbolism, as loaded and nebulous as the term is, was one that permeated all three semesters, perhaps most markedly in the Boston City Hall studio. Form as symbol, as well as the symbolism of program, was something each student wrestled with, wittingly or not. Shuangjing Hu and Mengshi Sun began the semester by recognizing that some of the administrative spaces and functions of City Hall are intertwined with the momentous occasions in our everyday lives. Births, deaths, and marriages are all events that require documentation, the kind that is often procured in the architecture of City Hall in the form of licenses and certificates. Their project was an attempt to remind us of that by proposing a series of multipurpose indoor/outdoor spaces that could support both the administrative functions of civil servants as well as ceremonial events in the lives of Bostonians. In contrast, Eunil Cho and Roberto Jenkins had a different take on form and symbolism. Their project was designed as an all-encompassing hub that incorporated government functions, hotels, commercial spaces, and subway infrastructure into one large overarching form. The notion that the functions of government are on an equal formal— and therefore symbolic—footing as shopping was provocative and induced in their final review the kind of debate we always hope for at semester's end.

Drawing and modeling, two of the architect's most basic tools, are also important topics in the studio. Scanning through the work in the book will quickly show a mix of representations, not excluding those drawn and made by hand. Our discussions about representation in the studio have always privileged drawing and making as tools for identifying problems as much as representing the perfect solution—the act of drawing as a means to work

through a set of questions in order to provoke another level of inquiry. In fact, some of the most pleasant surprises of these Boston studios have been the conversations provoked by the tools of representation. The models produced in the Central Square studio were so incredibly useful (and large) that much of the final review discussion revolved almost solely around the models. The analysis work, such as one which paired BIG's sometimes glib presentation techniques with Rafael Moneo's solemn architecture was both critical and funny. The proposals for the "Instant City" exercise, a quick three-day problem we use to kick-start the studio, have been represented using everything from a single, dynamic rendering to a collection of drawings and short stories.

The Future

"In the looking, I found the cities within me."
— Suketu Mehta, *Maximum City: Bombay Lost and Found*

With this book taking its place as the second in a series about this studio, it's hard not to think about what's next for the Post-Professional Studio. Because, in the end, this book is as much a reflection on our own time as critics as it is on the body of work produced by the students. The truth is that the question with which this essay began— and with which we often begin the semester—is also a provocation for us as teachers. Why do *we* return, twice a week, every fall, to teach this studio? Why do we resurrect each year the problem of "City"? The answer may have something to do with a fascination with the specific architectural and urban issues implicit in all the work presented here. It is certainly motivated by a belief that the themes raised in this studio are important within the discourse of architecture as well as for the education of an architect. But probably the real reason we keep coming back is simply for the thrill of asking questions—questions about the city, the students, our education, and ourselves. It has been a good reason to return to Boston, and is always a good excuse to come back to New Haven.

Boston Development Trends

Kishore Varanasi

Bostonians have never been known to sit back and wait for change. For over three hundred years, we have continuously reinvented ourselves and our city. We are a small city, with just a three-mile radius, with great ambition, and we always have been. Today's innovative urban design and development is no exception. That being said, there is still great opportunity for Boston to grow in the future, particularly with respect to the city's public realm.

Back in the seventeenth century, Boston was just a small, swampy town (not even a city, yet). But as Boston's population and influence grew, so did its boundaries. Indeed, Boston gradually annexed and added land over the next three centuries. Perhaps the most interesting of these additions did not start off as land at all.

Throughout the nineteenth century, Boston leveled its topography to expand its footprint. In the first half of the century it reduced three peaks near the waterfront to just one lower peak: today's Beacon Hill. The excavated land was used to extend the hill south towards today's Charles Street. It was also used to fill in Mill Pond, literally laying the groundwork for the creation of the Bulfinch Triangle. This historic district was designed by the well-known Federalist architect Charles Bulfinch. Back Bay, which was actually a bay in Boston's early days, was filled in during the middle of the century. Wide tree-lined streets and neat row houses were added to create one of the country's most remarkable examples of nineteenth-century urban design.

Similarly, the Seaport was created through further infill towards the end of the century, representing the continuously pressing need for buildable land in Boston.

Much of this infill coincided with an age of rapid industrialization in Boston. The Bulfinch Triangle, for example, became a major railroad hub and home to a bustling manufacturing industry. The city also experienced an influx of immigrants at this time, particularly from European countries such as Ireland and Italy. This meant that a number of city neighborhoods were quickly added or adapted to accommodate these additional residents, often in poor or even dangerous conditions.

These dense neighborhoods, however, inspired close-knit communities and a unique urban culture. When leading urbanist Jane Jacobs visited Boston's Italian North End in the late-1950s and early 1960s, she was struck by the vitality of this supposed "slum." She notes in her book, *The Death and Life of Great American Cities* (1961), how the neighborhood's mix of uses and tightly clustered buildings created a sense of safety and community. Children played in the streets and passersby stopped to visit on the sidewalks. Yet, the neighborhood's density and demographics caused many outsiders and city officials to dismiss its best qualities.

This mistaken perspective of such neighborhoods speaks to the great misfortune and misunderstand-

ing of one of Boston's more recent land reclamation projects: the West End. Hailed as a victory over urban decay, Boston razed nearly its entire West End in the name of urban renewal. Characterized by a fine-grain urban fabric and thriving immigrant community like the North End, the West End was nonetheless also considered a societal canker. The neighborhood's small-scale row houses and residents were therefore removed by eminent domain to make way for new governmental centers and high-rise housing projects in the late-1950s.

Today, the city's desire to continuously reimagine and recreate itself is stronger than ever. However, it is now dedicated to a much more responsible form of urban revitalization. Just as the city responded to the need for railways and manufacturing spaces in the past, the city is currently building infrastructure for innovation in order to remain economically competitive and socially savvy in today's global world. This can perhaps be best seen in the Seaport area.

Characterized by a sea of surface parking lots and gritty maritime uses, the Seaport was a forgotten and disheveled district at the end of the twentieth century. Since then, however, the area has experienced significant growth and investment related to the thriving global innovation economy. Numerous biotech and finance giants have broken ground on new headquarters and urban offices. Cultural and educational centers such as the District Hall public innovation center, the Institute of Contemporary Art (ICA), the Blue Hills Bank Pavilion, the World Trade Center, and the Boston Convention and Exhibition Center act as critical community anchors. And an ever-increasing number of rooftop bars, waterfront restaurants, and, of course, the Harpoon Brewery keep the district young and alive. Recent development has included more and more housing

TOP   Boston West End prior to redevelopment.
BOTTOM Boston West End at the start of urban renewal. Courtesy Lowery Aerial Photos/West End Museum.

as well, helping the district to transition into a true live-work-play community.

However, the recent spur of development in the Seaport highlights one of Boston's consistent shortcomings in urban planning: its lack of a continuous and compelling public realm. As is true in so many Boston neighborhoods, the Seaport's public spaces are small and distinct. Separated from the rest of the community by major roadways, bridges, and industrial infrastructure, it is remarkably difficult to access those small public spaces that do exist in the area. Furthermore, the blocks, streetscapes and surrounding architecture sorely lack acknowledgement of the human scale. Without many street trees or much ground-floor activity, the public realm and resultant pedestrian experience is lackluster at best.

This is strikingly inconsistent with the scale and significance of the rest of the development in the Seaport and suggests a strong and pressing need to reevaluate our public space planning and standards at the district, and likely city, level. While there are requirements for most large projects to provide public amenities, the quality, nature, and accessibility of these spaces can vary greatly. These efforts should not be piecemeal, but rather coordinated in such a way that that the sum of the parts is greater than the whole. This burst of development-related investment in the public realm should be leveraged collectively to deliver larger and more impactful public spaces. These spaces should be connected through streetscapes that naturally complement these projects, creating the continuous and compelling public realm that the city craves.

As we look to the future, there is also a larger opportunity to imagine the power of a porous public realm and open space network to connect the city more closely to the waterfront, natural world, and surrounding communities. Since its inception more than three hundred years ago, Boston has tackled just two major open space projects: Frederick Law Olmsted's Emerald Necklace in the second half of the nineteenth century and the Rose Kennedy Greenway at the turn of the twenty-first century. The socially, environmentally, and economically transformational quality of both projects is argument enough for thoughtful public space planning throughout the city. The Emerald Necklace provides invaluable urban habitat, connects the city's outer neighborhoods, and provides many disadvantaged communities with access to open and recreational space. The Rose Kennedy Greenway significantly reduces urban heat island effects in the heart of the city, creates critical visual and physical connections to the waterfront, and stimulates economic activity and investment downtown.

Perhaps it is time for Boston to make a name for itself for the next three hundred years by reinventing and reinvigorating not just its built environment, but also its natural one.

ABOVE *Precipice City* by Jason Kurzweil, Apoorva Khanolkar, and
Sofia Singler.

Instant City

Edward Mitchell

After establishing criteria for the evaluation of a city, that work was used to create an "Instant City." The title is derived from experiments in avant-garde urbanism of the 1960s, such as Archigram and Archizoom's provocations on the spontaneous eruption of countercultural alternative urbanisms within the confines of the official city. But the "Instant City" was also meant as a prompt to consider the problems associated with the impact of capital investment on the indigenous settlement patterns that precede the modern period. Beginning in the nineteenth century, particularly in the West, the quick rise of cities like Detroit could seem to be both miraculous and also culturally disorienting. Other "instant" cities are included in the precedent list —Roman military encampments certainly, but also festivals, factory towns or postwar bedroom communities, to say nothing of more obvious examples like the many new cities springing up in Asia.

While the idea of an Instant City may seem to mirror the current models of development which are radically changing the areas of the city that we studied, the exercise is intended to stimulate critical thinking in regard to what makes a city, both extensively and intensively. As a matter of extension the city should have metrics: population and density criteria, scale and measure, ratios of public to private use; as a matter of intensity, the city is also an event, liable to emerge at any given moment and to disappear without warning. Cities are made of both built matter and of rituals and happenings.

This weeklong exercise asked students to project ideas and values learned from the study of precedents into more visionary plans for a contemporary urban concept. The sole criteria for completing the exercise was establishing and justifying the required population, the physical size of the city, and the program or image that made their proposals "instant." While a majority of the Instant City sketches were somewhat conventional (centrally organized and adhering closely to traditional and transit-oriented development standards), several took on less immediately identifiable standards in identifying with the idea of networked relationships that could constitute contemporary interpretation of the idea of "city." Without a symbolic or singularly defining programmatic impulse, the problem of urban image comes into play. Potteries Thinkbelt, Broadacre City, and more contemporary enclave models are examples that represent the city as either dispersed or highly temporal—perhaps existing only as long as an overnight stay in a hotel, the itinerant carnival, the fairgrounds, or the short-term campaign of the military encampment. In keeping with the event-based strategies of groups like Archigram, these sketches suggested that the most minimal physical intervention might be sufficient to establish an Instant City and point to conceptual strategies that might reanimate the areas that we studied.

Perhaps the most evocative response comes from one group's fable of the *Gluttonous City*, a sad but resonant tale of a community visited by a traveling carnival. At first the carnival brings new life to the town, but soon the inhabitants devote all their wealth and energy into the carnival, to the detriment of the city itself, which begins to decay. The carnival, the Instant City, after it has drained the actual city of all its wealth, moves on to more lucrative destinations.

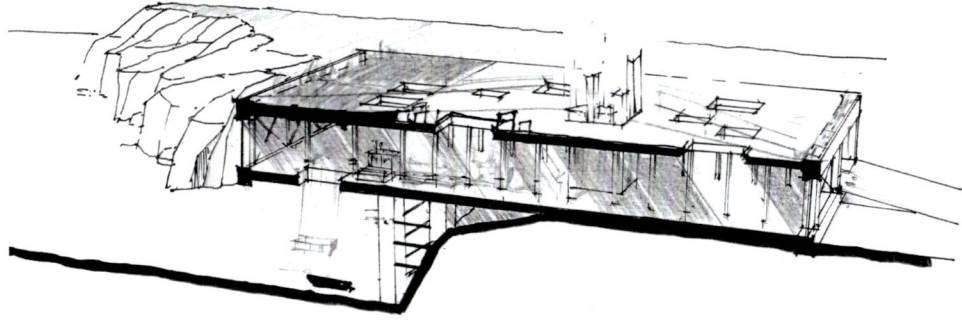

TOP LEFT *Precipice City* by Stephanie Jazmindes, Jospeh Yu and Peter McInish.
BOTTOM LEFT *Precipice City* by Stephanie Jazmindes, Jospeh Yu and Peter McInish.
TOP RIGHT *Precipice City* by Stephanie Jazmindes, Jospeh Yu and Peter McInish.
BOTTOM RIGHT *Precipice City* by Stephanie Jazmindes, Jospeh Yu and Peter McInish.

ABOVE *Instant City* by Karl Karam, Shuangjing Hu and Alicia Pozniak.

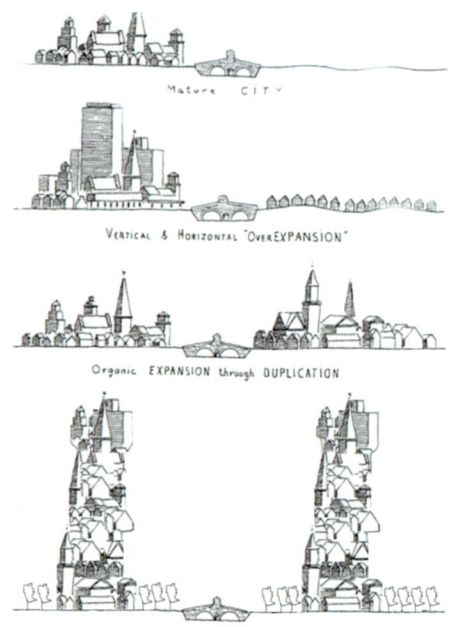

A.   B.   C.   D.   E.   F.

INGREDIENTS

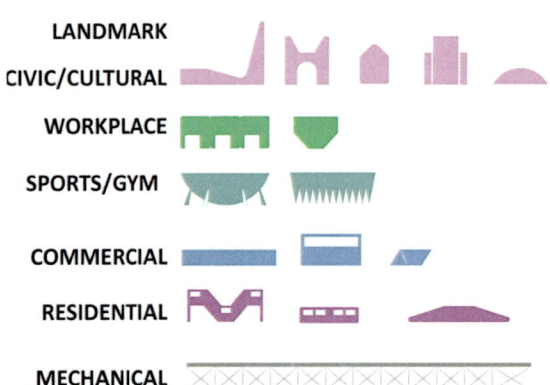

LANDMARK

CIVIC/CULTURAL

WORKPLACE

SPORTS/GYM

COMMERCIAL

RESIDENTIAL

MECHANICAL

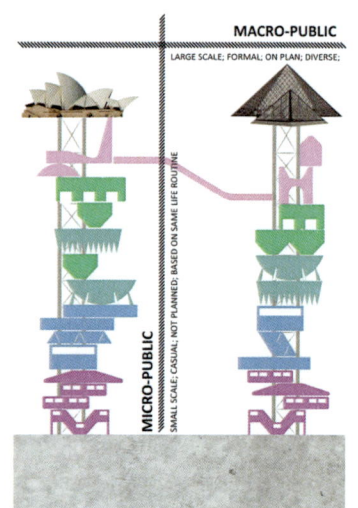

OPPOSITE Reinterpretation of Leon Krier drawings for the expansion of an Ideal City for *Instant City* by Eunil Cho and Jizhou Liu.
ABOVE *Instant City*, Colorado by Eunil Cho and Jizhou Liu.

THE GLUTTONOUS CITY

ARCHITECTURE 1022; POST PROFESSIONAL STUDIO_SKETCH EXERCISE_FALL 2013_
IAN * JULCSI * KATE * LAURENCE

1) PASTORAL

The town sits on the coast in a lush valley full of productive agricultural land. The needs of the townsfolk are more than met by the bounty of their farms, hunting in the surrounding hills, fishing, and their simple trade links with nearby towns. They live good lives, tending their gardens, tilling the soil, and building fishing ships. There are thriving craft workshops and schools. Their farm dwellings are humble but in the town itself there are solid public buildings and a noble temple. The routine of daily life is governed by nature: they rise with the morning sun and return home at sunset, at night they sleep and during the day they work the land. One day they see in the distance some strange shapes appearing on the horizon and seeming to approach their harbor.

2) DOCKING

The odd vessels are now all docked. They have bound themselves together into a sprawling mass along the shoreline, centered around a dense chaotic core. Each one is different and many are made from materials the townsfolk cannot identify in colours that seem most unnatural. At night, a magic light maintains an artificial day within the floating city. Initial fear has been replaced by great curiosity, all the more intense due to the odd noises and signs of mysterious preparations going on – scaffolding going up, the erecting of screens, construction of gangplanks. As yet there has been no communication between the new arrivals and the townspeople. The elders are suspicious. Apart from their wonder, however, the life of the townsfolk continues as normal.

3) EVENT

Overnight, flyers have appeared all over town advertising an event that night. The town is full of chatter and anticipation. Curiosity and an unaccountable attraction to the bright lights of the floating city have overcome the townsfolk's natural distrust of the new. The elders warn the people not to go, but they are, respectfully, ignored. The appointed time arrives and the whole town is gathered on the beach. Suddenly the peace of the valley is shattered by 100 decibels of amplified dance music and the sound of a spontaneous firework display. Simultaneously countless movie projectors switch on, neon shop signs illuminate, stores, bars and nightclubs roll up their shutters or throw open their doors. Overawed by the glittering spectacle the townsfolk rush in. They have never, in their quiet, untroubled lives encountered anything like this before, and their hosts, revealed to be charming, friendly and instructive people, are more than happy to initiate them into their sophisticated urban lifestyle. The townsfolk are entranced by the movies and intoxicated by the alcohol (in new and exciting flavours and strengths). They delight in the shops selling things they do not know the use for, but they have no money (they don't understand the concept). Luckily the retail assistants assure them they need not worry and give them their purchases on credit. They party, they dance and drink and in the early morning they are shown to eat kebabs and falafel.

4) THE DEAL

The townsfolk have recovered from the event. Their initial mortification at their own behavior has given way to a secret, nagging desire for more. They go to the floating city and request another event. The city people are happy to oblige, but they have run out of supplies and fuel. They explain that if the townsfolk can bring their produce they could re-start their city, besides the townsfolk owe them for their credit purchases anyway. The townsfolk agree, and the deal is done. They bring everything they can from their farms to the jetty, where it is all loaded onto conveyor belts and consumed by the urban processing vessels. That evening the floating nightlife starts up again.

ABOVE AND OPPOSITE *Gluttonous City,* a parable in eight parts for *Instant City* by Kate Lisi, Laurence Lumley, Ian Spencer, and Julcsi Futo.

5) CONSUMPTION

The needs of the floating city are becoming ever more demanding and it seeks to meet the townsfolk's rapidly increasing desire for new experiences, spectacles, more intense entertainment and more night-time excitement. Their appetite has become insatiable. The townspeople have discovered from the city dwellers that their time is precious and that they should spend their free time enjoying themselves as much as possible. The townspeople now understand that work is not quality time spent, but merely a necessity to fund their social lives. They get bored, which they never did before. They no longer wear the plain overalls they used to be content with, but now dress in endless new combinations of colourful clothes. They are learning to express their individuality. The youth have discovered from the city dwellers that they are 'cool', because they are without the burden of families yet. Their innocent parents accept this logic and work all the harder to satisfy their more and more exigent requests. Their new lifestyles have left the townsfolk out of sync with the natural rhythm of the day, and they are often too tired after a night of clubbing to get up at dawn and milk the cows. The farms are falling into disrepair. To keep pace with the needs of the floating city the land has been exploited beyond its capacity and production is starting to suffer. In response the city dwellers install their magic lights, so that after sunset work can still continue in an artificial day. The work they once found so fulfilling has now become a terrible drudge.

6) ABANDONMENT

The townsfolk have become greedy and mean. Crime has entered in where there was none before, and parts of town are lawless. The temple has long been abandoned and a general cynicism has set in. The floating city is dismantling its structures and is casting off. The valley is no fun anymore. The farms are nearly in ruins. The food has almost run out. The valley is quite ravaged and the harbor is full of floating trash, which is killing the fish.

7) DESOLATION

The ruin of the town is in its final collapse. Nature has started reclaiming the central square and the farms are long gone. There are very few of the old townsfolk left; most have died or fled. Those that remain scavenge for food like animals and fight each other for scraps. There is nothing of their civilization left now. Soon there will be no trace at all that humans ever lived in the valley. The floating city is far away.

8) NEXT STOP...

Meantime the floating city has traveled a long way and gotten a lot bigger. They want a whole lot more fun. They have spotted a new target in the distance…

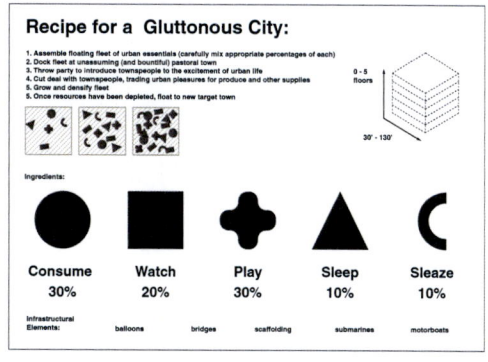

Fort Point Channel

Edward Mitchell

Boston, founded on a narrow peninsula in what is now the downtown government and financial center, was structured by its relationship to the water. Important historic sites such as the Old North Church, Fort Point Channel, site of the Boston Tea Party, and Paul Revere's house are destinations of the tourist trail that weaves through downtown. Despite huge changes, traces of the original street layout remain intact, constituting a fairly unusual fabric. Recently, the high cost of land outside the city made the downtown, as well as areas of South Boston, attractive for both business and residential development. The Big Dig, one of the last great infrastructure projects of the old Democratic regime, is the most obvious change in the heart of Boston. The project buried the Interstate and made better connections to the airports, leaving a public beltway between North and South Station. Recently, Boston has undergone a good deal of new development, including the construction of the Convention Center due east of South Station, the Institute of Contemporary Art (ICA) and many new commercial and residential buildings in South Boston. Downtown, office towers that take up full city blocks mix with colonial-era warehouses, reflecting the shift in economics from a colonial city seaport to a modern business center. The notorious urban-renewal-era Government Center sits at the central hub of streets that run to the waterfront and is connected to Back Bay and other areas to the south via Washington Street, one of the longest continuous streets in America.

The restrictive geography of the city forced massive changes to the original landscape, including leveling parts of Boston's three hills to expand the waterfront and fill in Back Bay. The Fan Pier area of South Boston, east of downtown across Fort Point Channel, is also largely infill. This area was once an important part of Boston's working waterfront and its rail yards serviced the central core. The name Fan Pier refers to the splay of railroad lines that ended at the port. Today, this area is largely a commuter parking lot, with only a six-block remnant of the old fabric, known as Fort Point, still intact.

Like many American cities, Boston suffered from urban blight during the decades immediately after World War II due to suburbanization and industrial decline. Under the policies of Urban Renewal, large areas of the traditional city were leveled in an attempt to revitalize the downtown and improve traffic flow to the core, which was limited by the colonial street layout and physical geometry. However, these interventions

OPPOSITE Fort Point Channel study area.

cut the city into distinct districts. Areas like the Bulfinch Triangle and the historic North End remain as vital memories of the historic city. During this period much of the job base and the population moved to the outer well-established suburbs. Unlike many cities, this second ring of streetcar suburbs, established early in the city development, constitutes some of the most desirable residential real estate in the metropolitan area.

The downtown, where it survived, became a mix of office buildings and tourist attractions. The studio looked at an area that is a central piece of an urban puzzle of parcels that makes up the South Boston waterfront. Each of these parcels has distinct problems of scale, character, and urban use. Our site surrounds Fort Point, a six- to eight-story former industrial fabric, similar to SoHo, New York. The main development parcel is one hundred acres of mixed-use development that has a large territory designated as an historic district and the area of the current Post Office, which is scheduled to move from its current location adjacent to South Station. Located to the immediate southeast of the one-hundred-acre study area is the Convention Center, linked to an elevated street, Summer, that ties into South Station. To the north is a waterfront parcel on Boston Harbor, Fan Pier, scheduled for 1.2 million square feet of new construction, which was considered in the preliminary analysis of the site, including: the Federal Courthouse; the ICA by Diller Scofidio + Renfro; Pier 4 also planned for 1 million square feet of new mixed-use development; and the World Trade Center.

Plans to move the Post Office offer further opportunity to speculate on the tangle of infrastructure that limits connections between South Boston, the Central Business District, Chinatown, and the Leather District. South Station, one of two

disconnected mass transit hubs seems an accident of circumstantial building campaigns rather than a major transportation center and entry point into the city. A number of projects, including the work of Cesar Pelli, have looked at redevelopment around South Station.

Students were asked to consider this site as a potential mixed-use development, capitalizing on the future need of office space, hotels, and new live/work opportunities in the downtown business district. Furthermore, consideration of how auto, bus, train, and water taxis might better connect the outlying areas into the center of the downtown were taken into account.

Early work was done to understand the urban scale. For example, the entire development of Back Bay could fit neatly into the area from Fan Pier back to the ragged development south. This kind of development would make real urban connections from the underutilized areas of South Boston to the waterfront. The Fort Point Planning District (100 Acres, as it is sometime called,) could become distinct and identifiable. Student Grant Scott's scheme, for example, takes this on as a real possibility, outlining a better-structured series of urban streets running north-south through the heart of the district. Similarly, students Eleanor Meacham and Craig Rossman use traditional methods like typological variation and more current tools like parametrics to weave a complex urban texture that transitions from the low-rise residential districts to the south into the high rises of the downtown. Others, like Alissa Hintz and John Farrace, or James Petty and Yoojin Han, monumentalize the transportation hub in order to better resolve the entry sequence into Boston. The most radical of these type of proposals is that of Jay Tsai and Miron Nawratil, who move South Station south to open up more

development territory in the CDB and to reorganize the transportation systems into a monumental new mixed-use structure. Others, such as Matthew Rauch's and Hochung Kim's series of large public courtyards, or Jie Tian's and Mengyao Yu's vision of a pair of intensive tourist hotel nodes, accept the isolated development strategy that seems to be the current trend, but amplify the city-within-a-city logic into memorable architectural statements.

While the political logistics of the site may in the end fail to integrate the bolder ideas of the studio, the discussions about the future of the city, its ma-jor point of entry, and the architectural and urban nature of a new central district remain provocative and projective.

ABOVE South Boston and Fort Point Channel from The *Boston Globe* Archive.

Retroactive Inevitability and Urban Design Advocacy

Tim Love

As an urban designer and architect who has done plans for the areas where Ed Mitchell and his collaborators have focused their Boston design studios, I thought it would be best to discuss the impact of the urban design studios on planning policy—both generally and in the specific locations of student proposals. Boston has long been a focus of academic speculation by urban planners and designers, perhaps most famously by Kevin Lynch, who used the city center as a laboratory to explore a psycho-spatial theory of urban analysis. Many have credited his reading of the mental maps of Boston's citizens as the impetus for Government Center because the former Scollay Square was singled out as the least imageable place in the city's fabric. In the early 1980s, Fred Koetter and Susie Kim's urban design proposals for the Charles River-facing edge of the Back Bay and surgical densification of both Chinatown and the Prudential Center (using a Nolli Map technique) had a direct impact on public planning policy. The underpinning of Koetter Kim's Prudential Center proposal—a lively pedestrian connection between the South End and the Back Bay—has been fully realized, even if it's lined with retail found at any shopping mall in America.

The Yale studios extend this tradition, but in a fruitful new area of the city: the borderlands between the Fort Point district, traditional south Boston, and the industrial port area on the eastern end of the South Boston waterfront. This former no-man's land, now being filled in with the kind of mixed-use commercial development favored by global REITs, has the same characteristics as the boundaries of Boston's neighborhoods, many of which have centers with a consistent character and structure, but soft boundaries. Some are clearly defined by transportation infrastructure or large open spaces. I-93 between the South End and South Boston is one example. Other boundaries are more diffuse. In many of these situations, remnant industrial areas, some now populated by big box retail, define this blurry line. Significantly, the Orange Line, Red, and Blue Lines, Boston's three high-speed transit routes, are located in these boundary zones. During the latest real estate development cycle, infill residential development has extended the existing neighborhood fabric up to the Broadway and Jackson Square stations, stops on two transit lines that are relatively close to the city center.

With this as a background, the Yale studios benefit

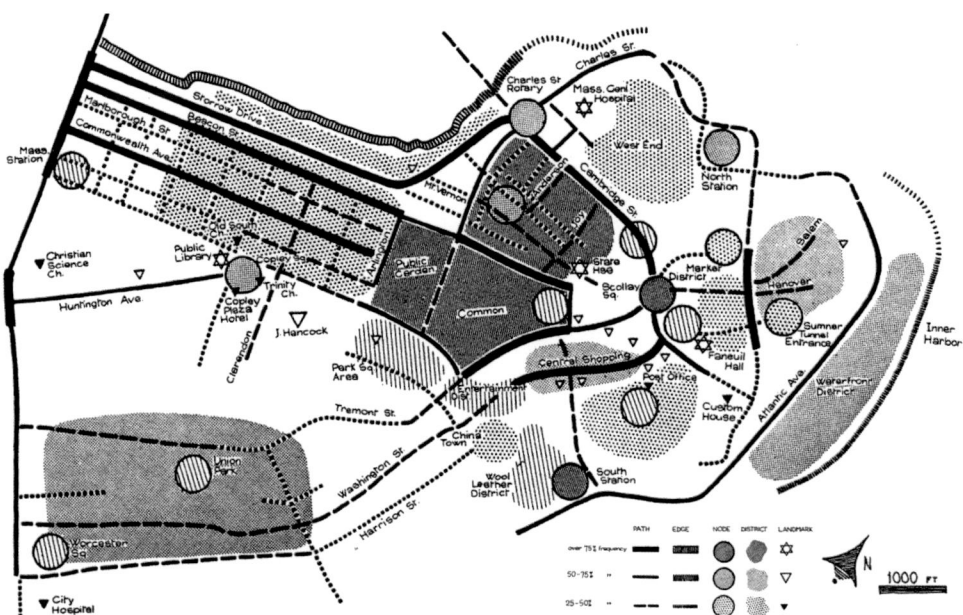

the public debate with the assertion that new centers should be planned for these boundary areas, and not only because transit stations are nearby. Instead of contextual "TOD (transit-oriented development)," most students propose unique and highly characteristic neighborhoods and public spaces that are as rich and memorable as the city's existing urban set pieces. As a result, the wonderfully ad hoc relations of Back Bay to Beacon Hill and Beacon Hill to Government Center is recaptured in the proposals. Rather than proposing the seamless transitions espoused by most planners, the Yale studios celebrate the way that Boston is an Epcot Center of urbanisms that, through their distinctive characters and ideologies, make the overall city a richer and more diverse place.

As a collective body of work, the proposals in Mitchell's studios make a case that twenty-first century urban interventions should be as assertive as the historical city-building initiatives that have shaped Boston. The best of the student proposals are both bold and retroactively inevitable. Retroactively inevitable proposals suggest an innovative new planning framework, typically with a memorable plan gestalt, that upon reflection makes all

previous plans seem unimaginative and unfulfilling. These are the schemes that, like the Koetter Kim proposals, have the highest chance of functioning as unofficially sanctioned master plans. For a proposal to be retroactively inevitable, it needs to frame existing problems differently or pose a new problem to solve. This is why the fuzzy area between traditional South Boston and the shiny new Seaport is such a fertile territory. Several plans exist for this area, most notably Cooper Robertson's 1999 Seaport Public Realm Plan and the Boston Redevelopment Authority (BRA)'s follow-up 100-Acre Plan (authored by the BRA's Kairos Shen and CBT, a local commercial architecture firm). Both officially sanctioned plans deploy streets and blocks, modeled on Cooper Robertson's two successive master plans for Battery Park City, to blend existing urban fabric with the new development areas. The result is the "good urbanism" promoted by the Congress for New Urbansim, city-planning departments, and the large architecture and planning firms that have dominated professional urban design practice for the past twenty years.

But "good urbanism," with its carefully considered suturing of old and new, does not capture

ABOVE Kevin Lynch, "Boston image as derived from interviews," from *The Image of the City*.

the official or public imagination like retroactively inevitable proposals. In the case of Cooper Robertson's proposals, the inevitability of the solution is predictable, thus eliminating the aesthetic, rhetorical, and political benefits of effective surprise.

Two projects from Mitchell's studio highlight these strategies and effects. The first, conceived and designed by students Michael McGrattan and Mansi Maheshwari, propose a new canal that links the southern terminus of Fort Point Channel and the Reserved Channel just north of West First Street. This area, currently a fuzzy boundary between the historic wood-frame building fabric of South Boston and a remnant industrial area, has been the focus of ad hoc development activity in the past ten years. Rather than blend the existing and new neighborhoods, McGrattan and Maheshwari's proposal converts the South Boston industrial area and waterfront into an independent island. This is a potent idea given the contentious relationship between South Boston's elected officials and the proponents of growth along the waterfront. Importantly, McGrattan and Maheshwari's proposal treats the canal as a new center rather than an edge. Their nostalgia-tinged renderings, bringing to mind a 1980s proposal to convert Fan Pier into an island as much as Schinkel's views of Berlin, make a convincing case that the canal would be the center of a humanely scaled neighborhood. Their approach suggests that the Good Urbanism tool kit won't work along the First Street Corridor because it's too far from both the waterfront and Broadway, South Boston's bustling commercial corridor.

Like the canal scenario, Jay Tsai and Miron Mawratil's proposal for a relocated South Station, and associated development, includes the same kind of initial bold move, substantiated by residual benefits. The southern half of Fort Point Channel is dammed and drained in order to create space for the relocation of the tracks that currently terminate at South Station. Since the tracks would now be below street level, new city fabric can connect the Fort Point neighborhood with the Leather District across both the channel and existing rail yard. The new station head house would be in a more dramatic location in the city: facing a series of parallel bridges where Boston Harbor meets Fort Point Channel. Tsai and Mawratil's scheme, if realized, would make arriving in Boston as dramatic as the view from Venice's train station.

I was on Mitchell's final reviews and saw Tsai and Mawratil's proposal at the same time that I was helping a public agency figure out how to incentivize the relocation of a large postal facility that needs to move in order to allow for the expansion of tracks at South Station. In order to broaden discussion and possible approaches, I wrote a blog post about Tsai and Mawratil's scheme and sent the link to public officials at several agencies that were involved with the discussions. As a result of the power of their proposal, state officials made a case to the real estate advisors of the U.S. Postal Service that a station expansion was not necessarily dependent on the sale of their parcel, despite the myriad engineering, environmental, and financing issues raised by the plan.

The best proposals from the Yale studios stick in the imagination of public officials precisely because they have been worked out to a relatively high level of architectural detail. The aerial and eye-level renderings convey the potential character of proposals as much as the intended density and scale. Jorge Silvetti and Rodolfo Machado called this approach "unprecedented realism," and acknowledged the role that their detailed two-point perspectives (drawn by hand in the 1980s and

1990s) played in legitimatizing their urban proposals. Their work and theory suggests that retroactive
inevitability is only possible if a proposal is fleshed
out enough to provoke a desire that transcends
problem-solving in the public officials and thought
leaders that make the key planning decisions.

Rather than consider the proposals generated by
urban design studios personal artistic statements,
schools should encourage student's in these studios to embrace the impact their work can have on
the future shape of cities like Boston. In the case
of Mitchell's studios, what the student schemes
inspire is an embrace of strongly conceived and
highly differentiated interventions rather than the
carefully feathered urbanism favored by professional practice. And if the planning strategies, if
not the specific design proposals, are adopted by
public officials as intriguing alternatives, so much
the better for the city and the academy.

Endnotes

1. Rodolfo Machado, *Floridian Follies,* 1986 (reprint-
ed in K. Michael Hayes, *Unprecedented Realism:
The Architecture of Machado and Silvetti*, Princeton
Architectural Press, 1995, pp. 14): "This rudimen-
tary technique is somehow based on the technique
of collage, inasmuch as it draws bits and pieces
from various heterogeneous systems of objects
and buildings. This causes an immediate theoretical problem, that of establishing the difference – or
the nature of the relation – between unprecedented
realism and surrealism. . . . the issue of tectonics
is of importance in establishing this difference. By
tectonics, we mean the weighty presence of reality,
of the obstinate corporeality of things that makes
the fusion of materialities an impossibility, even if
that fusion were buildable, that tangibility that will
inform the design with "an odor of reality" or with
the "possibility of happening," effects in which surrealism was not interested."

CarPark
Fort Point Channel

Alisa Hintz + John Farrace

While South Station marks a significant urban entry into the downtown, there are still a large number of commuters and visitors who enter the city by car. A large area to the east of Fort Point Channel is currently dedicated to surface parking. Development schemes for these areas typically include structured parking buried within individual parcels. This project chooses to celebrate the car using a strategy reminiscent of Louis Kahn's plans for Philadelphia, which also featured monumental parking towers ringing the downtown civic core.

Driving is turned into a positive urban experience as green pathways lead from the parking towers to the city. Long vistas to the downtown choreograph the procession of commuters who enter the city from long subgrade approaches. Like a parkway in the sky, the shifts within the parking towers animate the driving experience, and the pedestrian connections from car to the city proper are envisioned as event-filled promenades with visual connections to the waterfront, ample green spaces, and food carts lining the path to and from work.

Clustering the parking into a larger commuter hub would reduce city traffic so that new development in the South End is less restricted by the car.

ABOVE Section through Fort Point Channel.
OPPOSITE BOTTOM Rendered view from highway.

TOP Macro site plan.
BOTTOM Model.
OPPOSITE TOP Rendered view from project interior.
OPPOSITE BOTTOM Rendered view looking towards South
Station.

Stitching South Boston
Fort Point Channel

Eleanor Measham + Craig Rosman

The development of difference within an urban system is claimed by two different camps within architecture, those who see architecture as a language and those who see it as a product of functionalist analysis. Typology and code are the two tools that typically describe these approaches.

But linguistics and digital code are related. The team that initially represented opposing positions worked to establish rule sets which would constitute the kind of rich typological fabric that makes up many of Boston's most compelling urban neighborhoods and districts, from South Boston to Beacon Hill. One member of the team worked on orchestrating a complex area of flats, each adjusting its basic typology

to various factors, ranging from corner to inner-block parcel to the varying sections within the Fort Point Channel district. The other wrote algorithmic scripts that incrementally transformed the fabric by allowing for higher density micro-zoning as development works westward into the Central Business District and the Leather District.

The promise of both methodologies was that the urban fabric could be described systematically from building mass to detail without succumbing to the banality of repetition, and, though the study and analysis of the subject was not complete, the proof of concept was evident in the complex and resolved grain of the proposed fabric.

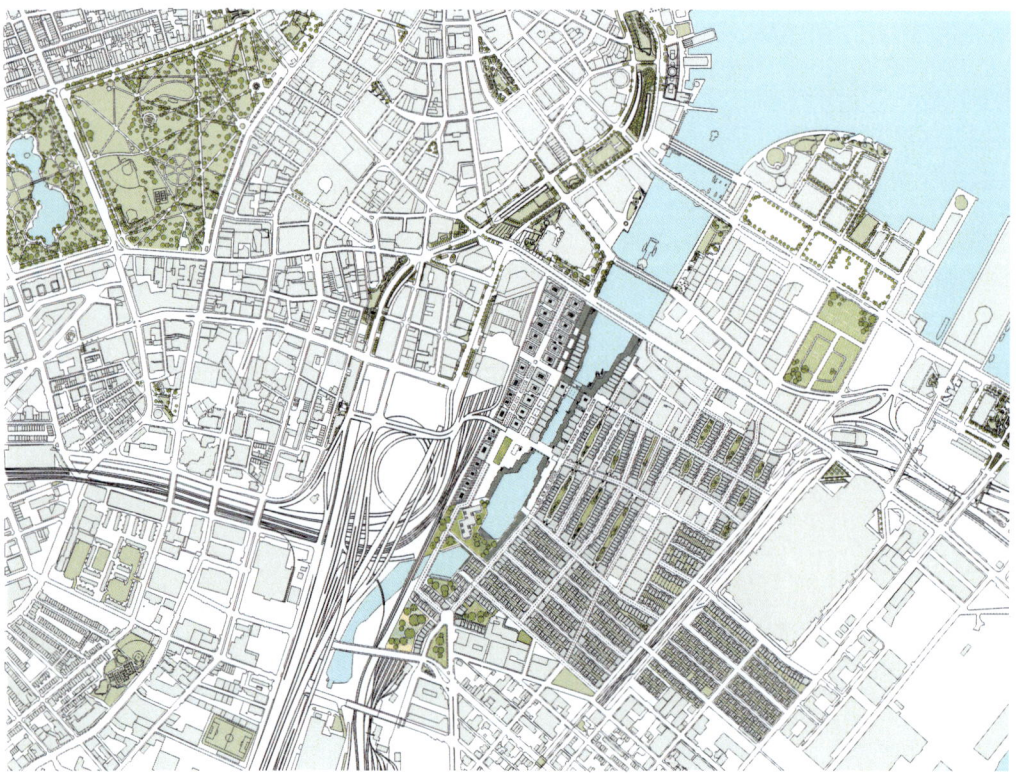

ABOVE Site plan showing proposed new district and public space framework.

OPPOSITE TOP Analysis of building clusters near T Stops.
MIDDLE LEFT Neighborhood fabric and public buildings.
MIDDLE RIGHT Buildings along major arterials.
BOTTOM LEFT Major buildings and institutions.
BOTTOM RIGHT Superposition of grids.

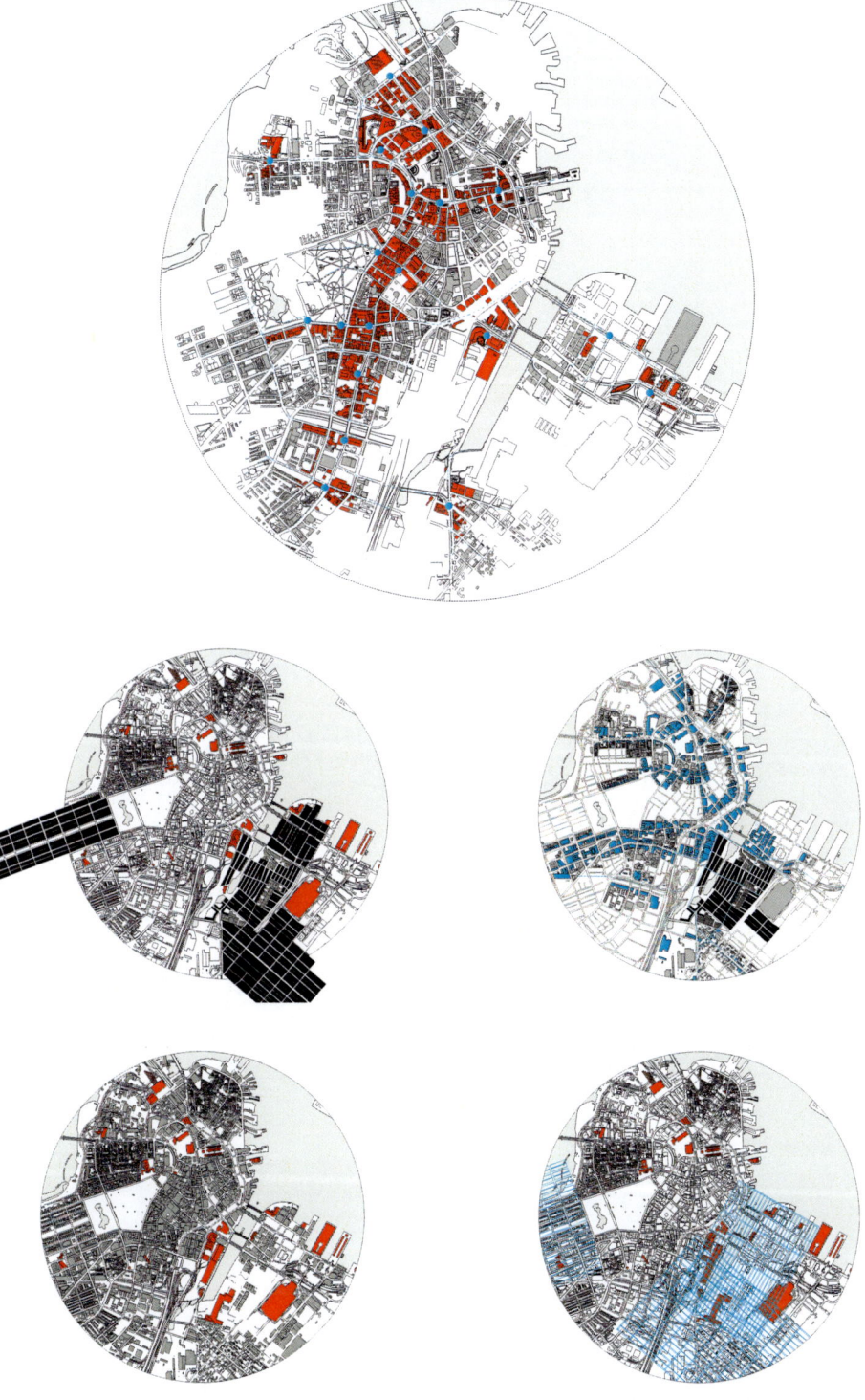

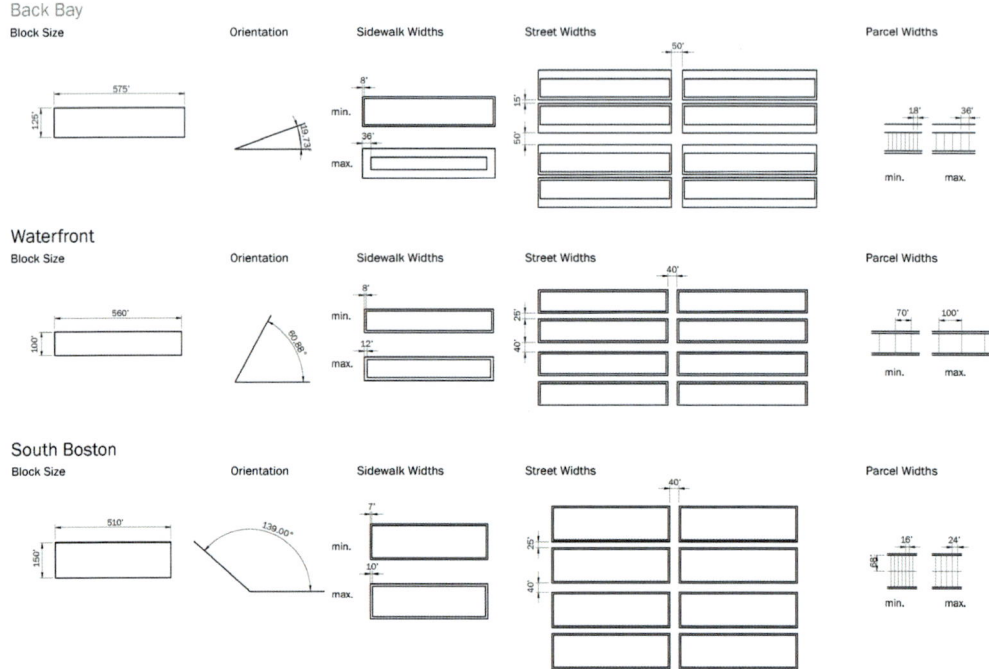

Back Bay

| Block Size | Orientation | Sidewalk Widths | Street Widths | Parcel Widths |

Waterfront

| Block Size | Orientation | Sidewalk Widths | Street Widths | Parcel Widths |

South Boston

| Block Size | Orientation | Sidewalk Widths | Street Widths | Parcel Widths |

TOP Analysis of Back Bay block structure.
BOTTOM View of proposed fabric at Fort Point Channel.

Boston Pattern: Row House Block Structure

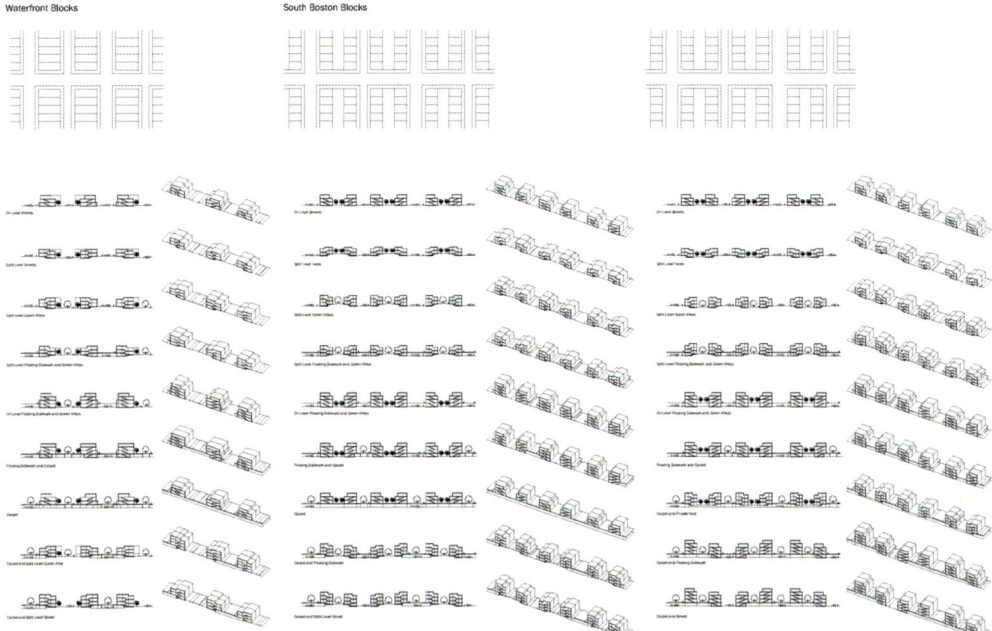

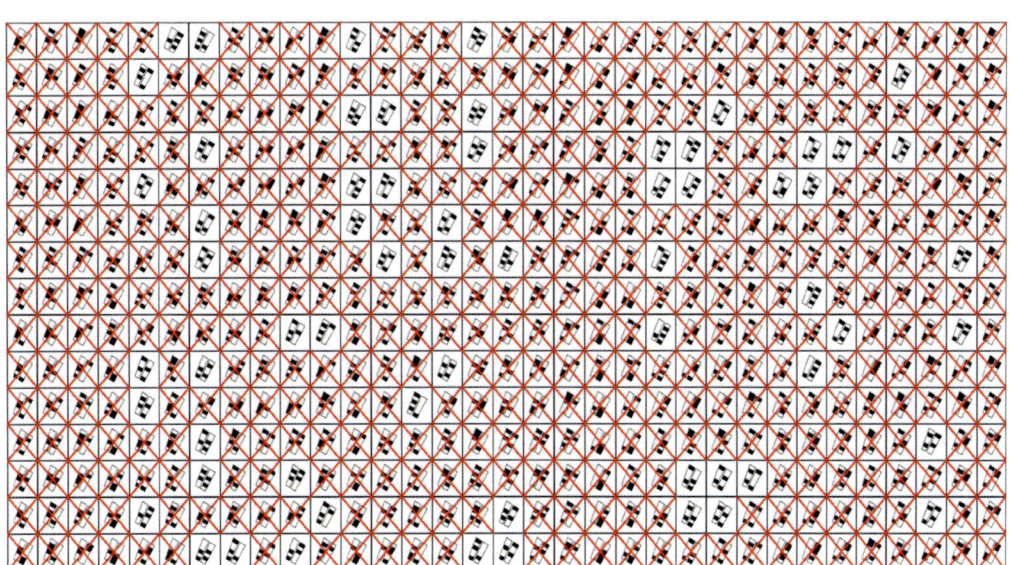

TOP Boston patterns. Row house structure.
BOTTOM Generative algorithimn of potential block structures in the
100-Acre parcel.

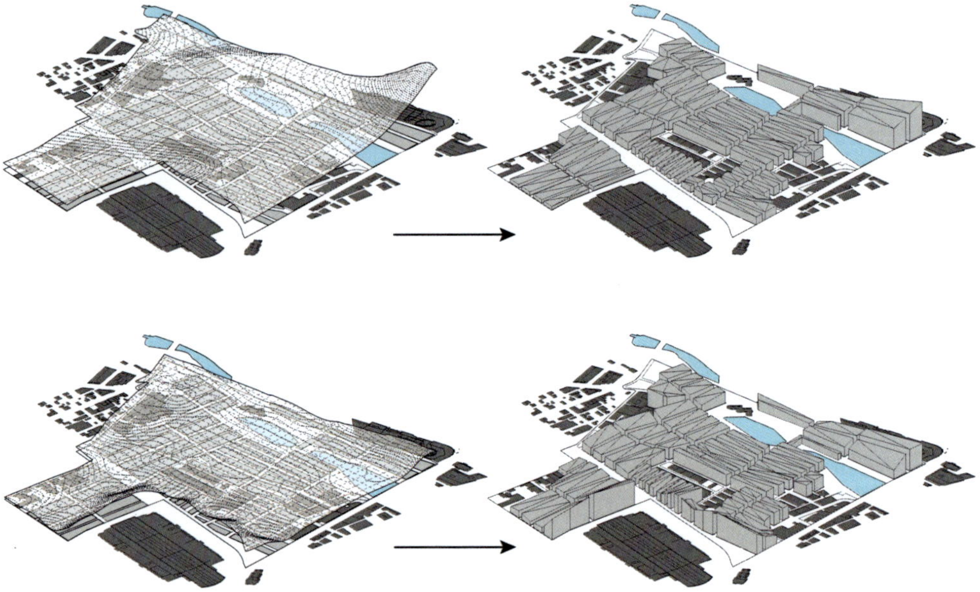

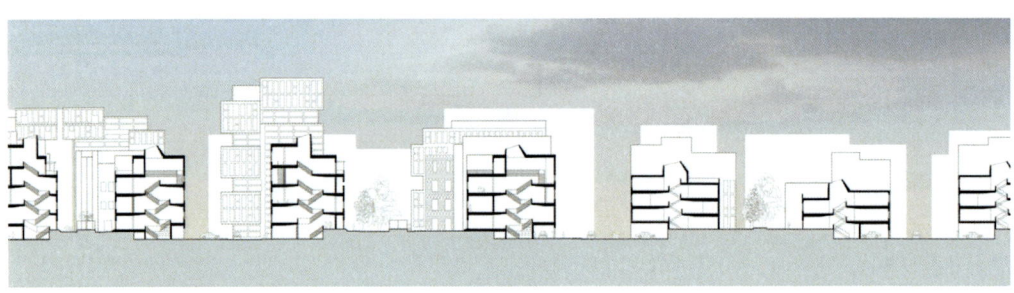

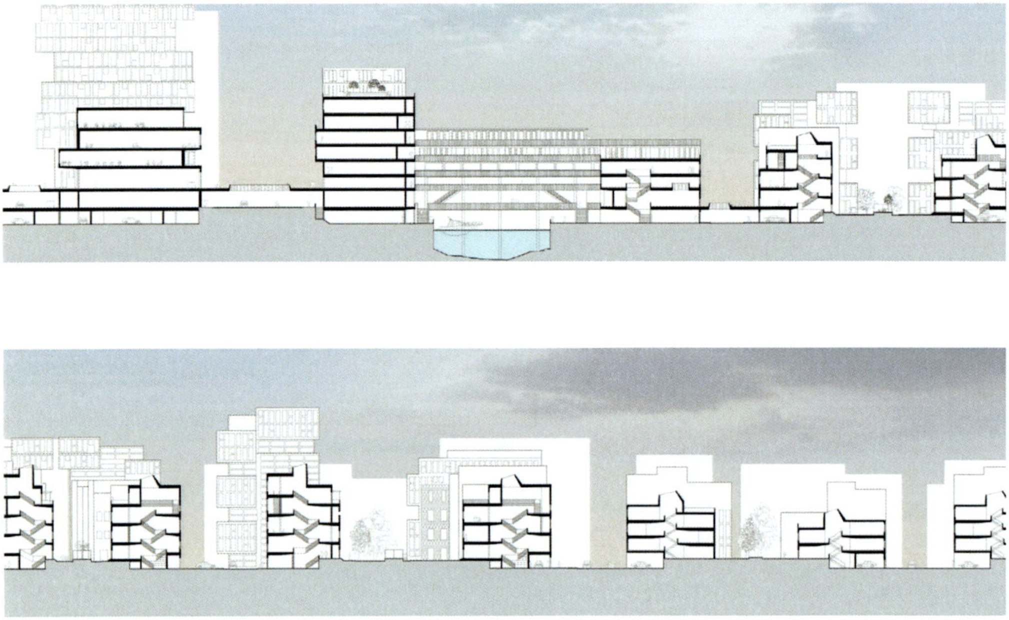

TOP Determination of density factors and zoning
envelope for 100-Acre parcel.
BOTTOM Sections through Fort Point Channel and
through the proposed neighborhood.

OPPOSITE TOP Study for townhouse variations as
determed by changing FAR values.
OPPOSITE BOTTOM Figure/ground drawing of
proposed finger blocks.

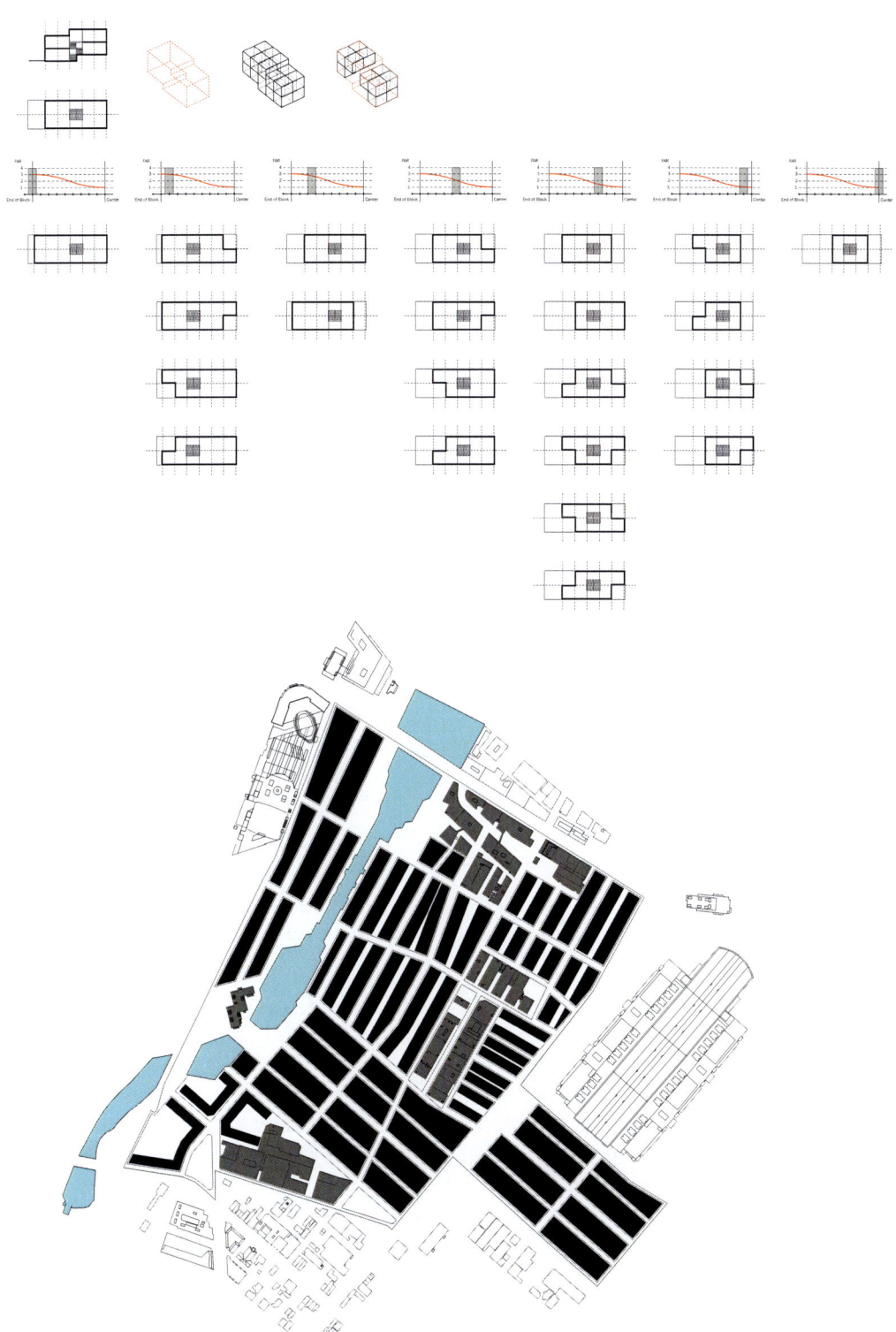

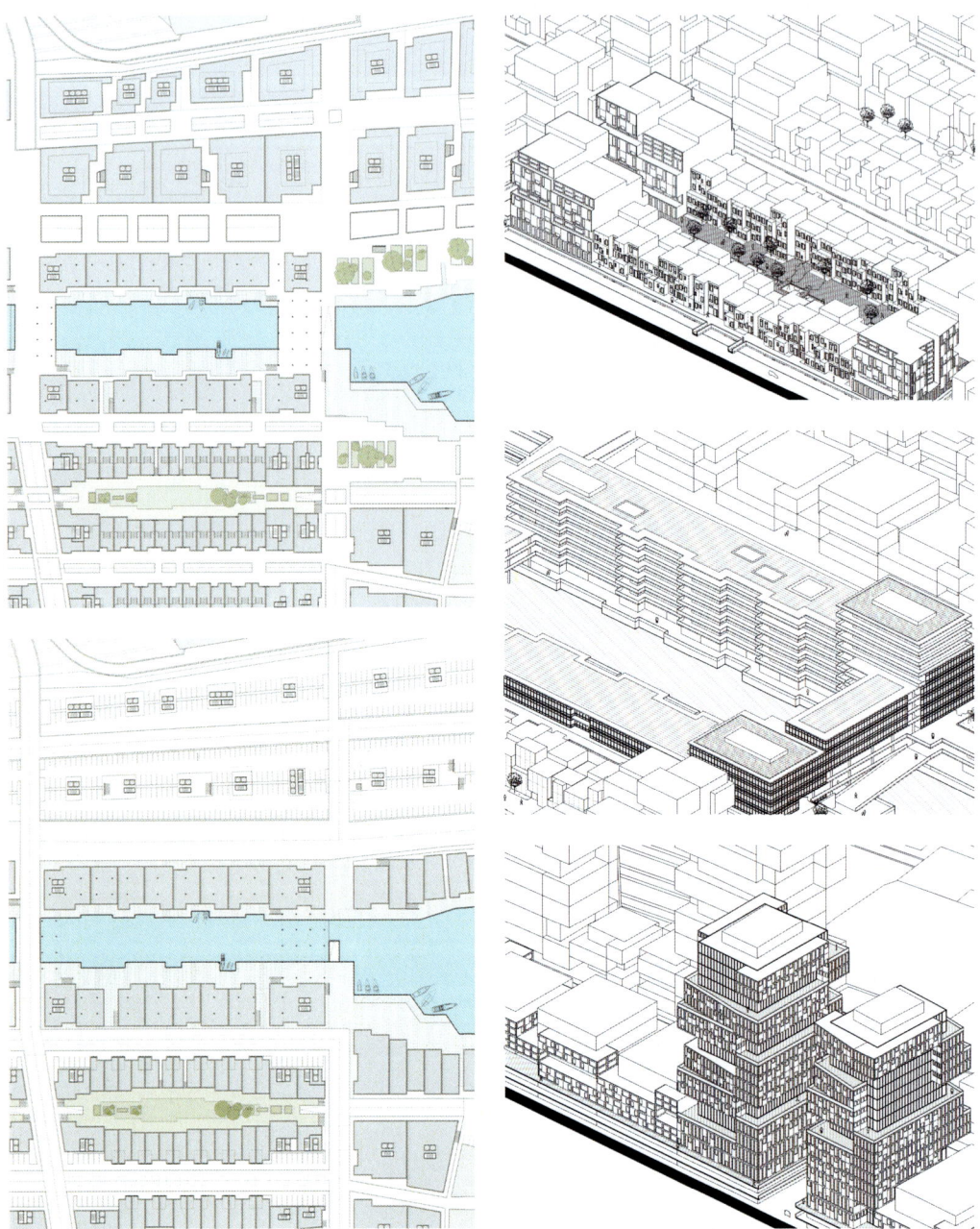

ABOVE LEFT Ground (bottom) and upper (top) floor plans.
ABOVE RIGHT Axonometric drawings of key moments.
OPPOSITE Corresponding rendered views within same key moments.

Extension to the Greenway
Fort Point Channel

James Petty + Yoojin Han

James Petty and Yoojin Han saw the site as the termination of the southern rail system, the end of the Rose Kennedy Greenway and the Emerald Necklace. If development were to happen around Fort Point Channel, the tangle of infrastructure currently inhibits meaningful connections to South Boston.

The major move shifts the train tracks east so that commuters exiting the train station have views straight up Fort Point Channel, making a more theatrical entrance to the city. Summer Street then acts as a dam to the Canal. By making the shift, a larger area of land becomes available in the Central Business District. Like other schemes, the fabric above the new tracks is envisioned as a mid-rise, flex office space. Passengers exit the tracks below ground and emerge through daylighted slots in the new fabric. The new fabric on the former rail yards culminates the Greenway. New urban courtyards include public spaces, restaurants, and public facilities which can be used by office workers, train passengers, and the residents of the Leather District.

The grain of the fabric runs predominantly north and south, but a second system takes advantage of the section of the site which drops a full story across the canal, allowing pedestrians to move unimpinged across the large urban mat, making for better urban connections. The eight-meter-wide building structures are based on the rhythm of the tracks and platforms below. Every other space between the buildings is either a path for pedestrian access to the buildings, or a light well illuminating the station below. Access to the station is achieved through various points and intervals throughout the new fabric. These direct paths into the city become part of the procession between the destination and the platform. They contain supporting businesses and shops for the users. Visitors to the city are greeted with the sky directly above them, leading them to the paths, which take them into the city.

The placement of the station at the head of the channel is an opportunity for high-rise development, giving the station an iconic marker that orients visitors. Part of the original channel is left intact to create a promenade for both the new urban fabric and the existing Boston Harborwalk.

While the scheme may have benefitted from a more conventional system of smaller cross streets and more defined blocks, the invention of shifting the rail tracks towards the channel would be feasible both as a phased construction idea and would resolve several current problems associated with the multi-tiered transportation tangle that currently limits connections in this part of the city.

OPPOSITE Photograph of the model.

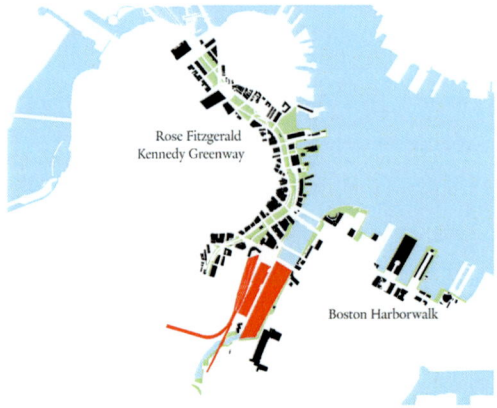

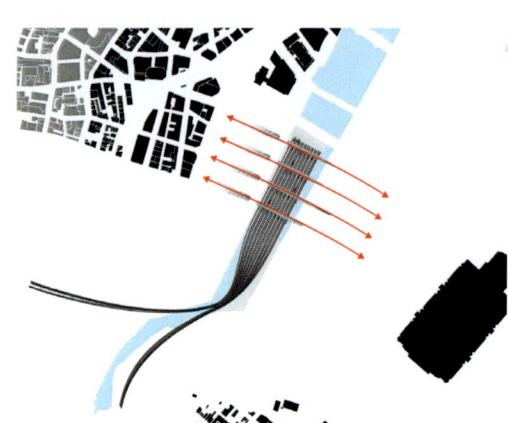

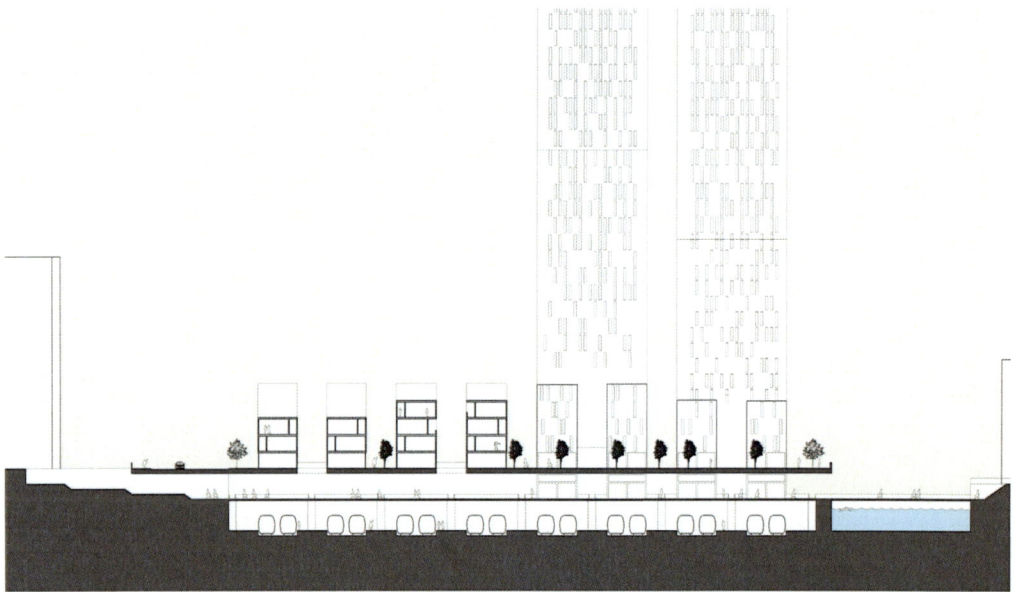

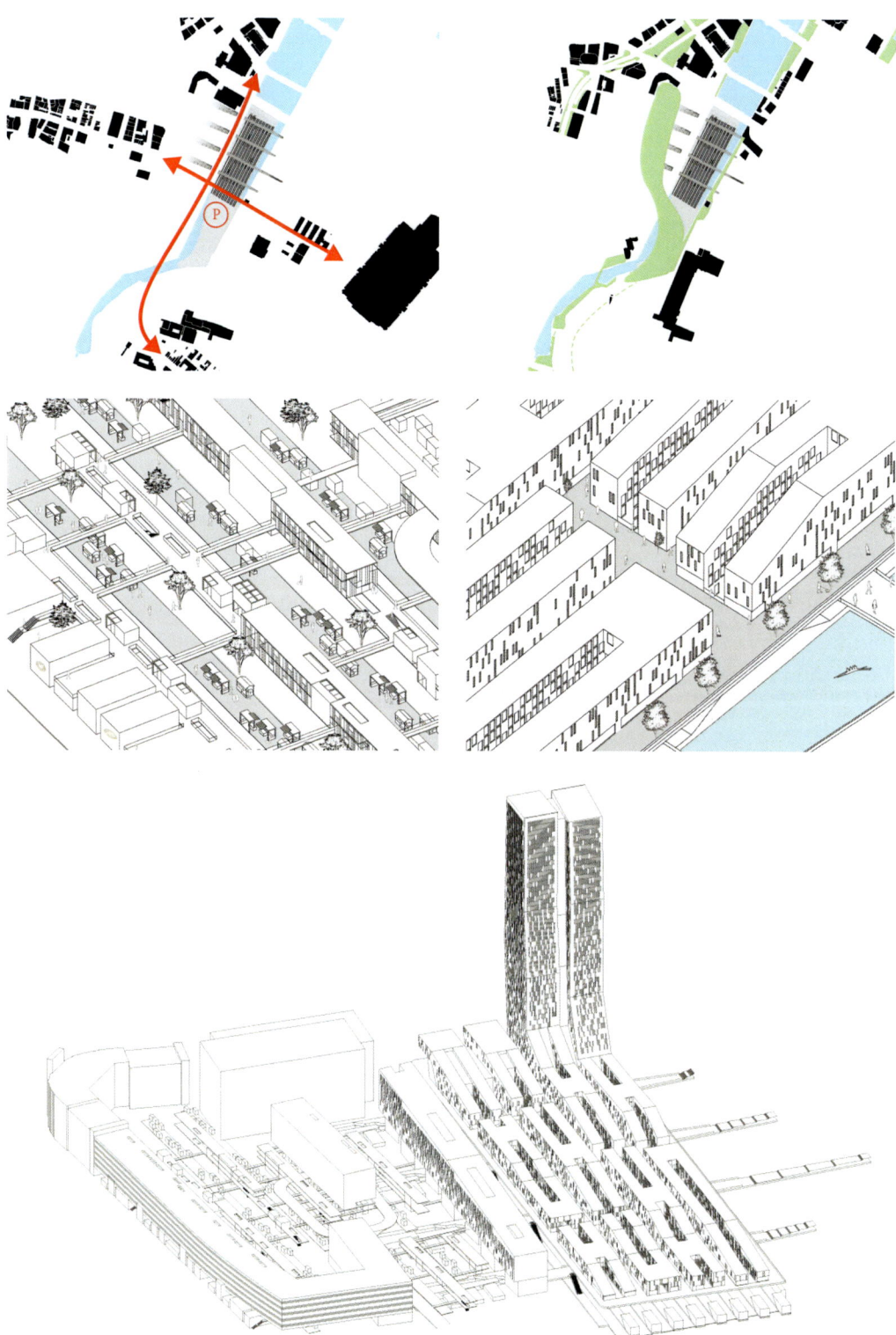

OPPOSITE TOP LEFT Figure/ground diagrams of proposed connections to the Rose Kennedy Greenway and Harborwalk.
OPPOSITE TOP RIGHT Proposed shift of rail yard over Fort Point Channel.
OPPOSITE MIDDLE Section cutting transversally through Fort Point Channel.
OPPOSITE BOTTOM Site plan.

TOP LEFT New road connections.
TOP RIGHT New extension of the Greenway though the site.
MIDDLE Axonometric drawings of new proposal.
BOTTOM Axonometric of the proposal, old South Station to the left and new station to the right.

TOP Renderings taken from Seaport Boulevard.
BOTTOM Rendering from the train tracks up to the new towers.
OPPOSITE TOP Aerial rendering of proposal.
OPPOSITE BOTTOM Perspective section through the former area
of the Channel.

This is a Hybrid
Fort Point Channel

Jie Tian + Mengyao Yu

Boston is a transportation hub connecting it to the Eastern coastline by rail in just under two hours, the eastern half of the United States by car in one day, and the rest of the world by air in one day. Historic Boston's center was a result of a nexus between water and road, but if we see that Logan Airport—equal in scale to the downtown CDB—is part of a new configuration of the city, then the bay itself is the new center between the airport, the CDB, and the Convention Center District. This new transportation hybrid of plane, ferry, taxi, hotel, convention center, and office space is the new core of a globally oriented, metropolitan Boston.

The proposal studies the potential links between these physical nodes and develops a temporary city for international business with two new hotel/residential centers on either side of Fort Point Channel and makes stronger intermodal connections between the currently disconnected transport infrastructures. The site is made up of a series of loops for high-speed international business, taxi and auto connections, and a pedestrian extension of the Greenway across the site.

The two new hotel/residential complexes act as cities within the city, home to a new population of international visitors and part-time residents who will take advantage of the banking industry, new research centers, and entertainment venues that make up the new metropolis.

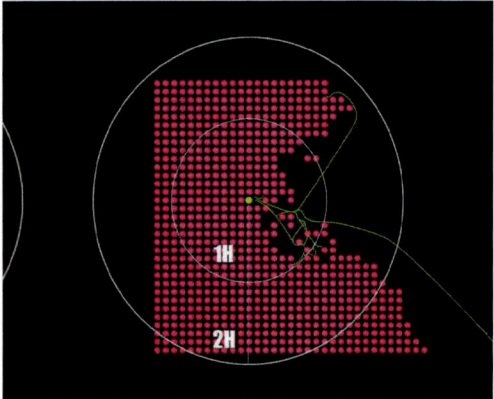

TOP Coastal areas linked to site by mass transit in one and two hours.
MIDDLE Area reached by automobile in three, six and twenty four hours.
BOTTOM Area reached by plane in six, twelve and eighteen hours.
OPPOSITE TOP Links from the site to the airport, ferry terminal and major highways.
OPPOSITE BOTTOM Vehicular connections through the site.

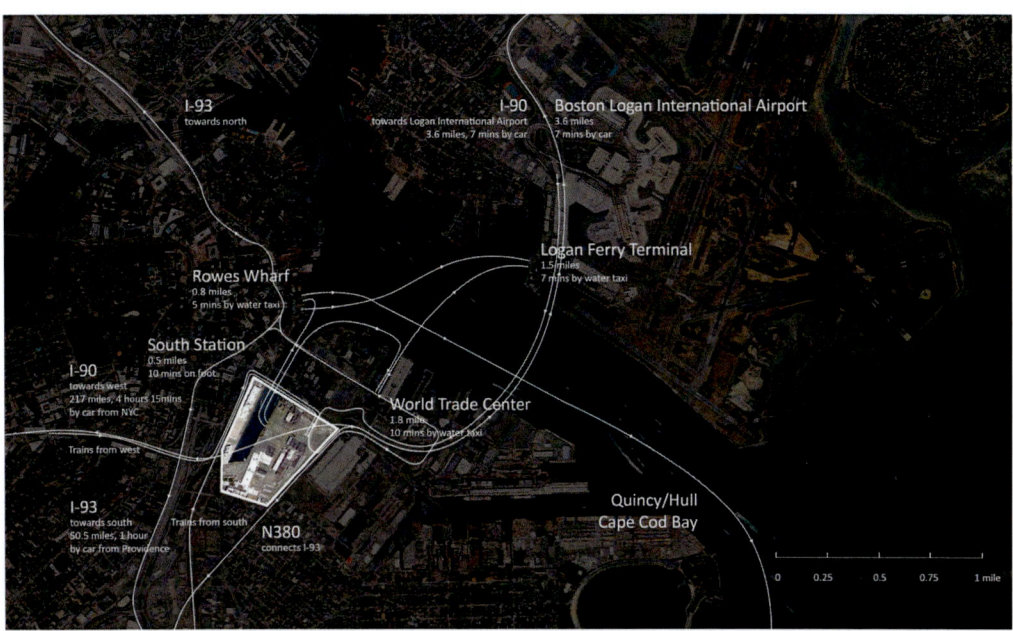

I-93
towards north

I-90
towards Logan International Airport
3.6 miles, 7 mins by car

Boston Logan International Airport
3.6 miles
7 mins by car

Logan Ferry Terminal
1.5 miles
7 mins by water taxi

Rowes Wharf
0.8 miles
5 mins by water taxi

South Station
0.5 miles
10 mins on foot

World Trade Center
1.8 miles
10 mins by water taxi

I-90
towards west
217 miles, 4 hours 15mins
by car from NYC

Trains from west

I-93
towards south
50.5 miles, 1 hour
by car from Providence

Trains from south

N380
connects I-93

Quincy/Hull
Cape Cod Bay

0   0.25   0.5   0.75   1 mile

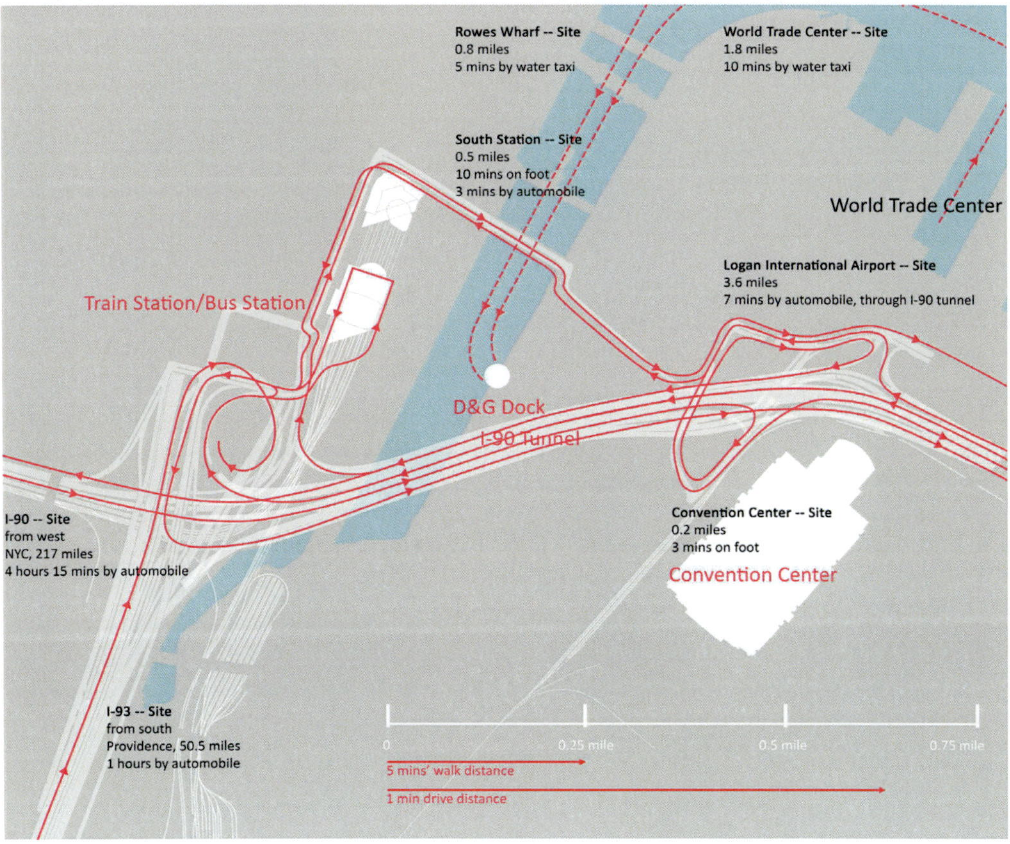

Rowes Wharf -- Site
0.8 miles
5 mins by water taxi

World Trade Center -- Site
1.8 miles
10 mins by water taxi

South Station -- Site
0.5 miles
10 mins on foot
3 mins by automobile

World Trade Center

Logan International Airport -- Site
3.6 miles
7 mins by automobile, through I-90 tunnel

Train Station/Bus Station

D&G Dock
I-90 Tunnel

I-90 -- Site
from west
NYC, 217 miles
4 hours 15 mins by automobile

Convention Center -- Site
0.2 miles
3 mins on foot

Convention Center

I-93 -- Site
from south
Providence, 50.5 miles
1 hours by automobile

0   0.25 mile   0.5 mile   0.75 mile

5 mins' walk distance

1 min drive distance

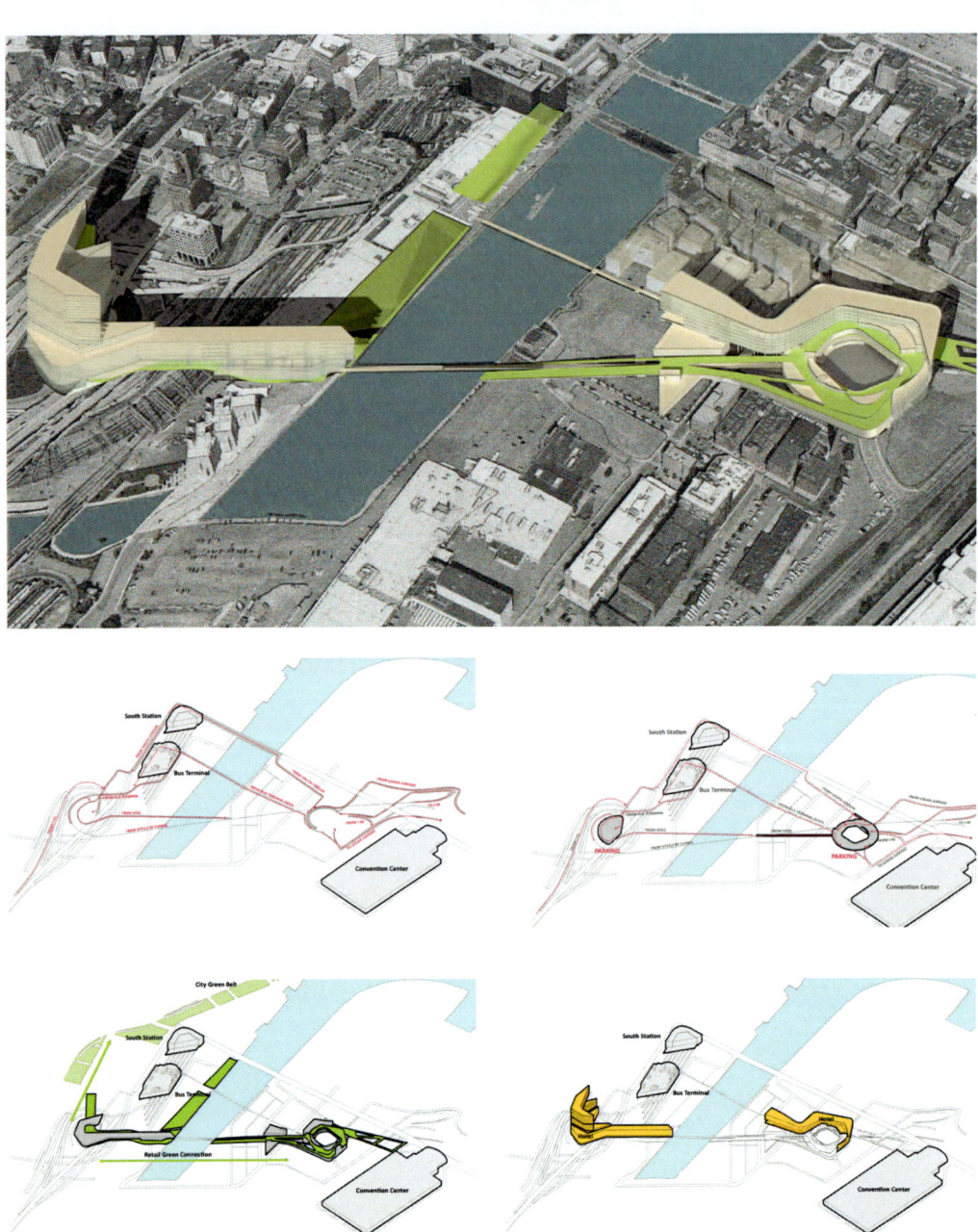

TOP Rendered aerial perspective of the two major sites and their
urban relationships.
MIDDLE Diagrams showing high-speed (left) and pedestrian (right)
access.
BOTTOM Diagrams showing pedestrian connectivity to context
(left) and vertical treatment of each site (right).

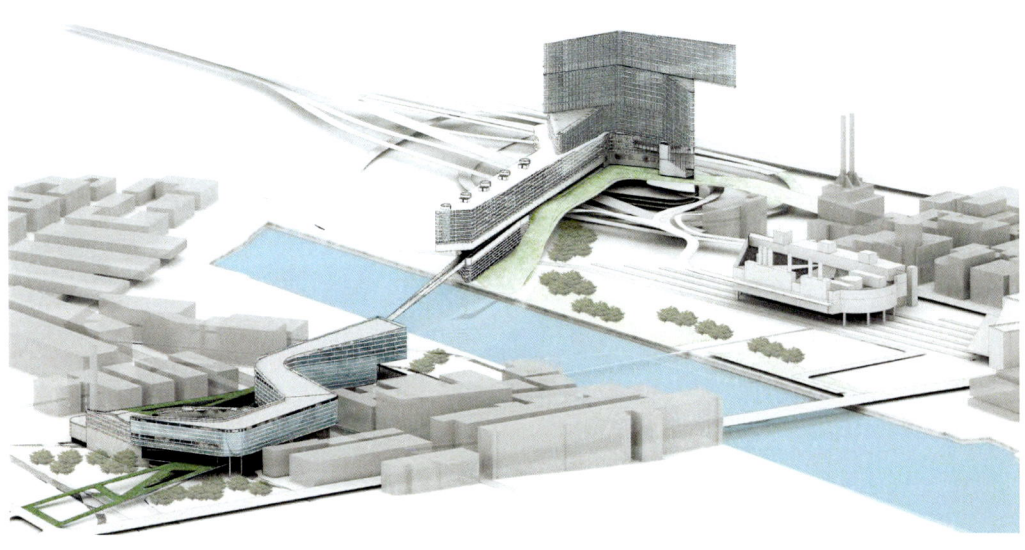

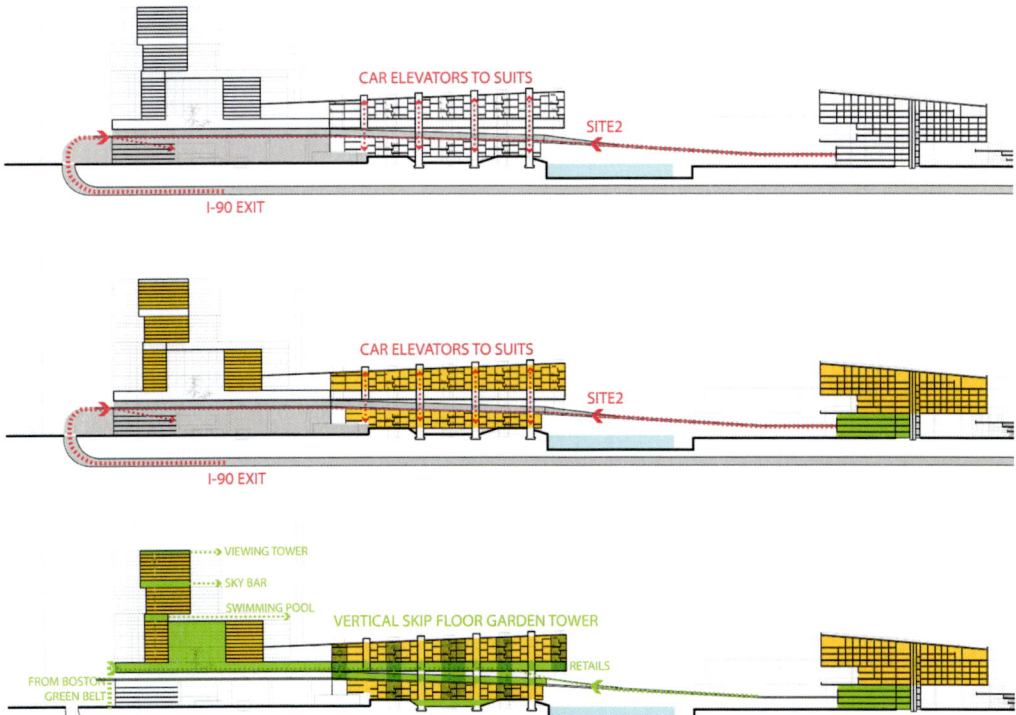

TOP Rendered perspective of Site 1 building.
MIDDLE TOP Diagram of vehicular access.
MIDDLE BOTTOM Diagram of driver access to building.
BOTTOM Diagram of vertical skip-floor gardens and building
program.

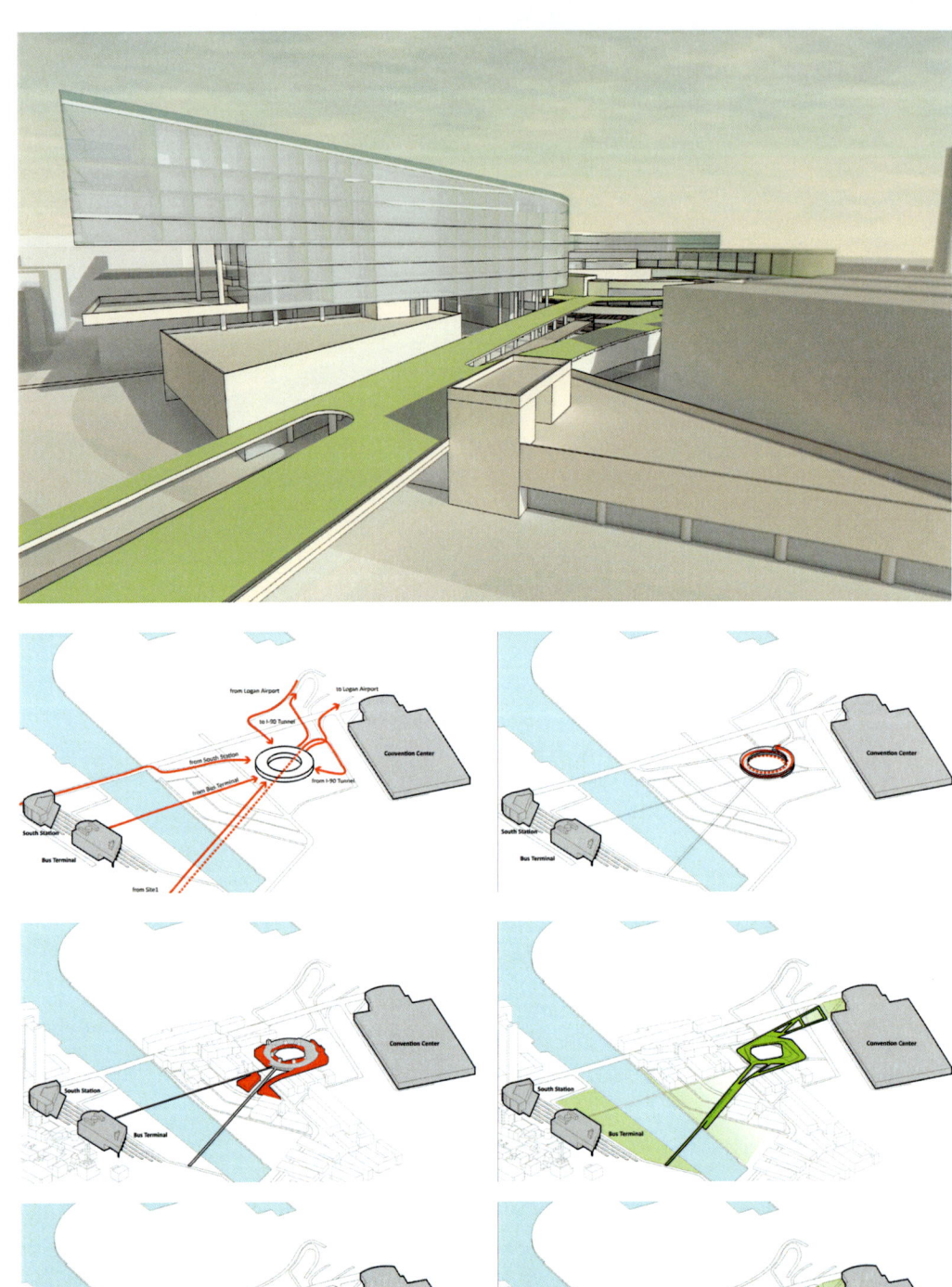

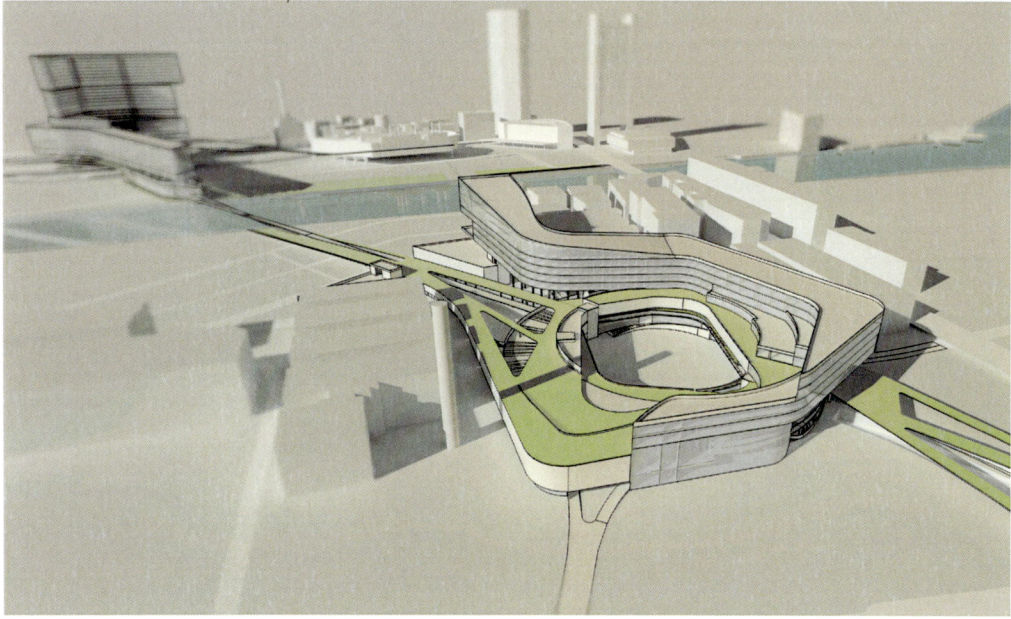

OPPOSITE TOP Rendered perspective of Site 2 building.
OPPOSITE MIDDLE TOP Diagram of vehicular access (left) and
parking (right).
OPPOSITE MIDDLE BOTTOM Diagram of commercial zoning
relationship to parking (left) and the new green connection (right).
OPPOSITE BOTTOM Diagram of retail zoning (left) and hotel
(right) connection to new green spaces.

TOP Rendered perspective of one hotel with South Station in the
foreground.
BOTTOM Rendered perspective looking west across Fort Point
Channel.

Super Courts
Fort Point Channel

Matthew Rauch + Hochung Kim

Recent developments changed the scale of the South End. While older industrial buildings like the Gillette factory and the dock-front warehouses are also of large scale, the typologies near Fort Point Channel conformed to a traditional block structure. Beginning with the Convention Center, the area's new fabric consists of stand-alone buildings with limited street connections. The planned extension of the Convention Center could further exacerbate what some see as a problem—single-tenant, single-use buildings which lack the flexibility of the older fabric.

Matthew Rauch and Hochung Kim see this new scale as an opportunity. With a few impactful interventions they create a new urban fabric of big set pieces linking a new South Station Plaza to the Gillette facilities, to the southern addition to the Convention Center, to a new large-scale hotel with a courtyard, and finally to the Seaport World Trade Center. The chain of big building forms are cities within the city. Each large building, in turn, is also a city onto itself. At each scale, from greater Boston to the new Convention Center Complex, each enclave contains elements of a complete urbanism—housing, market, meeting spaces, retail, and offices.

The big scale completes an urban idea in one phase but allows smaller "pilot fish" to feed off and complement the financial "whales" of the urban fabric. The team envisioned the surrounding fabric to be developed by smaller players, giving texture to the big scale, and weaving though the larger mega-complex.

The analysis shows that most of this land area, infill from the industrial era of the city, is vulnerable to flooding. Tidal rise and recent storm surges, already cause problems around the Convention Center. Water infiltration is a major factor in new development in this area. The scheme's bigger moves essentially make islands within the floodplain. The drawings show how the design might account for storm surge and flooding. The project, despite its enormous scale, has a flexible fabric that can handle surges and still function as a lively urbanism.

ABOVE Site plan.

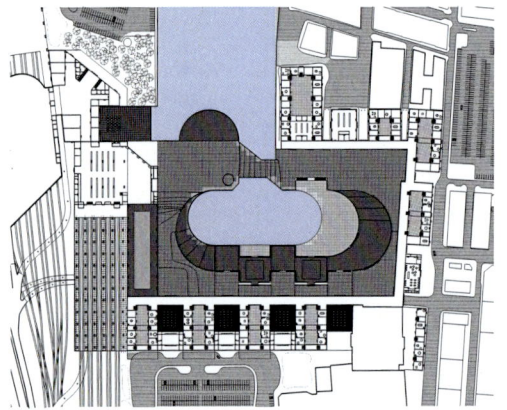
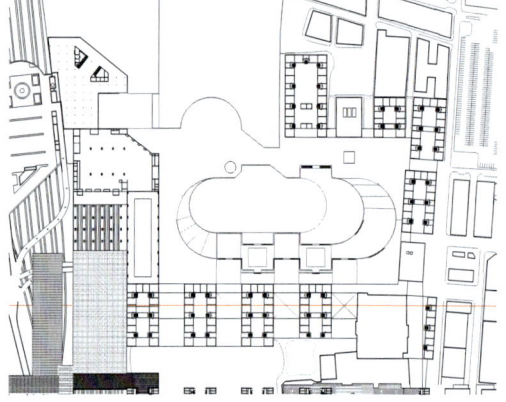

TOP Perspective looking north showing, from left to right, South
Station and the new plaza, the Gillette complex, a new business
courtyard, the extension to the couryard and then, north, a new
courtyard hotel and the Seaport World Trade Center.
BOTTOM Ground (left) and upper (right) plans of South Station
Plaza.

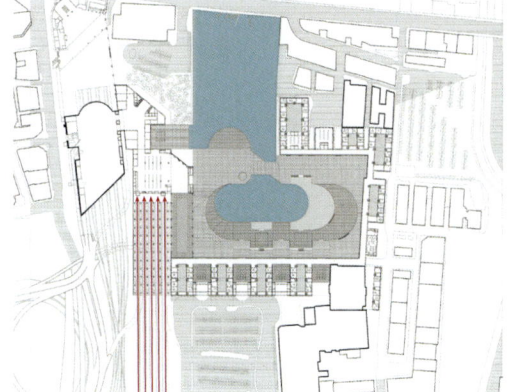

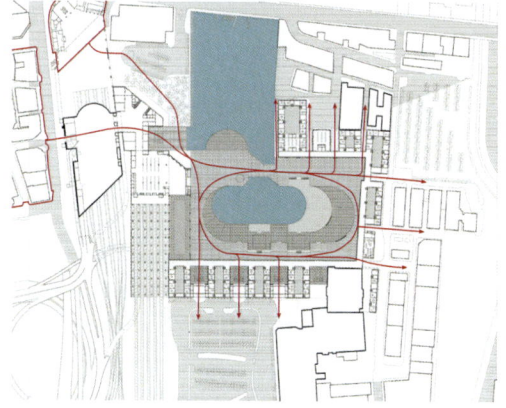

BOTTOM LEFT Rail transit lines leading into South Station.
BOTTOM RIGHT Pedestrain connections from South Station
across the plaza.

ABOVE AND OPPOSITE Rendered simulation of tidal flooding and
its effect on the new proposal.

TOP Perspective looking northeast across the plaza.
BOTTOM View across the main plaza.
OPPOSITE Rendered composite of aerial view from South Boston.

Channel District
Fort Point Channel

Mengran Li + Grant Scott

These schemes represent two variations on the same basic premise. Rather than trying to connect east-west across the Channel, the team considered that the area running from Summer Street to West 4th Street between the Convention Center and the Channel is an area roughly equivalent to Back Bay. A major urban street forms the central spine through this district. Existing early signs of commercial development make it a logical connector running north-south through the district, with the historic Fort Point Channel buildings to the north making one anchor and the commercial end of West 4th the southern termination of the street.

Grant Scott's scheme develops green bands to connect across the Channel which simultaneously break the scale of the Channel into a "blue" commons between new higher density developments around the perimeter. To the east, against the Convention Center, he proposes larger commercial building types to mediate the scale of the Convention Center to the new mid-density core of the district. The variations in types allows for a smooth transition between the currently disparate scales on the site in order to retain a mix of housing stock that mimics the historic residential fabric of South Boston and to accommodate mixed-use development required for a more robust commercial district.

Mengran Li works the west side of the scheme by extending the green bands across the Chanel and through the rail line in order to connect the Leather District and Chinatown into the new Fort Point District. Like several other schemes, the complex sections for this area require vertical connections from Atlantic Avenue over the tracks. Two towers on Atlantic act as gateways to a deck built over the tracks and designated as a commercial and business district for commuters. The waterfront properties then have a complex mix of public and private tiers facing the water. Though slightly hidden in the urban scheme, this area could potentially be developed as a mega-project suitable to a larger commercial tenant or financial office complex with convenient access to train and subway and an internalized park system for the tenants.

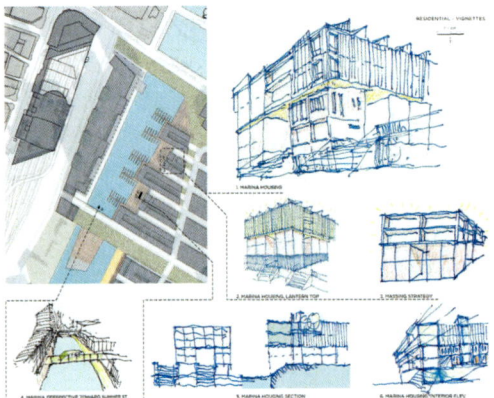
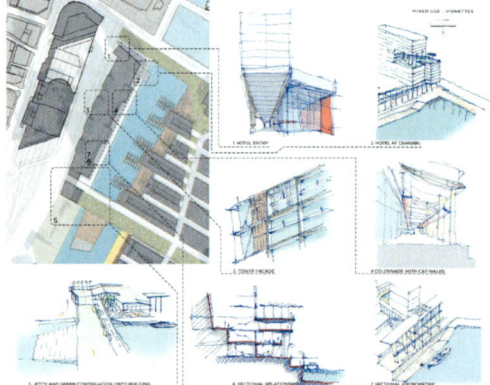

ABOVE Sketches of building massing and facades for Fort Point. Channel district. Grant Scott.

TOP Massing model of the district looking towards downtown.
BOTTOM High-rise study at South Station site.

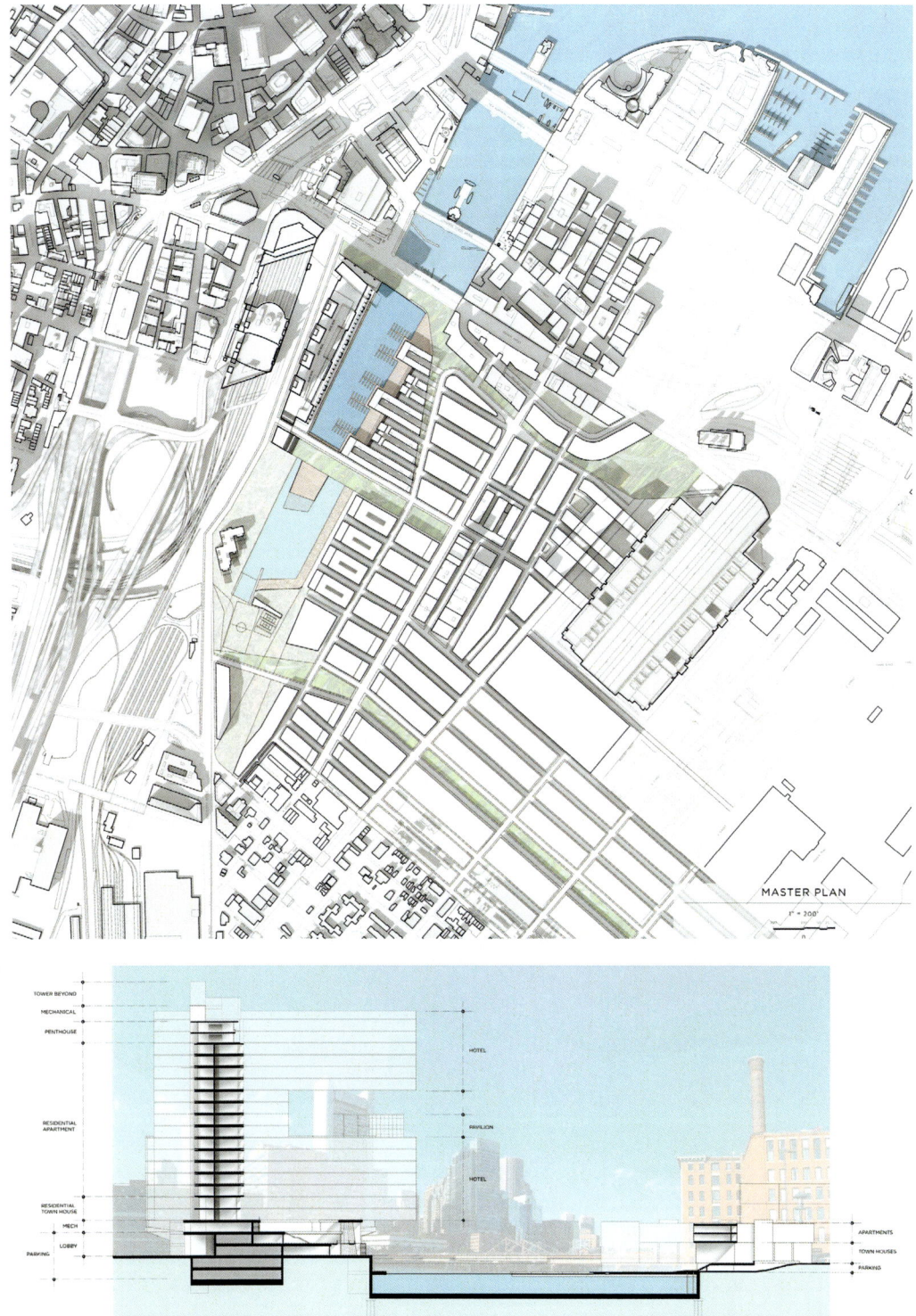

OPPOSITE Diagrams for attractor buildings, site zoning strategy, green connectrions, street spine, combined green and commercial spaces, block layout designated by use, area for second phase development, an expanded South Boston.
TOP Site plan.
BOTTOM Section through the Channel.

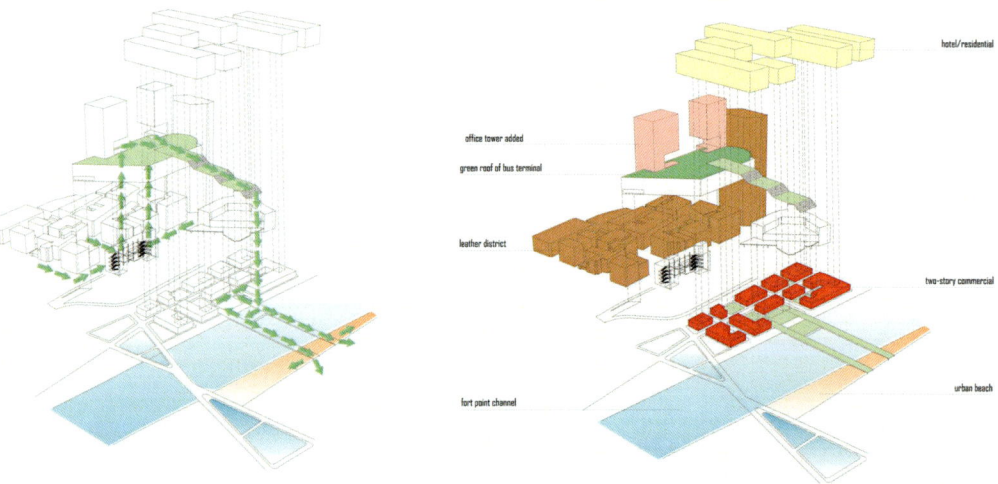

TOP AND MIDDLE Figure-ground diagrams describing new connections
between adjacent neighborhoods and new proposal.
BOTTOM Axonometric circulation (left) and program (right) diagrams.
OPPOSITE TOP Site plan.
OPPOSITE BOTTOM Ground floor plan.

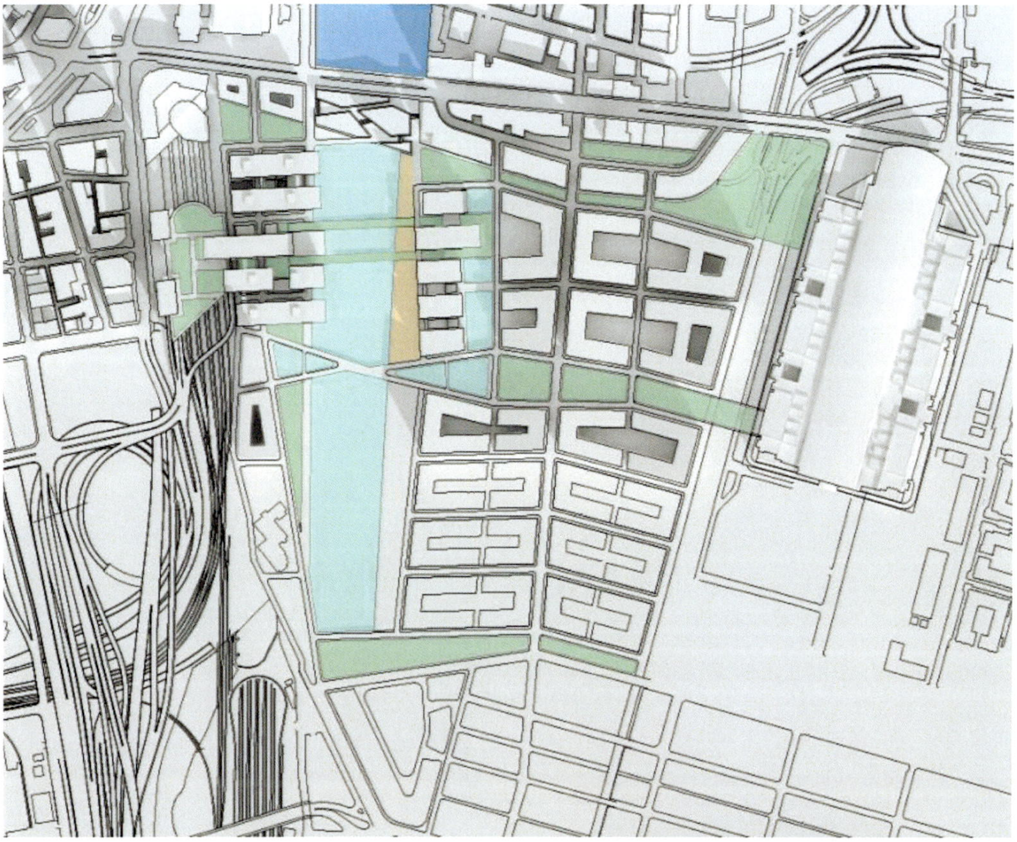

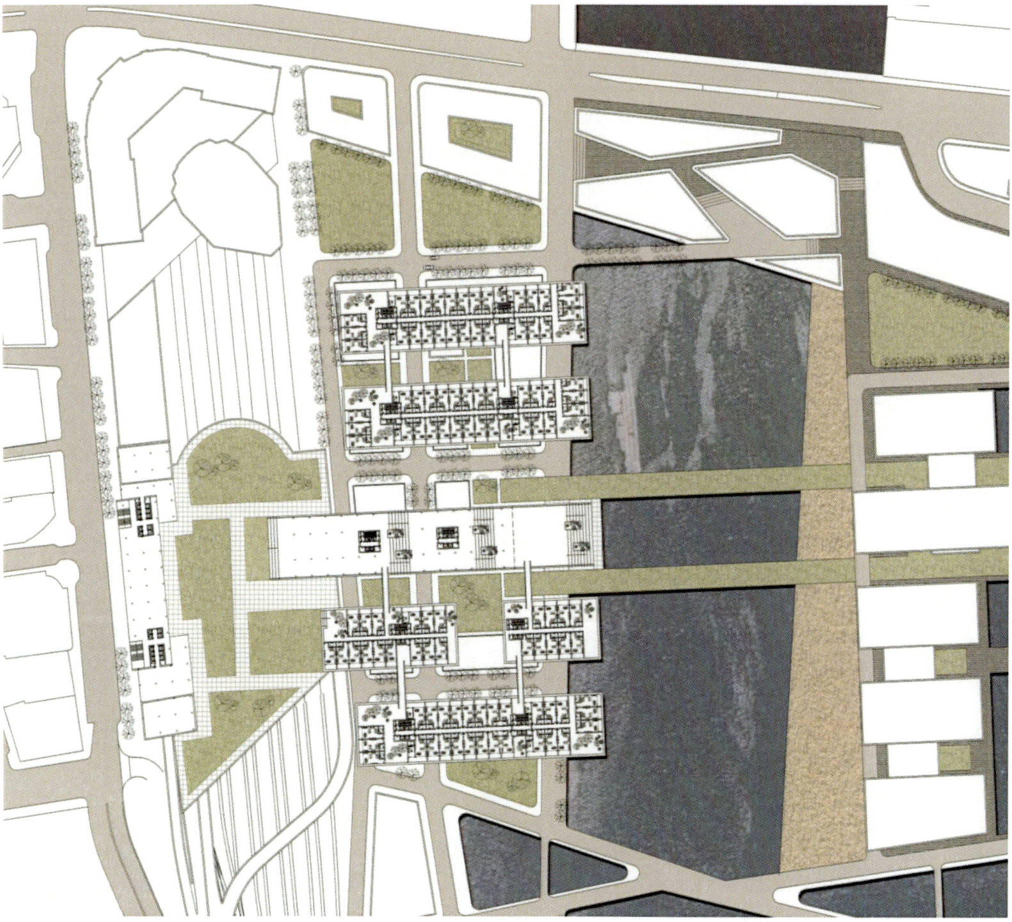

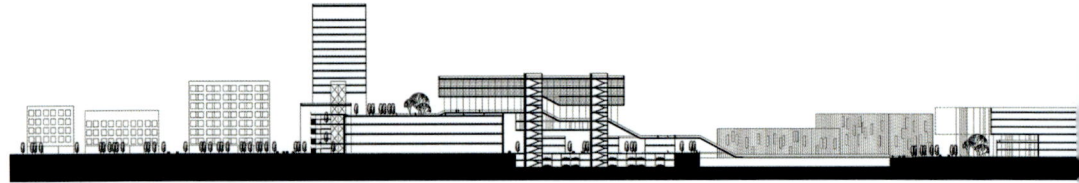

TOP Massing study at Fort Point Channel.
MIDDLE Terrace level at area above rail yards.
BOTTOM Section through the Channel.

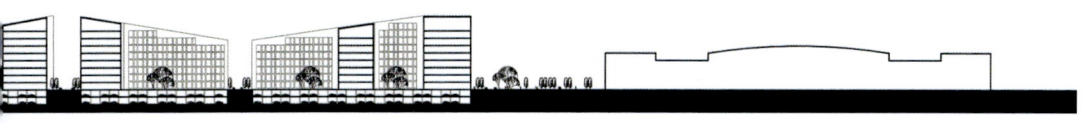

TOP LEFT AND RIGHT Massing at area west of the Channel.
MIDDLE View through upper level above the tracks looking west
towards the Leather District.

Very Big Data
Fort Point Channel

Swarnhab Ghosh

Because of the depth and richness of its knowledge infrastructure, the Boston metropolitan area witnessed a steady growth in the number of technology start-ups in the late-1990s and the early 2000s (It has since given up its title of the second largest "start-up ecosystem" in the country). This growth motivated the creation of the Innovation District initiative by former Mayor Thomas Menino at the turn of the century.

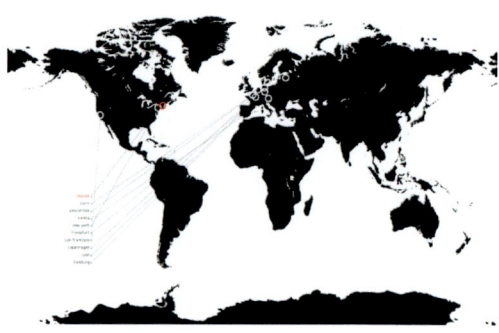

This proposal builds upon this legacy and projects an alternative future for South Boston and the Fort Point Channel District. Taking lessons from the monolithic architecture that has come to define data centers, this Information Technology (IT) installation seeks to provide office space and network infrastructure for Boston's fledgling Innovation District in one massive building. With the capacity to house nearly all of the proposed Innovation District, the project also accommodates on-site data centers—the lifeblood of large-scale computation—in the integrated, water-cooled structure that spans the Fort Point Channel, and is resistant to the most pessimistic long-term flood projections, connecting South Station and the Boston Convention Center.

2012

Water from the Channel will be used to cool the servers and the resultant hot outflow will be harvested, filtered, and returned to the Channel to create a wetland machine, further purifying and cooling water before it returns to the harbor. This wetland—warm, moist, and lush, and punctuated with intermittent puffs of steam—will function as a park with its own exotic microclimate, extending the Boston Harborwalk into the Fort Point Channel. By operating as architecture, ecology, and infrastructure, this project visualizes the spatial implications of ubiquitous cloud computing—a diffuse, abstract, and omnipresent contemporary phenomenon whose incomprehensible spatio-temporalities belie its sheer physical monumentality. By flattening the distance between its workers and its vast infrastructure, this project proposes a radical yet resilient reconfiguration (and aggregation) of the spaces that make up the IT sector and the systems that attend to it.

2092

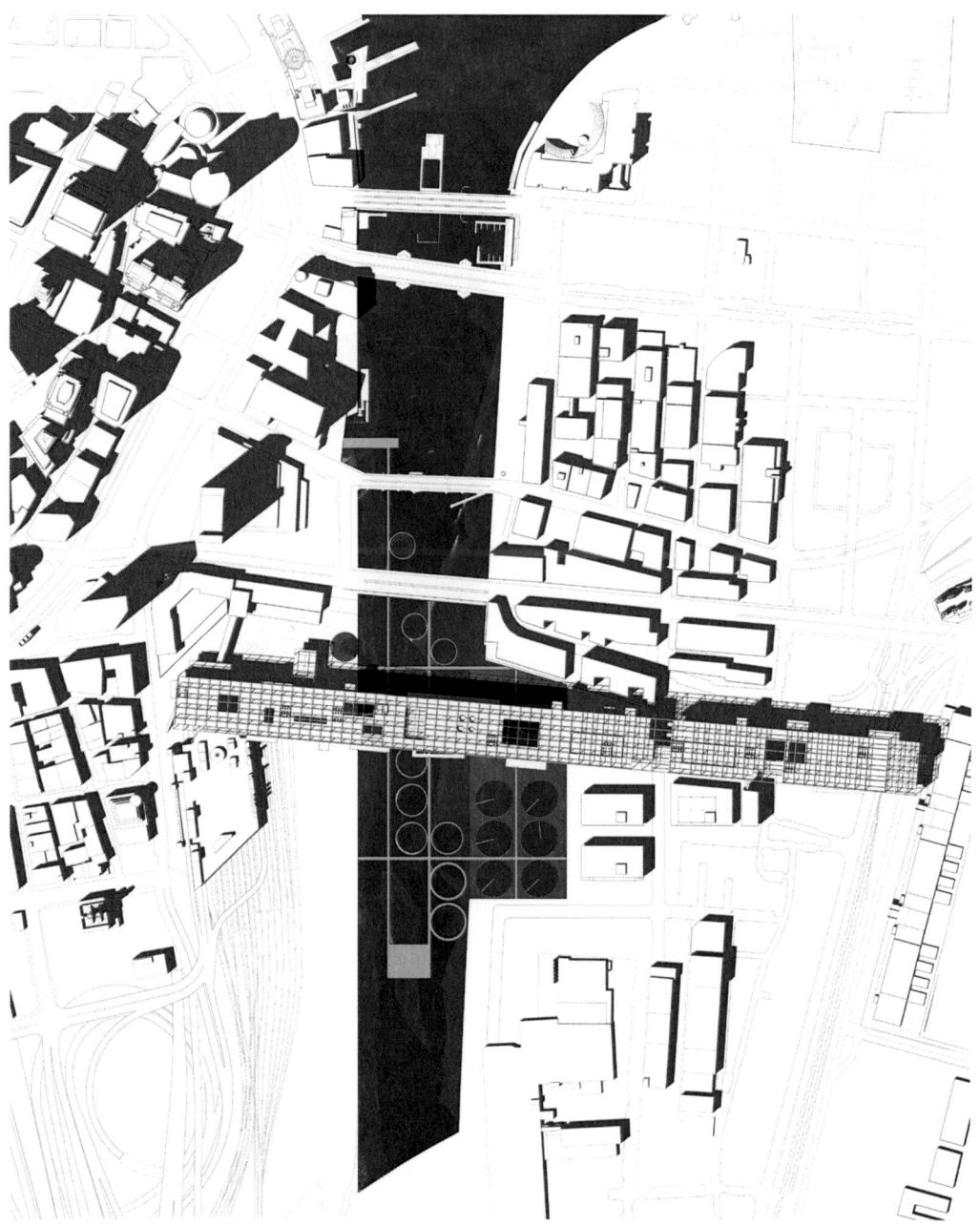

OPPOSITE Start-up diagram, flooding diagrams.
ABOVE Site plan.

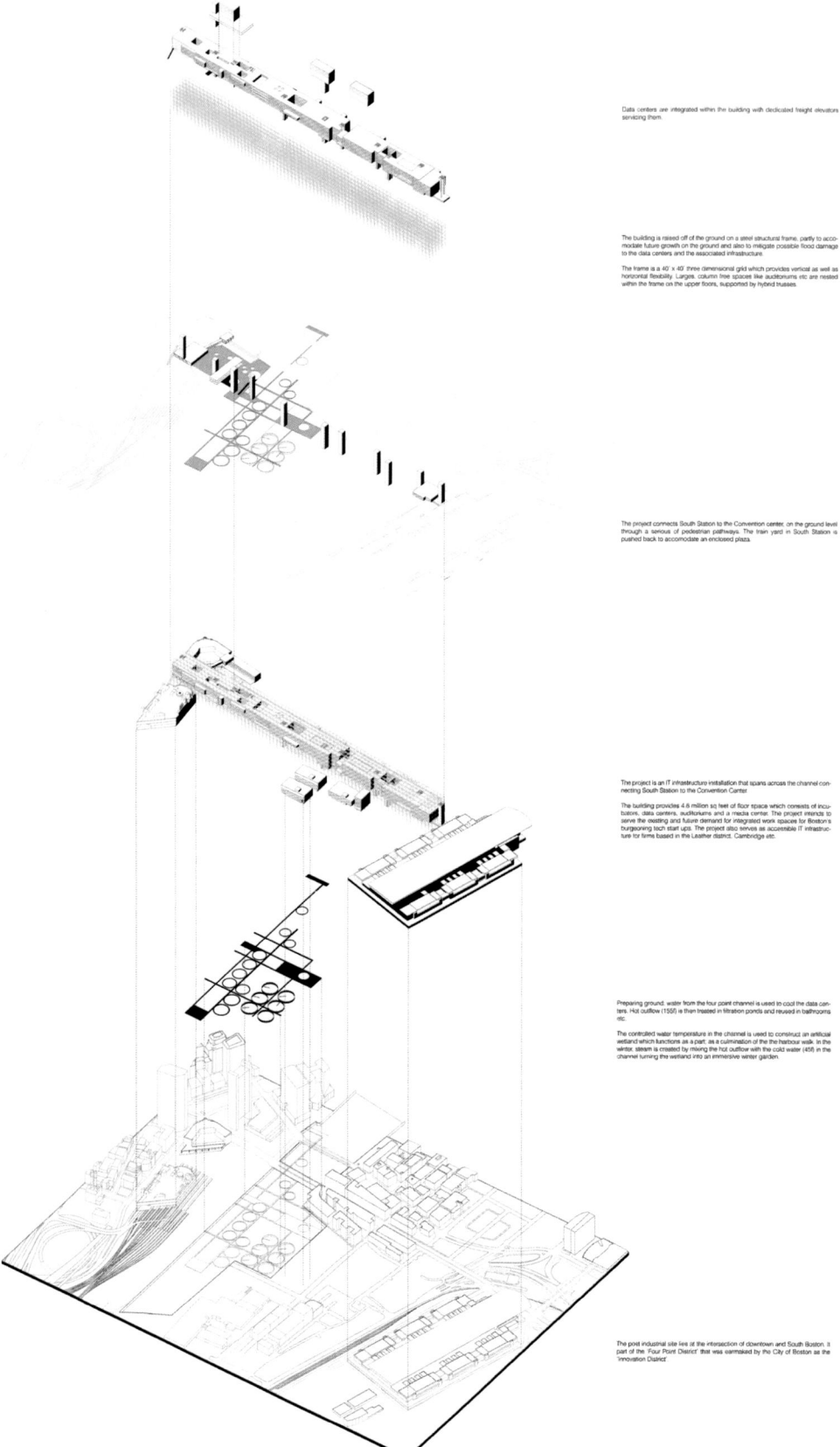

Data centers are integrated within the building with dedicated freight elevators servicing them.

The building is raised off of the ground on a steel structural frame, partly to accommodate future growth on the ground and also to mitigate possible flood damage to the data centers and the associated infrastructure.

The frame is a 40' x 40' three dimensional grid which provides vertical as well as horizontal flexibility. Larger, column free spaces like auditoriums etc are nested within the frame on the upper floors, supported by hybrid trusses.

The project connects South Station to the Convention center on the ground level through a serious of pedestrian pathways. The train yard in South Station is pushed back to accomodate an enclosed plaza.

The project is an IT infrastructure installation that spans across the channel connecting South Station to the Convention Center.

The building provides 4.8 million sq feet of floor space which consists of incubators, data centers, auditoriums and a media center. The project intends to serve the existing and future demand for integrated work spaces for Boston's burgeoning tech start ups. The project also serves as accessible IT infrastructure for firms based in the Leather district, Cambridge etc.

Preparing ground, water from the four point channel is used to cool the data centers. Hot outflow (150f) is then treated in filtration ponds and reused in bathrooms etc.

The controlled water temperature in the channel is used to construct an artificial wetland which functions as a part, as a culmination of the the harbour walk. In the winter, steam is created by mixing the hot outflow with the cold water (40f) in the channel turning the wetland into an immersive winter garden.

The post industrial site lies at the intersection of downtown and South Boston. It is part of the 'Four Point District' that was earmarked by the City of Boston as the 'Innovation District'.

ABOVE AND OPPOSITE Exploded and sectional axonometrics.

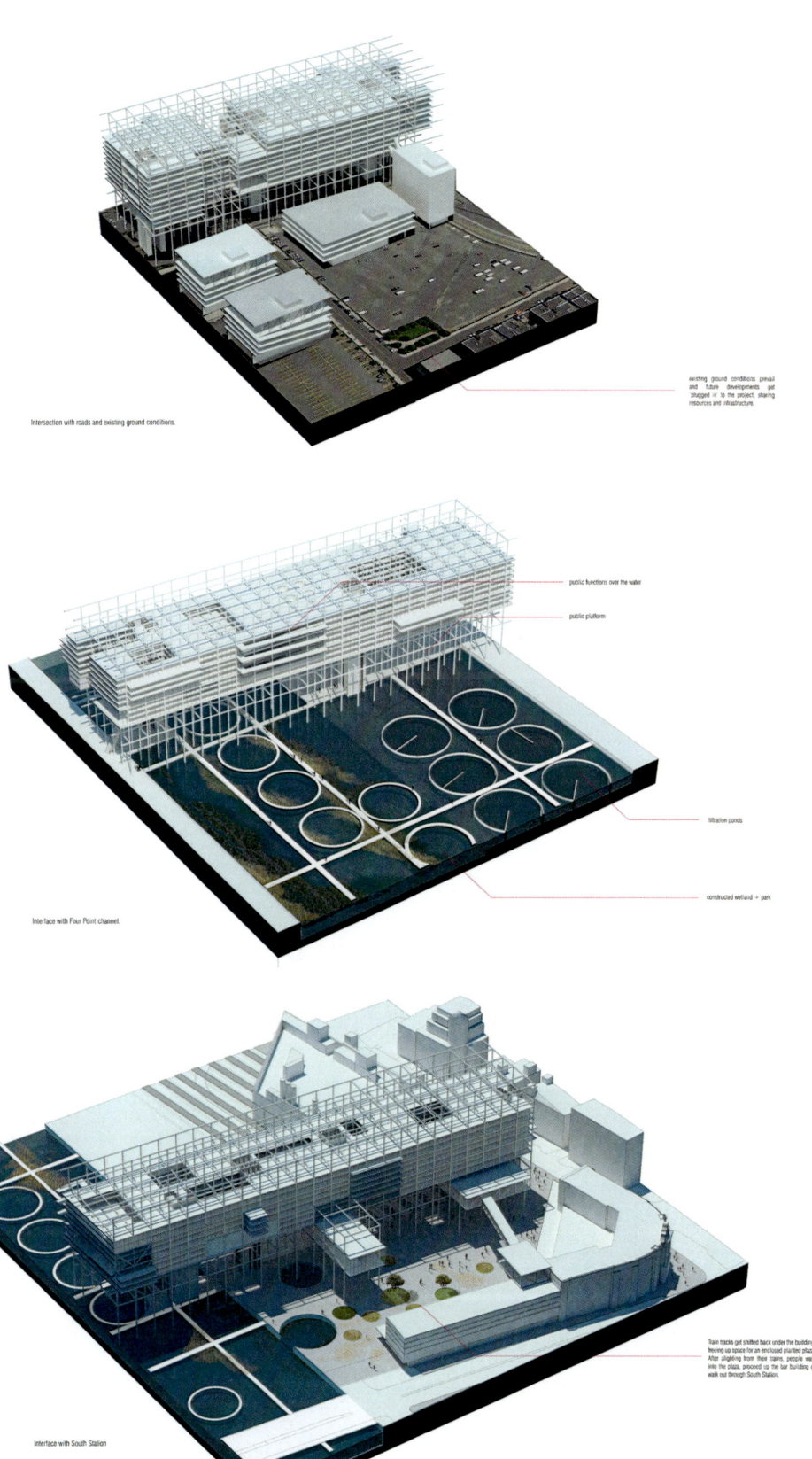

Intersection with roads and existing ground conditions.

existing ground conditions prevail and future developments get plugged in to the project, sharing resources and infrastructure.

public functions over the water

public platform

filtration ponds.

constructed wetland + park

Interface with Four Point channel.

Train tracks get shifted back under the building, freeing up space for an enclosed planted plaza. After alighting from their trains, people walk into the plaza, proceed up the bar building or walk out through South Station.

Interface with South Station

ABOVE AND OPPOSITE Rendered waterfront perspectives.

South Boston Canal
Fort Point Channel

Michael McGrattan + Mansi Maheshwari

Much of South Boston is landfill, and its adjacency to the downtown core once made it a logical place for freight and shipping connections into the core. But with the demise of the rail yard and the diminishing role of the port, the area has been largely a land banking opportunity dominated by surface parking. The two major channels, Fort Point and the Shipping Channel, are underdeveloped features. Both cut the district into smaller disconnected parcels, and the lack of circulation makes them less than appealing bodies of water. Furthermore, 1st Street, which operates as the service corridor for the Convention Center and the light industry that remains, makes a visible scar between the developing residential neighborhoods to the south and the emerging Convention Center business district. The major move in this scheme is to deploy an old real estate gambit, turning the least desirable area, 1st Street, into a feature around which new development might occur. The scheme boldly proposes connecting Fort Point to the Shipping Channel, which would increase water circulation through both bodies of water and operate as a linear "blue" parkway or canal that would make an attractive urban public space. The new canal would also help to manage groundwater in this area, which sits only a few feet above sea level.

The development of the plan then entails speculation on tactical maneuvers in section to incorporate tidal shifts and rising sea levels so that an animated public edge occurs along the new waterway. Critical speculation on this project asked how a large-scale strategy might be deployed. Either a large public commitment would be required to increase land values, or a hybrid might develop wherein private developers would be required to develop the public spaces according to a design code so that the scales of development that might be expected in the various locations might make intelligent but fiscally viable interventions to enhance the public realm.

OPPOSITE Rendered aerial view of the new canal extension.

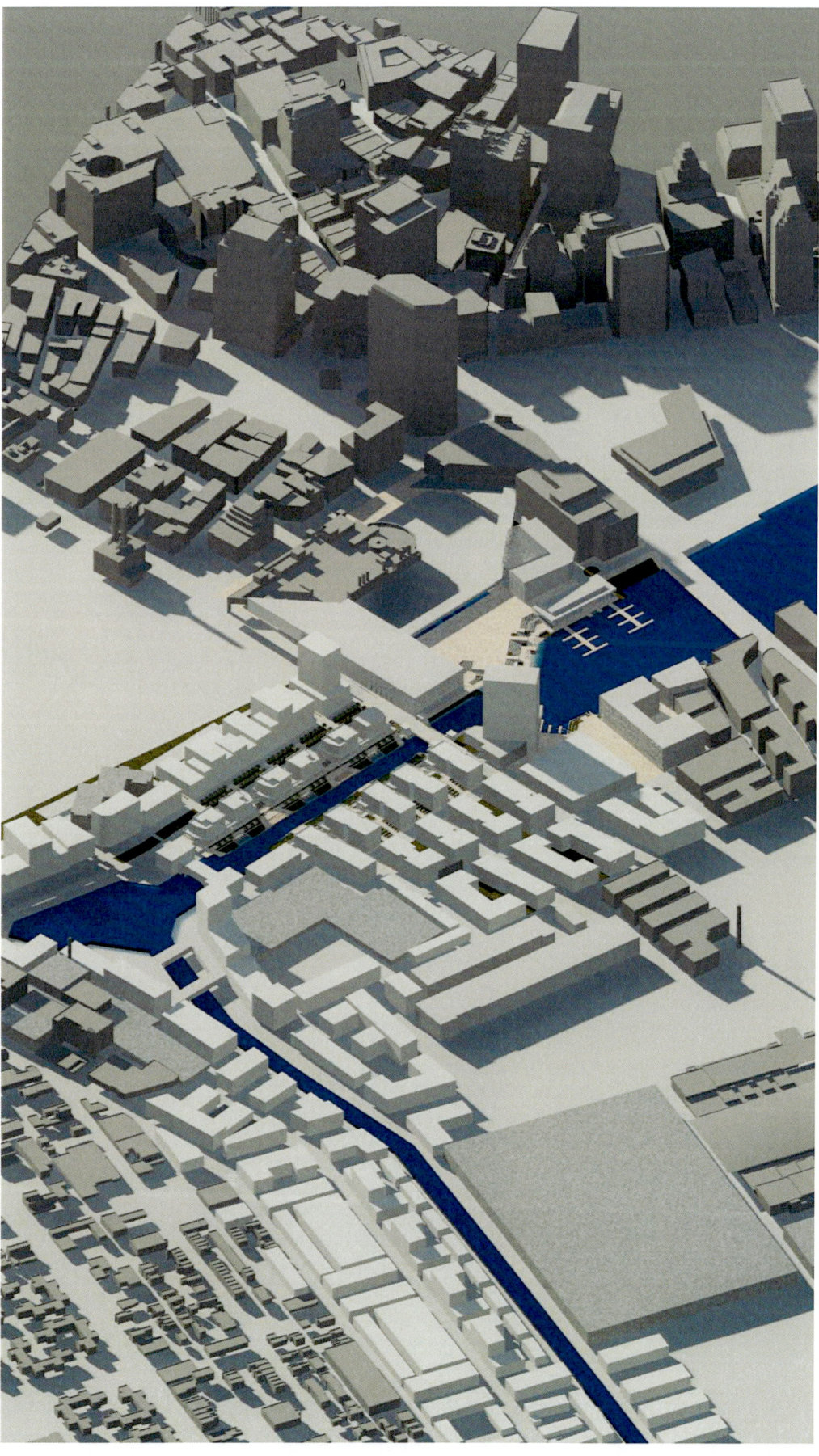

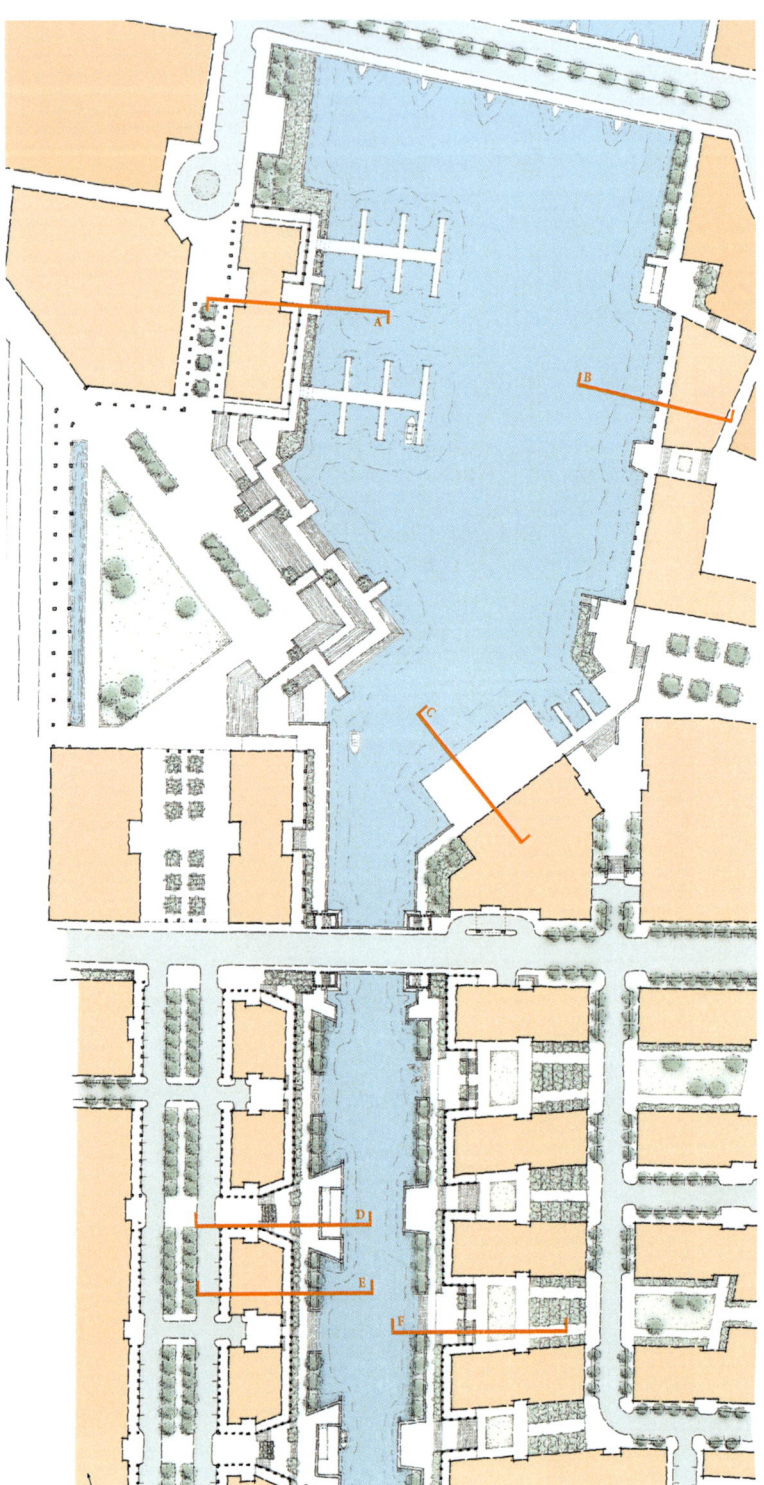

ABOVE Site plan.

OPPOSITE LEFT Sections through the district.
OPPOSITE RIGHT Diagrams reading top to bottom:
existing conditions, proposed canal connecting Fort Point to the
Shipping Channel, urban islands in the existing district, proposed
development sites.

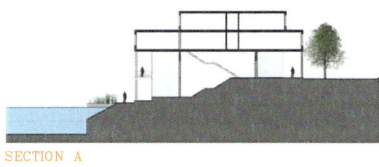

SECTION A

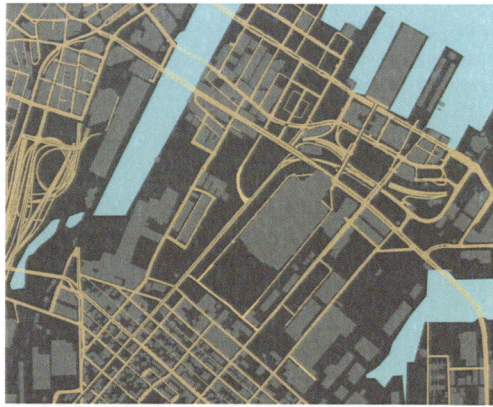

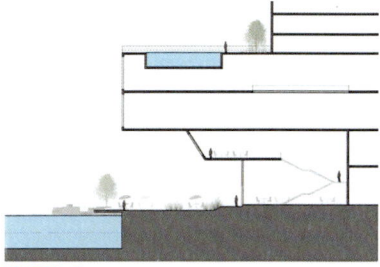

SECTION B

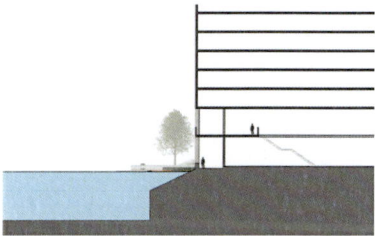

SECTION C

SECTION D

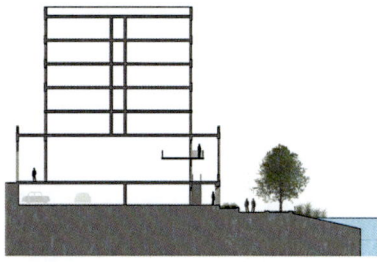

SECTION E

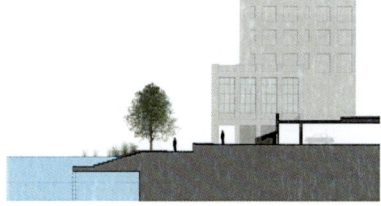

SECTION F
scale 1=20'

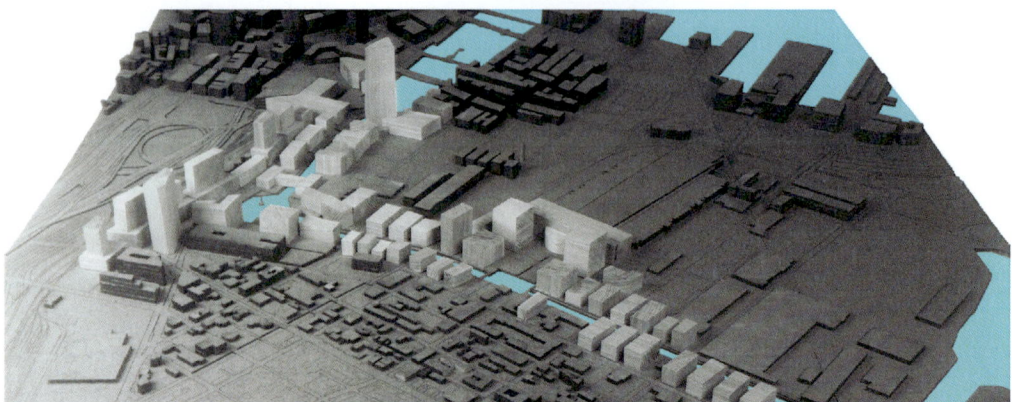

TOP Model photograph of new proposal.   OPPOSITE TOP Model photograph.
MIDDLE Views into the new business district.   OPPOSITE MIDDLE View looking north towards South Station
BOTTOM View north along the canal walk at Fort Point Channel.   OPPOSITE BOTTOM Canal walkway.

Great South Station
Fort Point Channel

Jay Tsai + Miron Mawratil

While South Station serves the purpose of a train station, it lacks the drama associated with great urban hubs like Grand Central Station or the old Penn Station in New York. In this project, like one other in the studio, the team decided to shift the tracks east into the southern area of Fort Point Channel so that the entrance to the city is a sequence of dramatic spaces leading from the tracks into a great hall facing directly into the channel. The parcel north of Summer Street is then configured as an urban beach that transitions the section of the city down to direct contact with the waterfront.

The hall itself is envisioned as a complex structure that at the upper levels mimics the scale of the existing urban blocks to the east and west of the site. These courtyard building forms are held up by a grid of massive columns that form a hypostyle hall that operates as the waiting room for the trains. Those buildings are designated for new office space conveniently located near the transport hub.

Traffic from I-93 is diverted around the two sides of the station complex, while I-90 is swung slightly south into a large commuter parking facility at the back of the complex. Above this southern portion of the scheme is a large hotel with cab drop-off for visitors coming from the airport. The underground T stop is simply shifted one stop south along its current path so that a new transit connection is made between the new South Station and a future east-west connection from South Boston across

the city running towards the research districts in Cambridge, well beyond the site.

Though the overall scheme appears massive, the manipulation of the roof line begins to add character and to mediate scales within the site. The complex then echoes the scale of the Convention Center but breaks down at the street level to the scale of the older parts of the city.

The canal, which currently acts as a barrier between the Leather District, the CBD, and South Boston now becomes the focal point for new urban development. Connections made along the west side of the canal then give continuity to the street grid and add a considerable amount of new real estate south of the CBD by bundling the transportation systems into a tight but extremely well worked out hub.

If Boston is to become a major metropolitan center, the need to upgrade its antiquated transit system, to add new real estate opportunities adjacent to the existing business districts, to weave the disparate downtown district together, as well as to provide a memorable urban experience, are successfully addressed in this ambitious scheme.

OPPOSITE Aerial rendering looking towards waterfront.

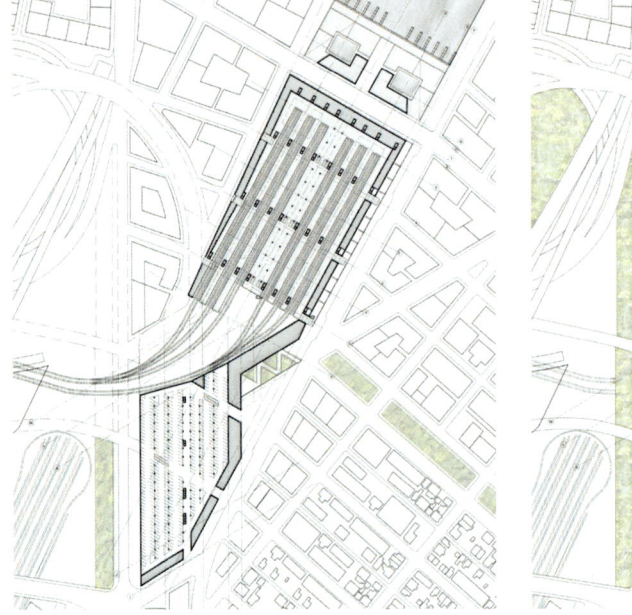
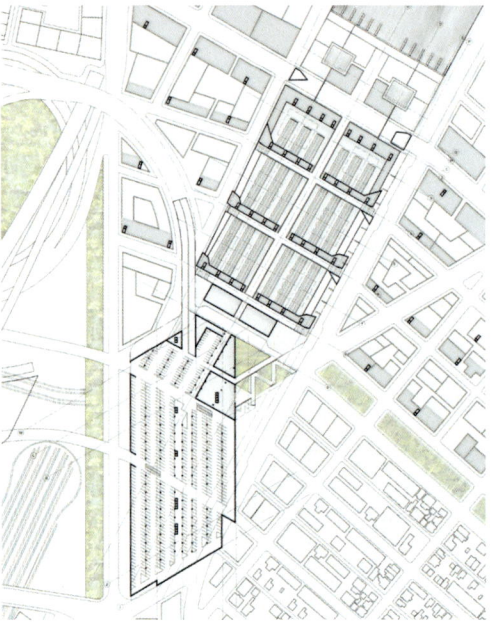

TOP Macro site plan showing new location of South Station at the
head of Fort Point Channel.
BOTTOM LEFT Ground floor plan.
BOTTOM RIGHT First floor plan.
OPPOSITE Roof plan.

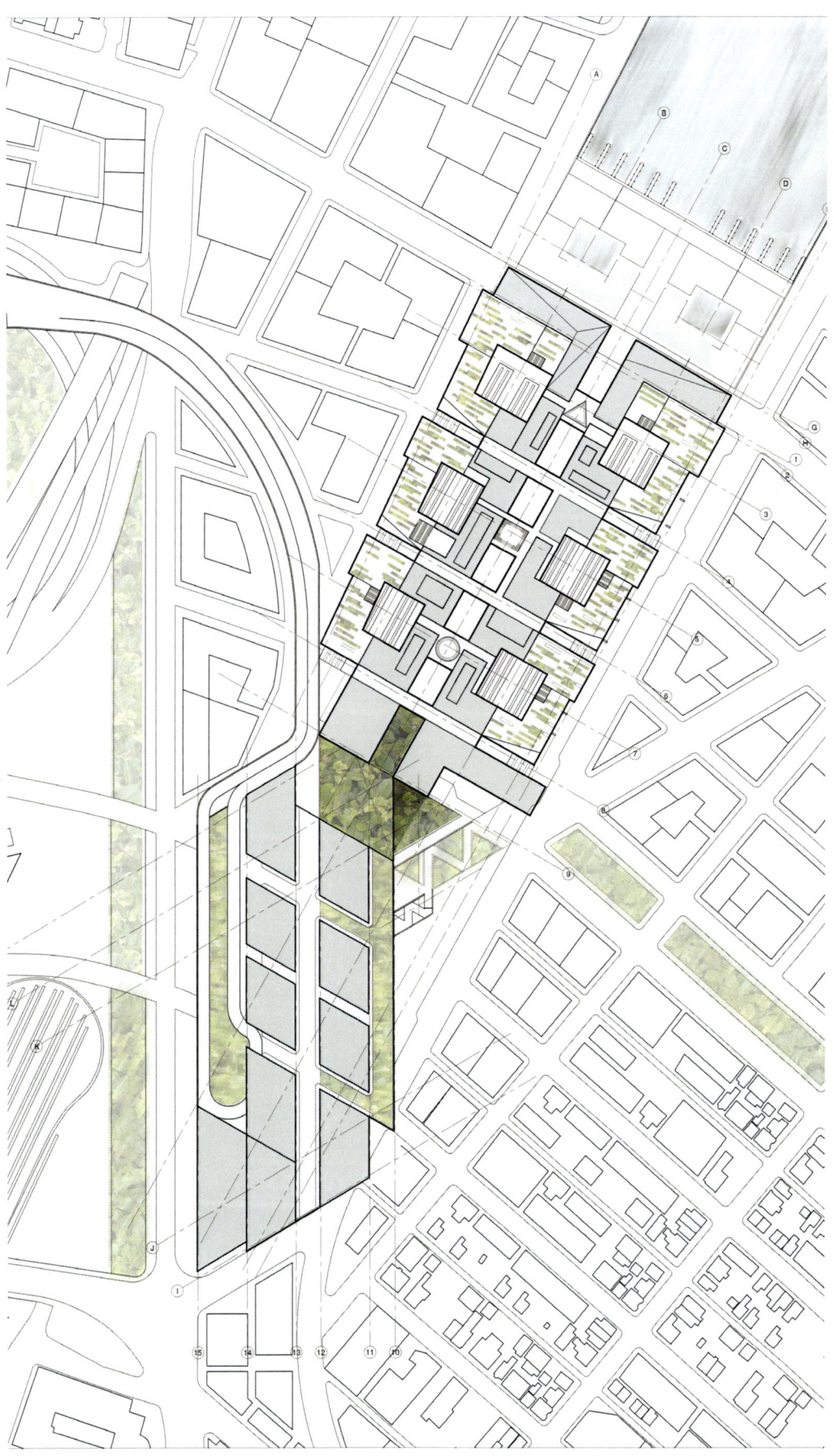

TOP Renderings of final scheme looking south from the channel
towards the urban beach.
BOTTOM Section perspective cutting through the building fabric,
with the train station and tracks shown below.
OPPOSITE Model photographs of final scheme.

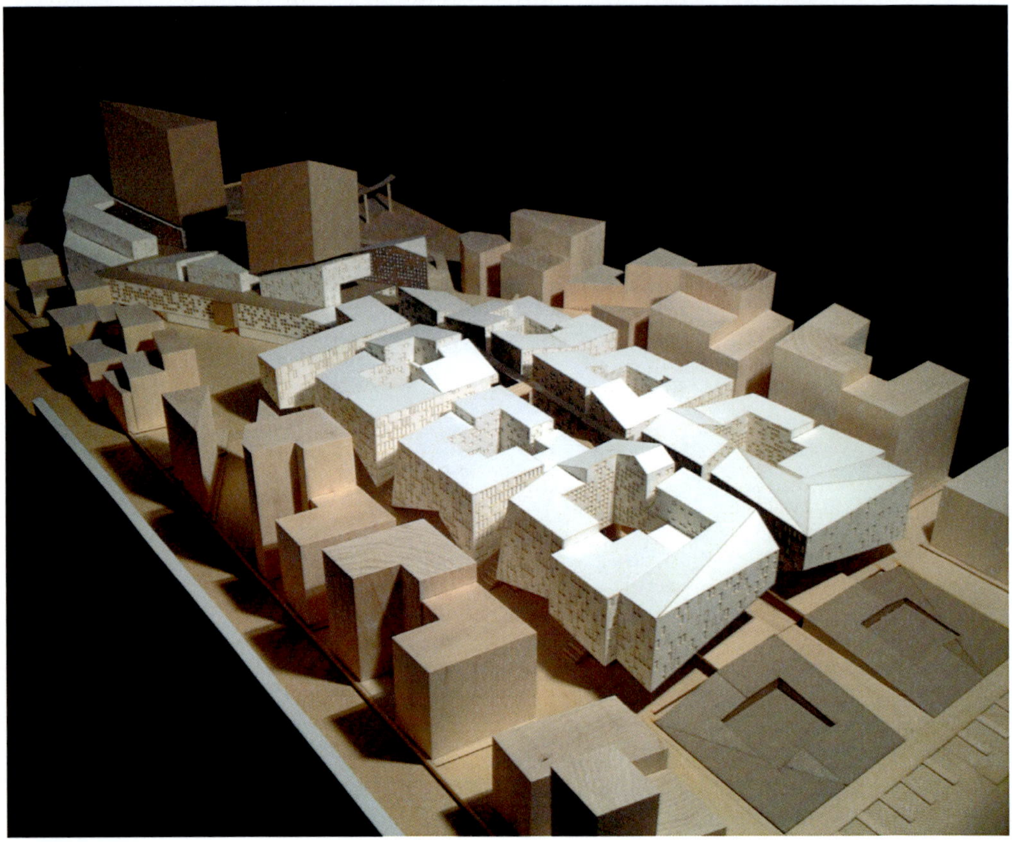

TOP Renderings through the new South Station hall.
BOTTOM Model photograph.

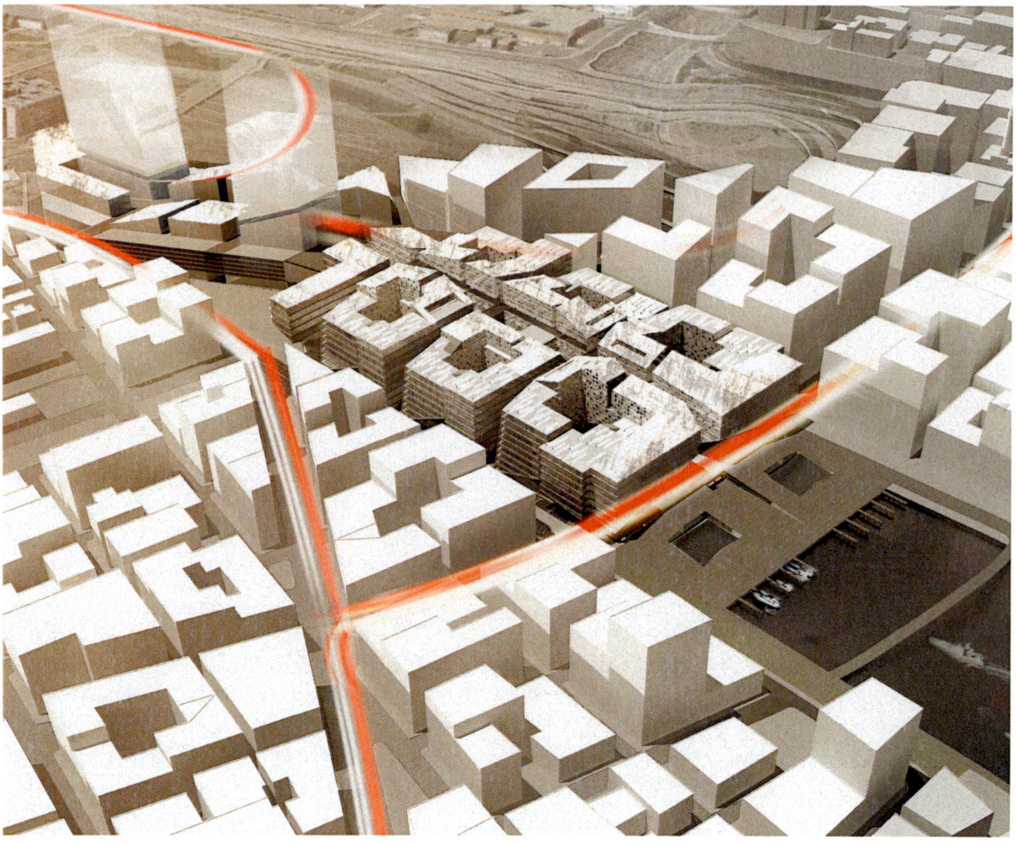

TOP Renderings through the new South Station hall.
BOTTOM Rendering of the project looking southeast showing major
road connections from the interstate and to the Central Business
District.

Central Square

Edward Mitchell

Central Square was a vital commercial center of Cambridge, but plans drawn up in the 1960s to run the Inner Belt (I-165) through the center of the community disincentivized landlords owning property in a once vibrant core. In the 1960s, the Department of Public Works (DPW) was promised ninety cents on the dollar, and plans were drawn up to modernize the city. Over 3,800 homes were scheduled for demolition until local groups made up of longstanding working-class residents, academics, and environmentalists protested the DPW's masterplan. The damage caused by the rumors alone, in some part, was already done. Even today it is somewhat surprising to find that one of the major thoroughfares in New England's most important city, one that connects the institutions of MIT and Harvard and leads directly into Back Bay, is a fractured fabric of mostly one-story commercial buildings. But cities are versatile, and despite the underwhelming nature of its architecture, Massachusetts Avenue is one of the most lively streets in the region, full of ethnic restaurants, coffee and book shops, and home to some of Boston's best night life.

Central Square is not immune to the changes taking place throughout the city and the region. Recent development pressures in Cambridge are due to a number of factors, including demand for lab and research facilities at MIT along Massachusetts Avenue, Harvard's plans for expansion into the Allston neighborhood, and increased demand for new housing throughout the city and across the region. Boston is in the midst of significant changes that could alter its somewhat provincial identity. This may transform the city fabric into that of a major urban center commensurate with its recent business development as a competitive global center for finance and technology.

The lab building is a particularly difficult urban typology with which to work. Its bulky massing is often in conflict with typical block sizes. Its singular program, and its security requirements, do not promote active street frontage or the easy evolution of urban life. When Koetter Kim made proposals for nearby University Park, they envisioned a mixed-use development of public spaces and active ground-floor retail. But, at the time, the commercial establishments along Massachusetts Avenue resisted this idea, thinking that additional retail and restaurants would draw off business from already struggling merchants.

OPPOSITE Site plan of Central Square.

More recent development in Kendall Square has more of a mix, but lacks strong street presence. Sometimes restaurants are pulled back from direct urban engagement and, perhaps in keeping with market trends, sequestered from the noisy hustle and bustle of the district's streets. Though a marked improvement from what had existed, Kendall Square lacks the funky street life of Central Square. Further expansion of labs into Central Square could diminish that urban energy, making a vital part of the city one more corporate campus.

Alex Twining, a graduate of our school, had options on several parcels in Central Square. With Kishore Varanasi of CBT, he approached us to study the area alongside their own efforts to conceive of a rich urban mix of, not labs, but housing and commercial real estate. Twining had already proven successful with similar ventures in Kendall Square. Recent zoning changes had enabled the financial equation to work, but, as with all well-intentioned public laws, the generalization of the rules required for equity limited the prospects of a more varied, eclectic, and textured development. In honor of the now-retired Fred Koetter, we chose to examine in depth the idea of the district, as opposed to a singular piece of architecture. How could an architect increase the density, in keeping with the goals of the region, while still providing a fabric that would keep the spirit of Central Square? Designing a good street or a good square proved even more complex than, and as difficult as, designing a singular work of architecture.

When discussing the nature of public spaces, we felt that the term "public space" itself was problematic, reducible on most plans to the green shaded area between buildings with little to no conception of how to activate, assemble, collide, and create a "public." We fixated on early images, not of "public space," but instead on the older New England idea of the Common. In particular we noticed that in historic images, the Common was depicted as a collage of very different activities—militia drilling in formation, livestock grazing, games being played by children, and exotic birds hovering above. Compared to contemporary renderings of joggers and mildly amused shoppers strolling along yet another series of forgettable shops, new images of Cambridge, and in particular, Central Square, we felt, needed a common or, better yet, an uncommom Common representation befitting the engaged residents and the neighborhood's eclectic and democratic self-image.

As with the studio on South Station, we asked ourselves, "What makes a city?" through the exercises to produce an Instant City, and researched the fabric of some of Greater Boston's best neighborhoods. We toured and explored the hidden courtyards and back alleys of the city, spoke with architects working in these neighborhoods, and spent time in the better haunts of Central Square. Our studio explored and extended the history of these critical projects on the city in both theoretical and practical terms.

In keeping with the trends in contemporary development, we critically engaged the very nature of today's consumer-based city. Boston may be in a renaissance. But though it is a job center, this is not solely because of the transfer of production from an industrial to a knowledge-based economy. Rather, the city is a self-reinforcing locus of consumption. As evidenced by the social media technologies coming out of Cambridge, the city is being reconstructed not just by the classic "citizen" but by a complex targeting of consumers. Public spaces may flourish in the near future, but they also inform and are informed by data-driven marketing and interfaces. Those schisms exist in the politics of redevelopment, between the political denizens of the old neighborhoods—the "People's Republic of Cambridge"—and the mass-customized micro-lifestyles of the new urban hipster. One of the Instant City exercises, *The Gluttonous City*, told the tale of a circus that comes to a sleepy town that at first excites and engages the citizens. But as the spectacle unfolds, the townsfolk begin to spend their hard-earned income at the fairgrounds until they are destitute, which then prompts the carnival to move down the road, leaving the inhabitants worse off than they had been before—a cautionary tale for the promises and

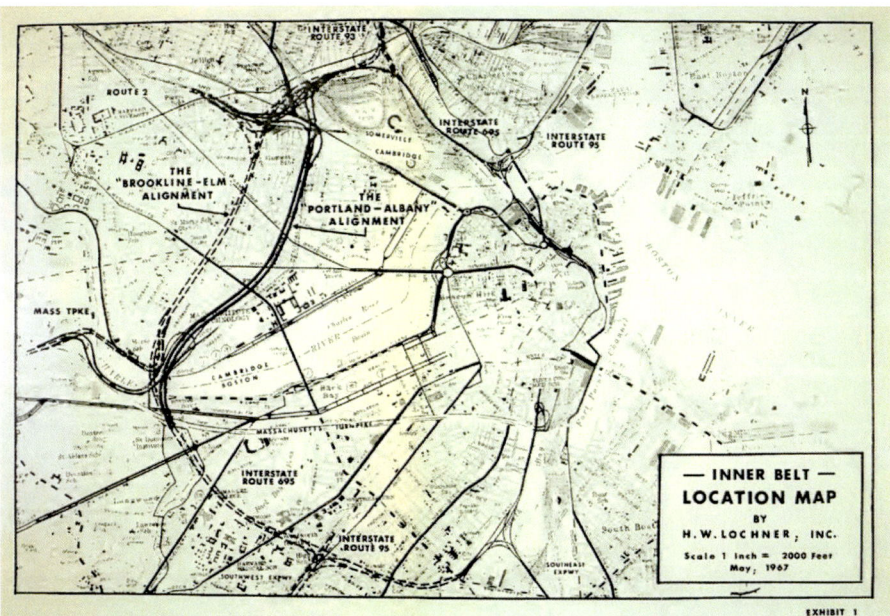

EXHIBIT 1

disappointments of the service economy. The real success of the studio was the willingness of the students to engage the developer's program, paying attention to the number of units required, servicing, market trends, and the economy of building types. But they were able to shift those requirements into a more active public provocation. Some projects, like Adam Wagoner's and Stephanie Jazmines's proposal, suggest a complex new avenue commensurate with the lofty ambitions of a metropolitan Boston. Others, like Karolina Czeczek and Kate Lisi, or Peter McInish and Laurence Lumley, try to raise the built area without losing the back-alley feel of the present fabric. And yet others, like Olen Millholland and Daniel Luster, saw that the amplification of the built realm and the need for real public spaces, our uncommon Commons, required a complex sectional resolution of traffic, green spaces, building forms, and activities that no zoning ordinance could ever script.

As the studio developed, an in-house competition began to develop, as one by one, large models of parts of the projects began to appear. Then, the detailed studies began to expand into the whole district. Model by model, the top floor of Rudolph

Hall was filled with large-scaled models of all of Central Square. One could literally climb into the spaces to anticipate what might be. As a disappointing and telling postscript, Alex Twining was so taken by the work that he and the principals at CBT offered to show the work in a Central Square storefront. Two truck trips were required to take the materials northward as Yale happily invaded the home turf of Harvard and MIT.

But when lawyers for our client saw the work, they closed the exhibit. They were concerned that the work looked too real and was too provocative, leading to one of two possibilities that were not in the client's interest. Either the citizens of the People's Republic would mount a protest against what appeared to be professional work with which they had no input, or rival developers, seeing the vast potential of Central Square, would pursue options on other properties, jeopardizing the possibility of a more coherent long-term planning and development process. So, though the exhibit was shuttered and the work given a return ticket to New Haven, we hope that these proposals might yet engage the community and the profession in the kind of speculation that might better determine our Common future.

ABOVE Location Restudy for Interstate Route 695, Inner Belt Highway, Boston, Cambridge, and Somerville. Prepared for the Commonwealth of Massachusetts, for the Department of Public Works, by H.W. Lochner, Inc., May 1967. Courtesy the Boston Public Library.

Listening to Squares: Keys and Counterpoints

Brian Healy

Small Cities with Small Squares

Cambridge is a city of squares. The main ones include Porter, Kendall, Harvard, Inman, and Central, but there are also 598 more intimate squares—mostly dedicated to veterans—scattered across the city. They are really just crossroads on paths that connect squares to other squares.

Cities can be evolutionary in an unscripted way, like Cambridge, which grew incrementally over time and continues to transform itself daily. Others are conceived in their entirety with a pre-conceived framework for their evolution, like Washington, D.C. or Chandigarh. The students in this studio looked at both strategies, and the projects presented here reflect typologies that try to incorporate the strengths and ambitions of each approach. In one, a floating cloud hovers overhead—one hopes benevolently—overlooking the entire neighborhood. Another inserts new fragments throughout the square—like new neighbors—adding to the existing melody of the place. Each approach reflects the constant energy and turnover of new residents that takes place annually in Central Square and throughout Cambridge. Each poses a critique of how cities and neighborhoods are formed and how they transform themselves over time.

Squares are made up of many differently scaled pieces that are sometimes closely linked, but often entirely unrelated. They reverberate off each other to create a type of melody that defines each particular place. These small, close-knit neighborhoods are organized by streets, parks, and sidewalks that are sometimes ordered with rigor but often just present themselves as a collage of unrelated parts from different periods and uses. They change continually across the day into the night, with each new season providing a backdrop for performance and spectacle.

I moved to Central Square from Brooklyn Heights back in 1986 to set up my first office. I knew almost no one in Cambridge and—with little work—I began to explore her streets, neighborhoods, and parks as a form of unscripted post-graduate study. It is in Cambridge and Central Square that I discovered the sounds of a small modern city, and I have spent my entire professional career here discovering how architects can create modern work that harmonizes with the melodies of this place. If we define "modern" as that which is progressive but still imbued with a strong sense of civic responsibility, then our city can be heard not just in its skyline, but in its streets, sidewalks, and squares. Just as Kahn recognized the city as the place of availabilities, Cambridge—and her squares—continue to show us how a city can shape one's future as much as it speaks to its past.

Cambridge has always been of its time—progressive—yet extremely conscious of its legacy in a manner similar to how music like the fusion of Miles Davis depended upon a keen awareness of the entire history of jazz. And—as with music—Cambridge has its own distinctive key where its neighborhoods and squares describe strong, clear melodies, against which contemporary architecture—through syncopation and counterpoint—can

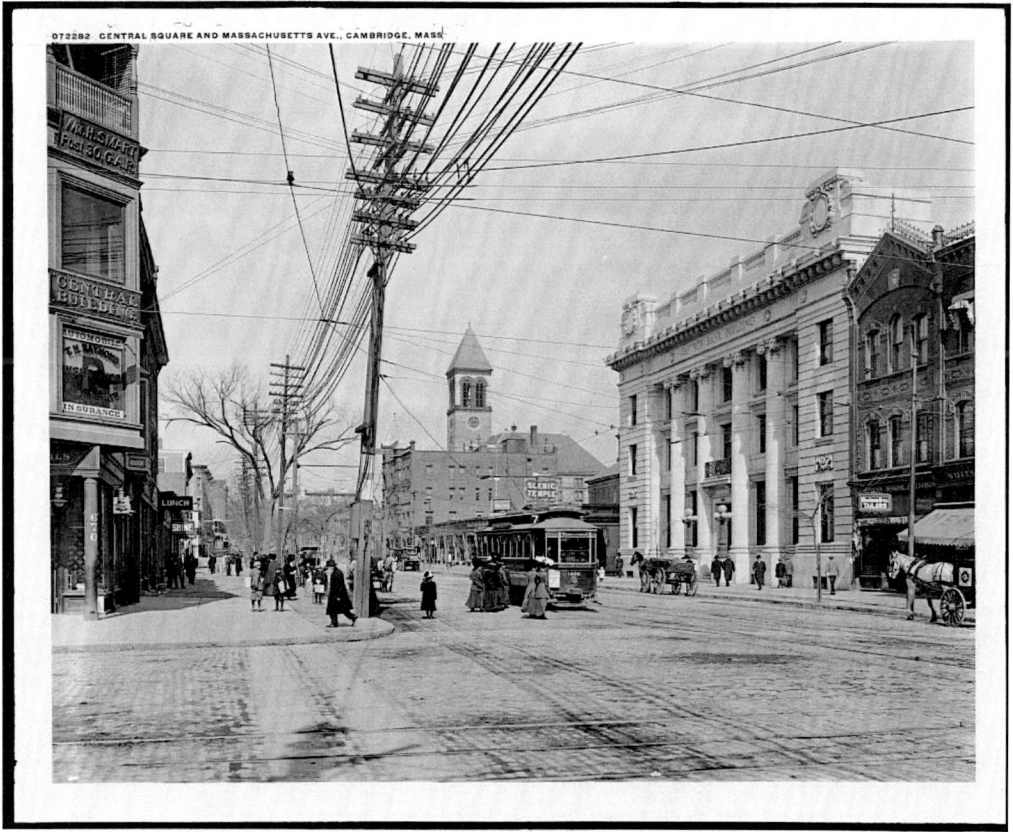

ABOVE Central Square and Massachusetts Avenue, Cambridge.
Circa 1910–1920. Detroit Publishing Co., publisher. Courtesy of the
Library of Congress.

harmonize. Central Square reflects this and has its own unique sound. As a modern place, it absorbs radical challenges to its structure, demographics, and geography, without ever losing a sense of itself. It can support the juxtaposition of old and new buildings, strengthening both through their adjacencies.

What we now perceive as Cambridge's current musical key—a radical and restless idea—did not start that way. Cambridge—which was known as Newtowne until 1638—was laid out in an orderly grid of streets where each family owned a house lot in the village with fields and a share in the Common. Eventually, they added a meetinghouse, a school, and a marketplace in today's Winthrop Square. By the time of the Revolution, it was a simply a quiet New England farming village with a Common and a College in what we now call Harvard Square.

That square was connected to Boston with the Longfellow Bridge in 1793, providing the first direct link between the two cities. Development along this path included new residential neighborhoods and during this process, Central Square grew to become the city's true downtown and government center. Each period had a distinct melody that still haunts the place while prompting new thoughts for how we can occupy and reimagine our neighborhoods and squares.

Architecture never stands alone. It is intimately connected to place, land, and community. Housing, streets, and neighborhoods are the ground from which a city springs. Its inhabitants' stories unfold in the streets, sidewalks, neighborhoods, buses, and subways. Cities are defined by these connections just as strongly as by their buildings and parks. The success of a building is locked to the life of the street and, therefore, great design can

galvanize a neighborhood.

As architects, designers, and planners, we need to create shared communal places and understand that a city—or square—is an ever-changing phenomenon. Places evolve, and the architect should contribute a forward-looking vision of what cities can become and how new interventions can add to and enhance what is already there. That requires design excellence, which can catalyze social engagement and foster community.

Cities are constantly changing and this puts tremendous pressure on architects, planners, and the community to create a coherent melody, one that resonates with us now even as it anticipates the other sounds that will follow. Inevitably, the endeavor is less a matter of individual inspiration and more of an honest acknowledgement that things could be done differently and that a different proposition could always be made. Academic studios like this one are based on this premise and they remind us of the power of an open and eclectic conversation that recognizes many voices in the growth of any place in real time.

The students understood this and their studio projects take a fresh look at Cambridge and Central Square. Their work continues to show how modern architecture from one generation can beget a new legacy of modern architecture for the next; and that what was once controversial is now simply another melody against which we can discover a new building vocabulary—or a new square.

Boston Neighborhoods

Edward Mitchell

The neighborhood studies represent a broad survey of different urban systems ranging from historic cities such as Timgad, Carcassonne, and Boston; utopian visionary plans such as Broadacre City, Erskine's Arctic City, 1960s French utopian fantasies; and architecturally scaled urban designs such as Aalto's Rovaniemi, Price's Potteries Thinkbelt, and Peter Calthorpe's Californian commuter centers. In analyzing the projects, the students were asked to provide documentation: a scaled figure-ground drawing, a table of values including the population and density, building and block types, the precedent's relationships to landscape, and descriptions of the political and economic structures of the proposals; analysis: interpretations of the expandable and mutable qualities of the projects which would still keep the core of the precedent intact, variations on the morphologies of the urban form that would allow for interpretation and variation within the type, and an account of the physical concept of the city. That physical analysis, it was proposed, might reveal that city structure and urban design strategies fall into three categories. The categories, as we interpreted them, were "Cities within Cities": enclaves or strongly defined architectural figures within a larger urban/rural pattern that tend towards self-referential closure; "Networked Cities": urban systems that relate parts at distances and which form dependent relationships between points in the network where the definition of physical links and connections is critical; and "Districts": areas that are prototypical of the general fabric of a city (neighborhoods, parishes, commercial centers) usually focused around a public program like a school of a mosque, but which are not necessarily self- sustaining nor the central organizing element of the city as a whole.

A successful city will often exhibit all three of these conditions. A city with only districts, but without the memorable symbolic characteristics of the City within a City, may not have an identifiable focus. Networked Cities, like suburban power centers, tend to lack either architectural focus or locally identifiable subgroups. The City-within-a-City strategy may produce a memorable architecture, but may be limited in its ability to adapt and survive. It may also knowingly reject the notion of the urban whole. By using precedents, the studios established common themes that could be discussed across historic and cultural differences while remaining vigilant that those differences were critical in evaluating the tendency to collage an historic paradigm into the complex context of any situation.

In addition to the more recognizable precedents, the students looked at regional examples, and analyzed and interpreted them as variations on the three themes established in the research. Students found: that the New England town green roughly corresponds, physically and politically, with cross-cultural paradigms like Roman military enclave agoras and the shared cooperative market squares of the Carcassonne cities; that industrial utopias from the Modern movement correspond with the limits and scale of actual industrial complexes like the Fall River mills; and that any projections of a future networked urbanism or sustainable ecological paradigm might learn lessons from the more intensive focus of polemical studies like Price's Potteries Thinkbelt and Erskine's Arctic City.

ABOVE Analysis of Beacon Hill alleyways and building typologies.
Boyuan Zhang and Elvira Hoxha.

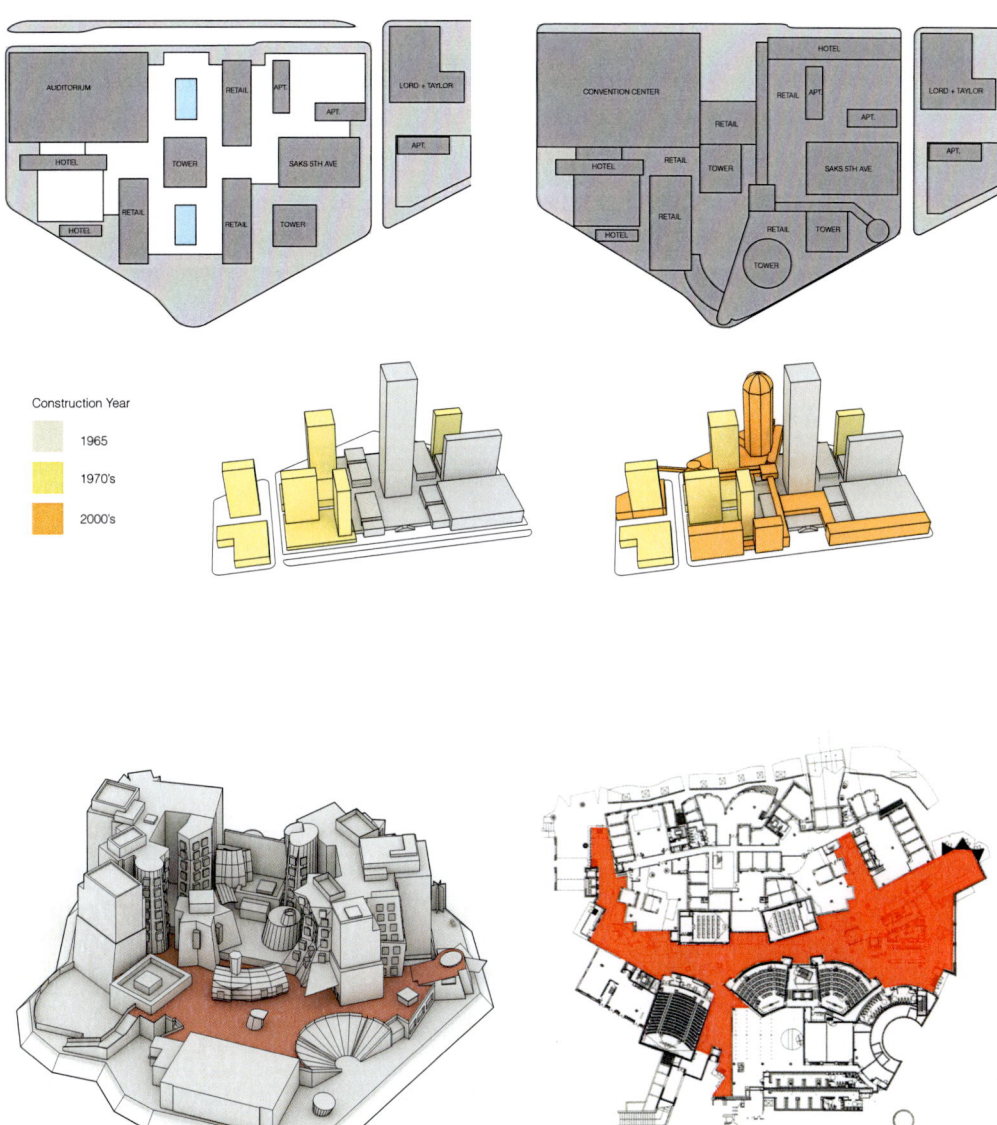

ABOVE Analytic drawings Cities within Cities: The Prudential
Center and the Stata Center, Frank Gehry. Amir Karimpour and Read
Langworthy.

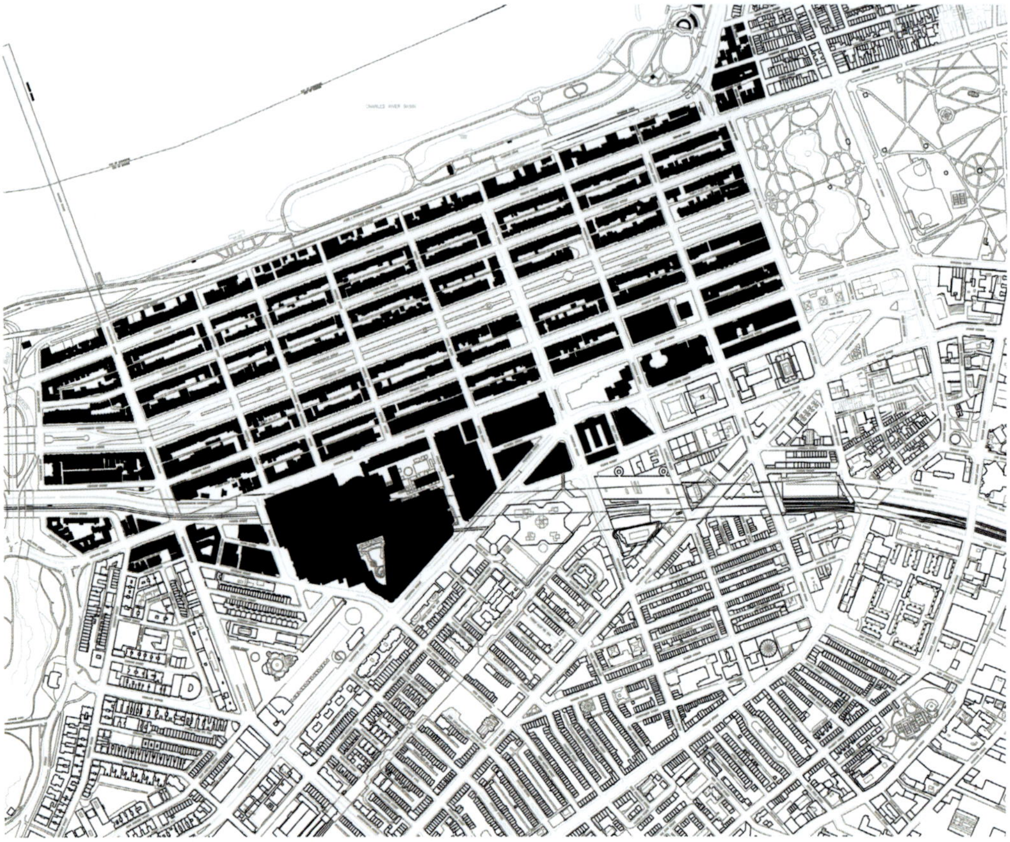

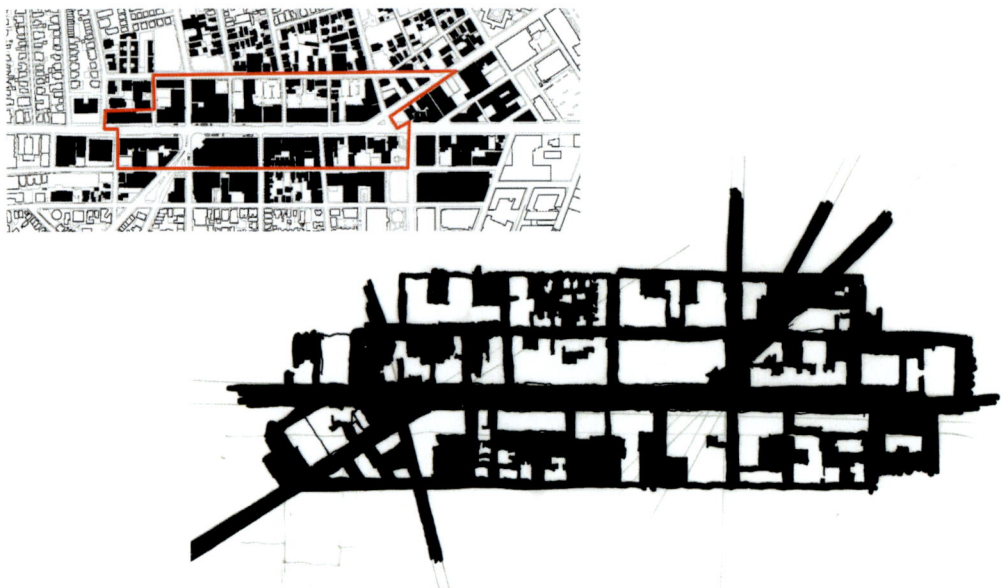

ABOVE Figure/ground analytic drawings of Back Bay. Katarzyna
Pozniak and Raphael de la Fontaine.
BOTTOM Figure/ground analytic drawings of Central Square. Katar-
zyna Pozniak and Raphael de la Fontaine.

Peter McIntosh + Stephanie Jazmindes + Kim Tak Yu

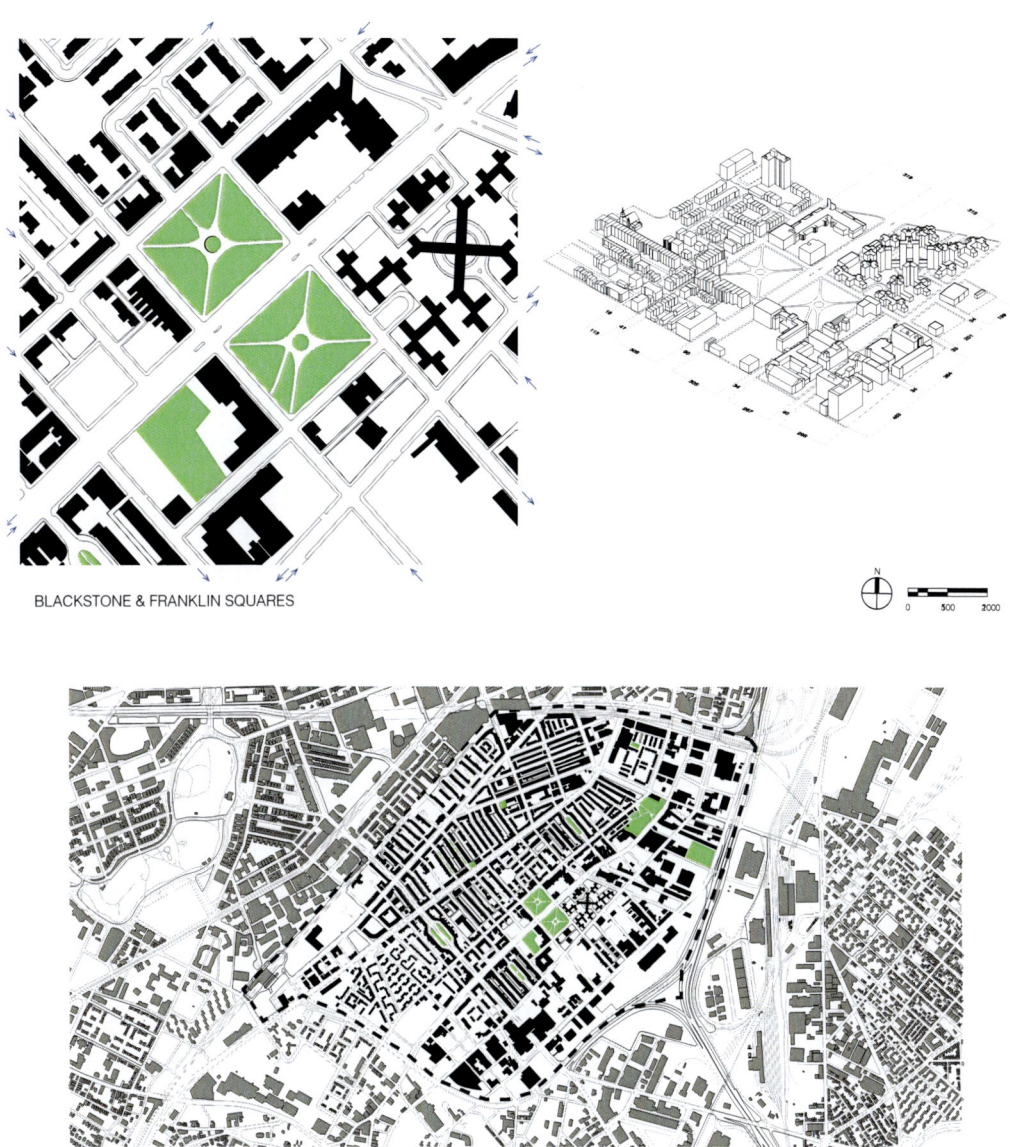

BLACKSTONE & FRANKLIN SQUARES

N
0   500   2000

FIGURE GROUND

N
0   500   1000

TOP Analysis of South End. Peter McInish, Stephanie Jazmines, Kin Tak Yu.
BOTTOM Analysis of South End. Peter McInish, Stephanie Jazmines, Kin Tak Yu.

The Grand Avenue
Central Square

Adam Wagoner + Stephanie Jazmines

While Boston and Cambridge are known for their more intimate residential streets, there are actually very few major commercial streets of consequence. Boston and Cambridge are patchworks of neighborhoods, not a hierarchical system of streets and avenues. The exception is in Back Bay where the imposed street grid has gradually fostered a lively commercial district along Newbury Street. Rumors in the 1960s of a major urban thoroughfare and the more recent competition from suburban commercial development reduced Massachusetts Avenue's once grand scale to a series of single-story commercial buildings. Future plans to densify the city will inevitably lead to a larger, more urban scale along the avenues. This project looks to restore Mass Ave to its former glory by organizing new development around the street edge on a plinth of parking, and bookending Central Square with a linear park to the south and a new urban square to the north. Penetrations through and over the parking plinth create a public pass-through that reconnects the main artery in Cambridge to its adjacent neighborhoods. An upper terrace parallel to the major thoroughfare provides a quieter, greener residential enclave with vistas to the avenue but distinctly separate from the hustle and bustle of the city.

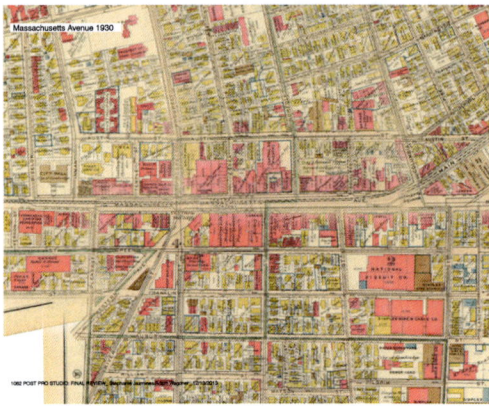

TOP Image of Massachusetts Avenue, circa 1950.
BOTTOM Map of Cambridge, circa 1930.
OPPOSITE Master plan of Massachusetts Avenue restored to its status of "good avenue."

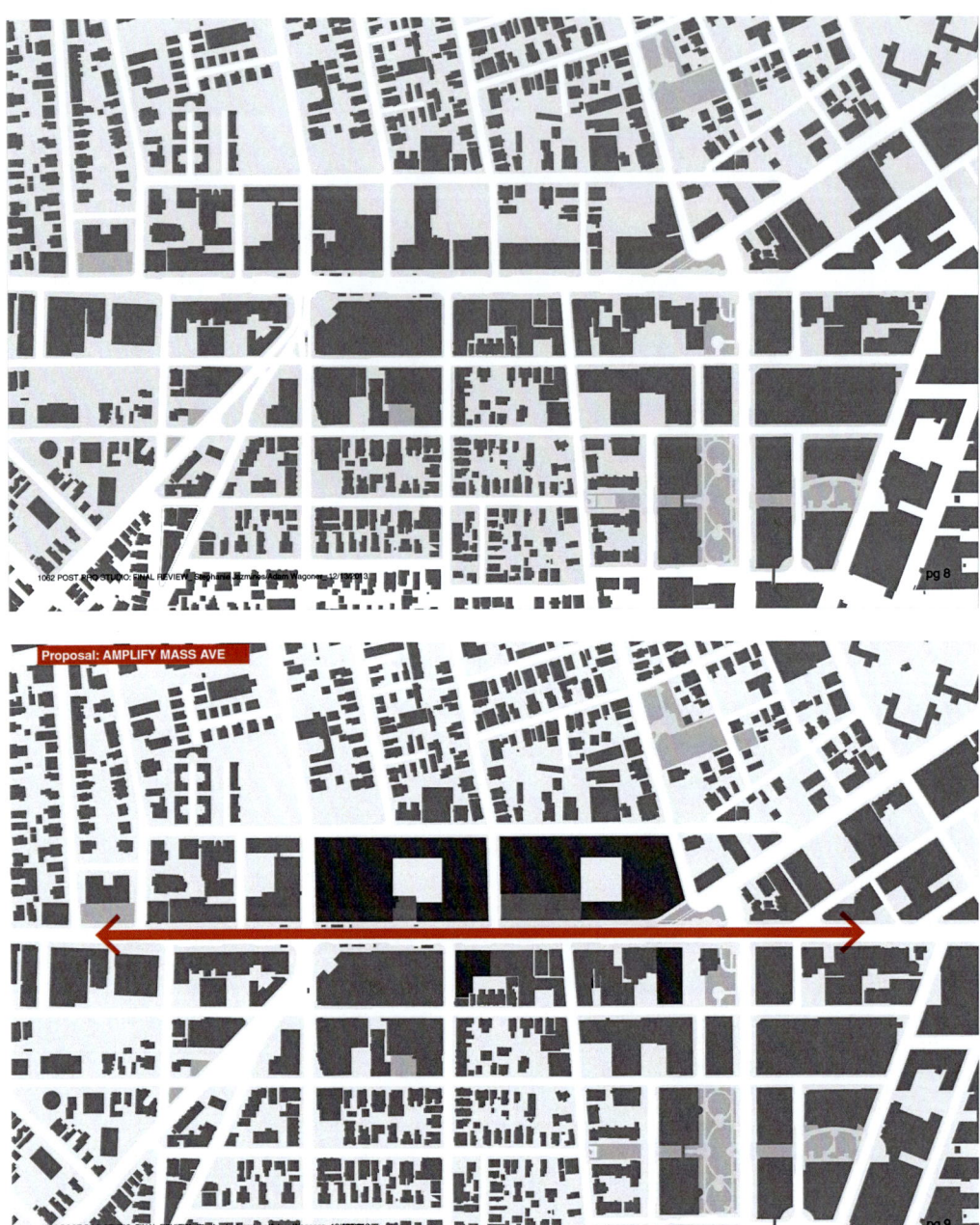

TOP Current figure/ground of Massachusetts Avenue.
BOTTOM Diagram of proposal to amplify the avenue identity of
Massachusetts Avenue.

OPPOSITE TOP Diagram of existing parks now linked together.
OPPOSITE MIDDLE Diagram of new connections to neighborhoods.
OPPOSITE BOTTOM Exaggerated bird's-eye perspective of the
new Central Square and park nodes created by the proposal.

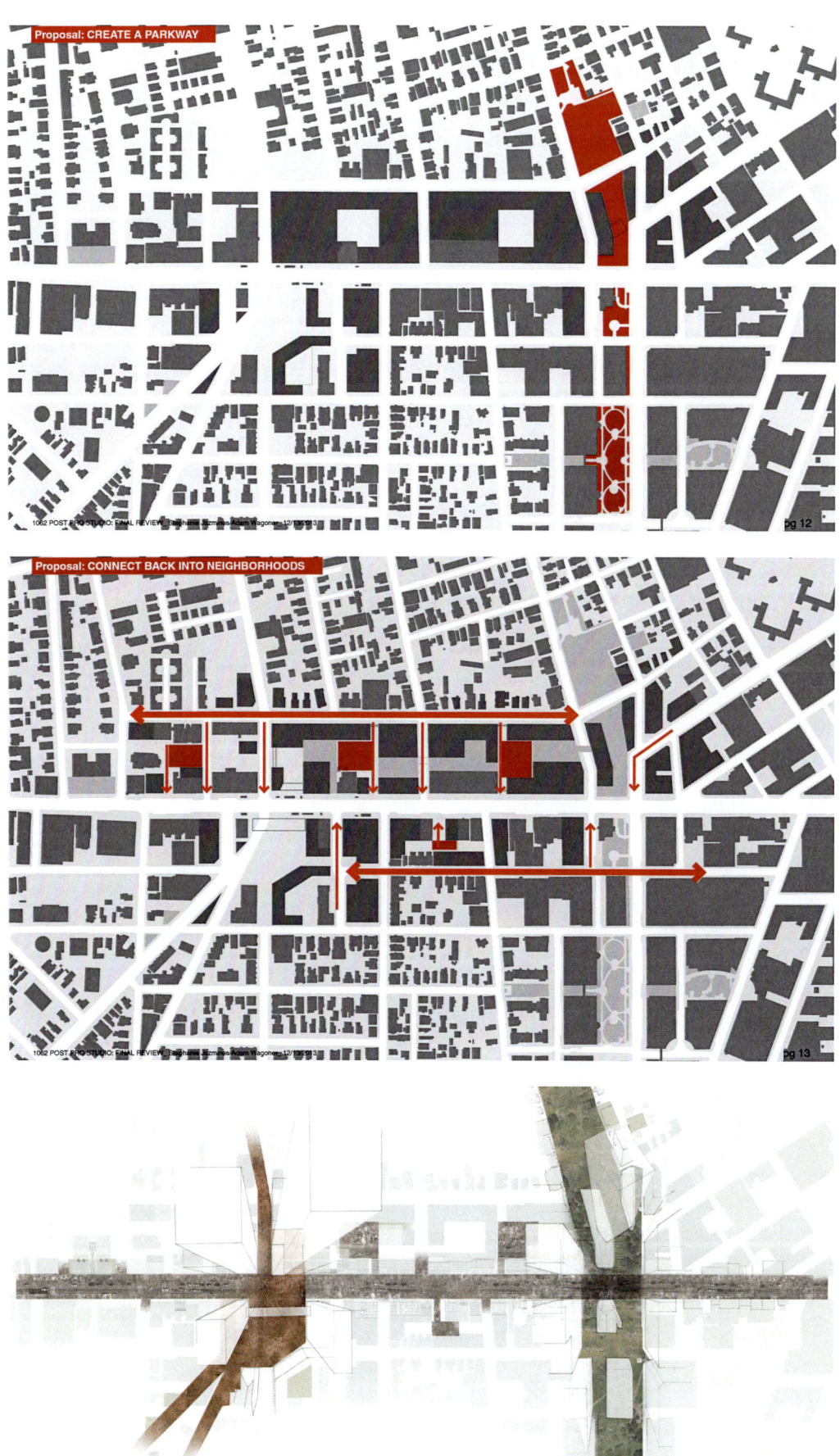

Proposal: CREATE A PARKWAY

Proposal: CONNECT BACK INTO NEIGHBORHOODS

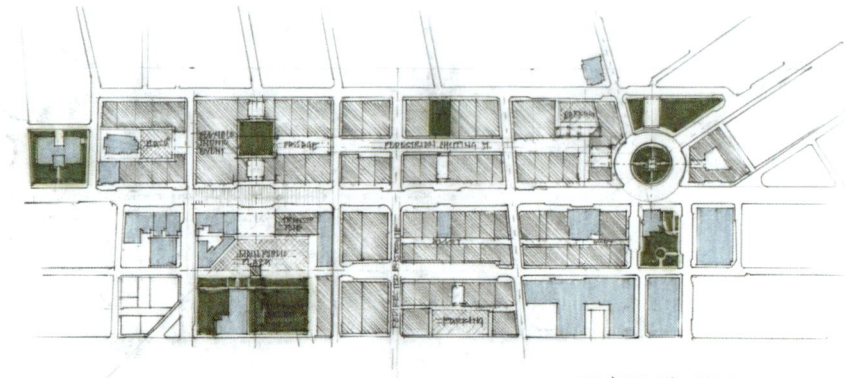

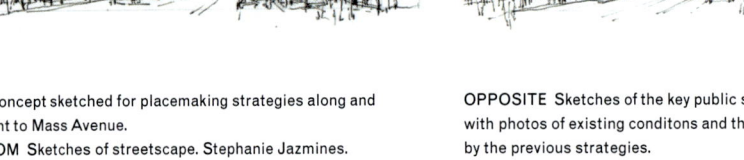

TOP Concept sketched for placemaking strategies along and
adjacent to Mass Avenue.
BOTTOM Sketches of streetscape. Stephanie Jazmines.

OPPOSITE Sketches of the key public spaces in Central Square
with photos of existing conditons and the same conditions amplified
by the previous strategies.

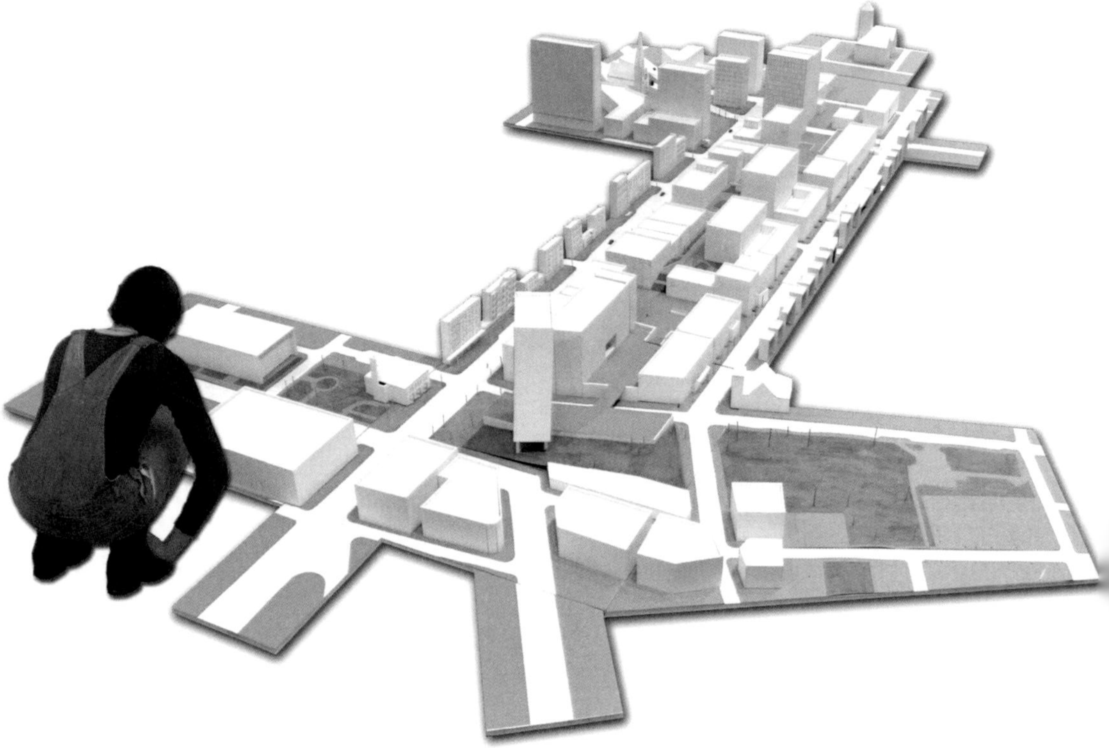

ABOVE AND OPPOSITE Model photographs of new
Massachusetts Avenue streetfront.

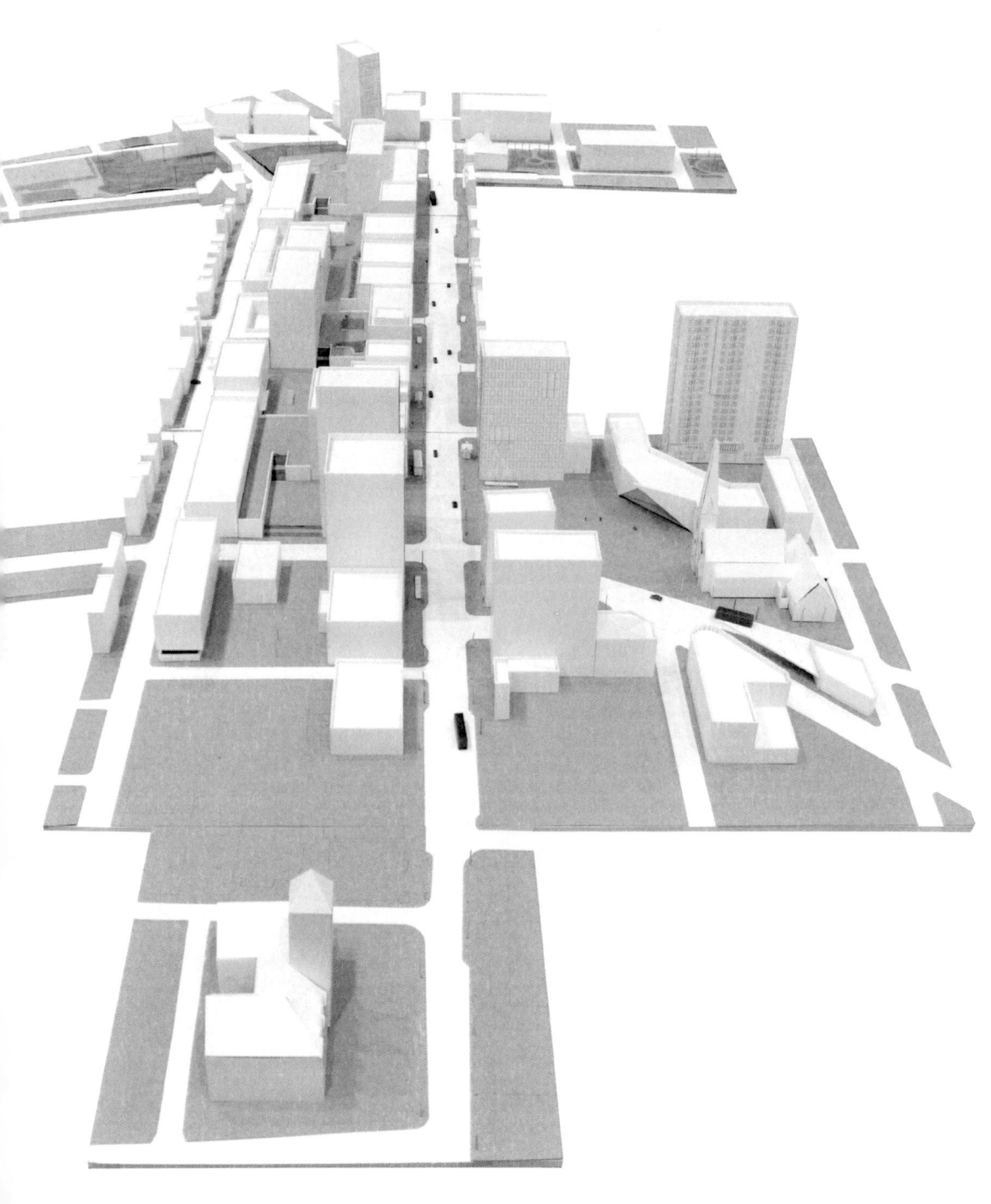

Courtyard District
Central Square

Amir Karimpour + Ian Spencer + Joseph Yu

ABOVE View of Central Square and Massachusetts Avenue
promenade from adjacent building.

While contextual arguments can be made for a mid-rise solution to increased density, this project makes no apologies for the use of two more typical development typologies—the low two- to three-story walk-up and the high-rise. Both types are products of the current economics of construction where the addition of a fourth floor increases structural expenses and adds the cost of elevators. This project proposes a courtyard district organized along the spine of Mass Ave. Inspired by the likes of Sert's Peabody Terrace Married Students' Housing at Harvard, a project undervalued by the greater community, the lower scale buildings integrate with the existing fabric of Cambridge. Each courtyard frames an existing public building, and the taller towers give specific identity to the urban blocks. These new open spaces restructure both the city and the public life around Mass Avenue. While the bar buildings engage the street, the towers provide Cambridge with iconic urban markers. Each block with its tower and public amenity adds up to an urban campus plan that makes clever adjustments to the context.

TOP Existing public space diagram and areas taken over as semi-public space in the new configuration.
BOTTOM Three views of Central Square and Massachusetts Avenue promenade from adjacent building.
OPPOSITE Aerial perspective.

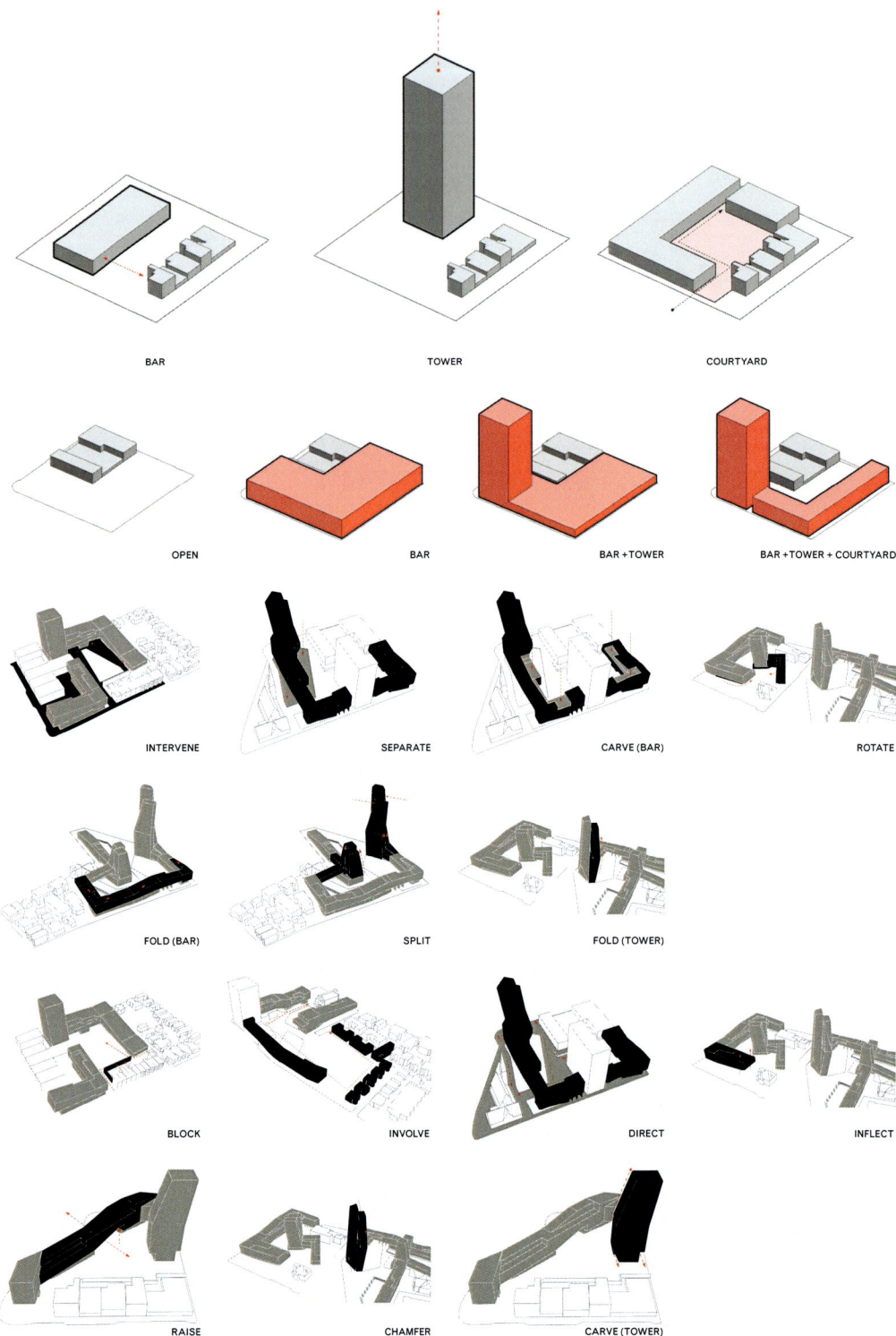

BAR   TOWER   COURTYARD

OPEN   BAR   BAR + TOWER   BAR + TOWER + COURTYARD

INTERVENE   SEPARATE   CARVE (BAR)   ROTATE

FOLD (BAR)   SPLIT   FOLD (TOWER)

BLOCK   INVOLVE   DIRECT   INFLECT

RAISE   CHAMFER   CARVE (TOWER)

TOP Established city-making tropes.
SECOND ROW Established tropes deployed at 4 FAR.
THIRD AND FOURTH ROW New tropes dissolving typological
boundaries.
FIFTH AND SIXTH ROW New tropes dissolving contextual boundar-
ies.

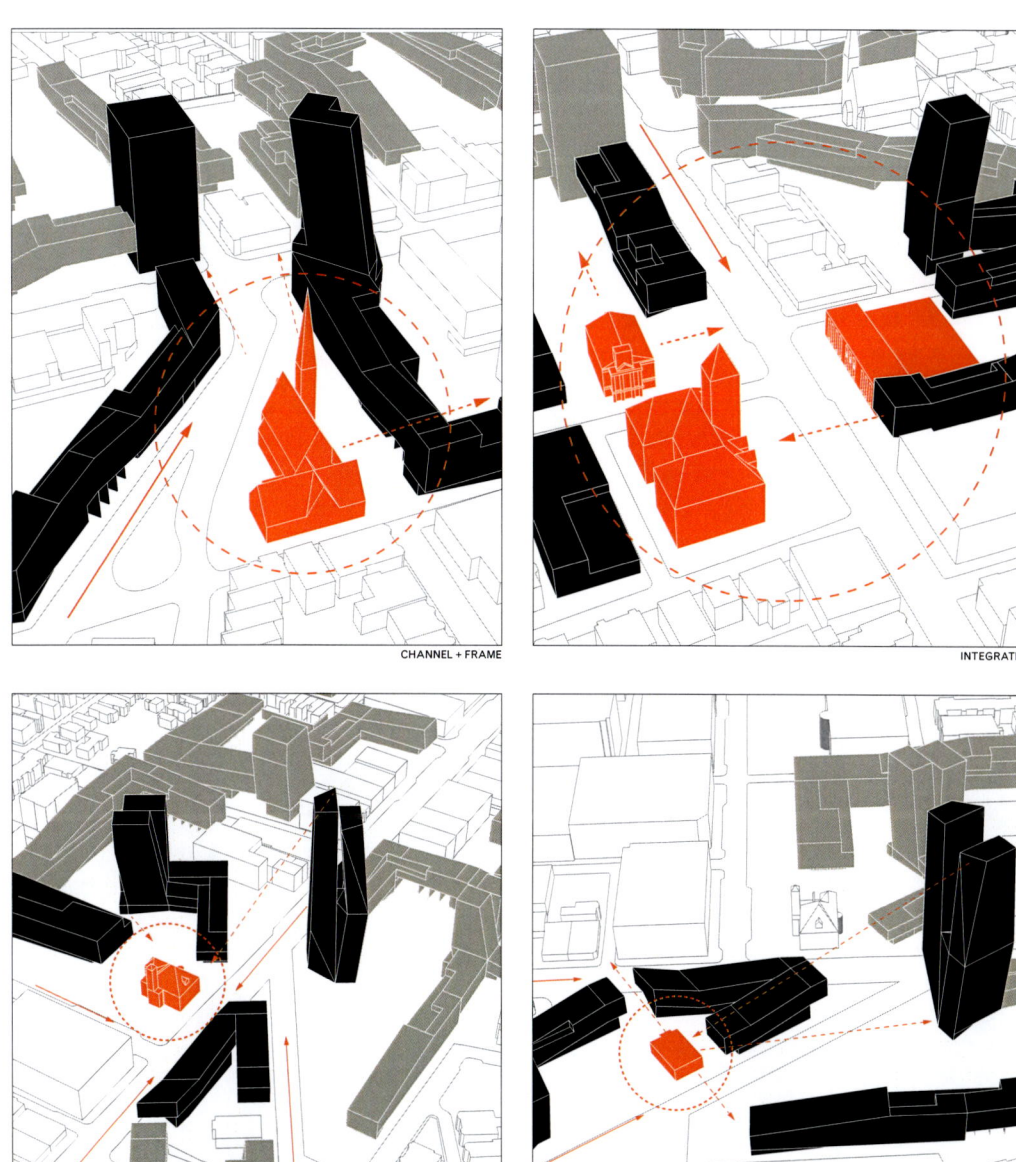

CHANNEL + FRAME

INTEGRATE

TRIANGULATE

ENCIRCLE

ABOVE Composite tropes that combine various new tropes.

TOP Ground floor plan.
MIDDLE Transverse section through firehouse tower facing Trinity
Church.
BOTTOM Longitudinal section through south courtyards looking north.
OPPOSITE Model photographs.

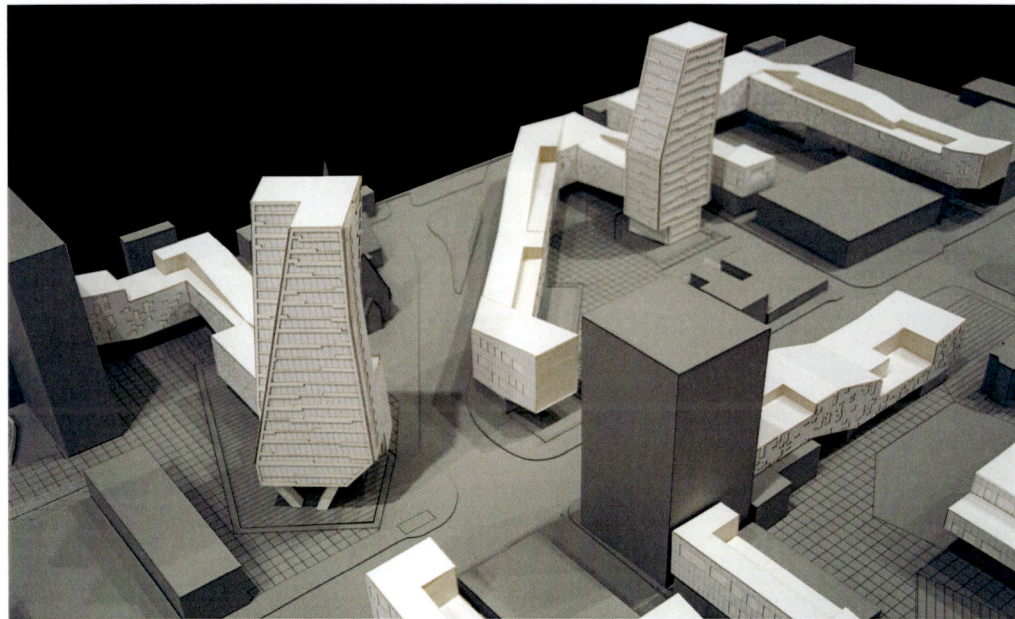

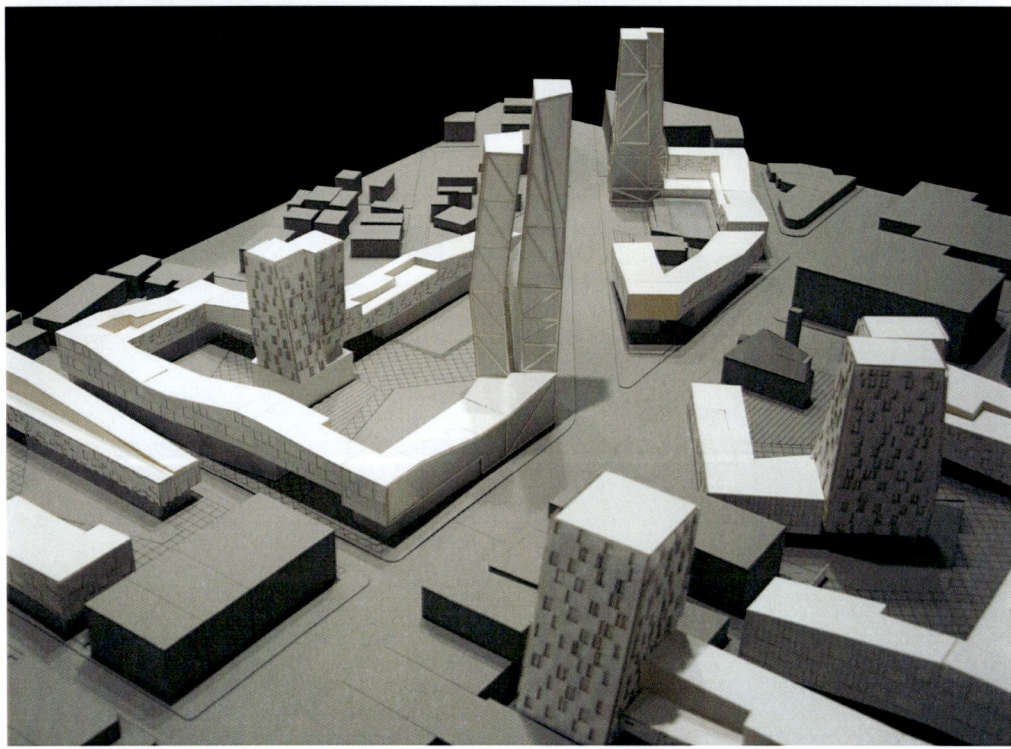

The Missing Nodes
Central Square

Boyuan Zhang + Elvira Hoxha

As a major thoroughfare through the heart of the city, Mass Ave is a public space more of motion than of rest. This project contends that any new development in this area should provide a series of public spaces for civic and cultural activities that draw on the energy of the Avenue. Anchored by two major public spaces on the north and south ends of the site, the new development fosters a collection of smaller semi-public spaces that drive the design of the new mixed-use development. To the west, the two diagonal connectors Western Avenue and River Street are terminated in a large ringed plaza over the T stop that quiets traffic and gives a

physical point of destination in what is now a rather confused intersection. To the east, Main Street's intersection with Mass Ave is enhanced by a large, framed market square. Building heights are raised to provide iconic new reference points from distances along the diagonal connectors. Mass Ave is then reinforced with street wall buildings that have rear courtyards that connect the streets parallel to the main drag, giving programmatic depth to the main artery.

ABOVE Rendering of cultural node.
OPPOSITE Master plan for new nodes.

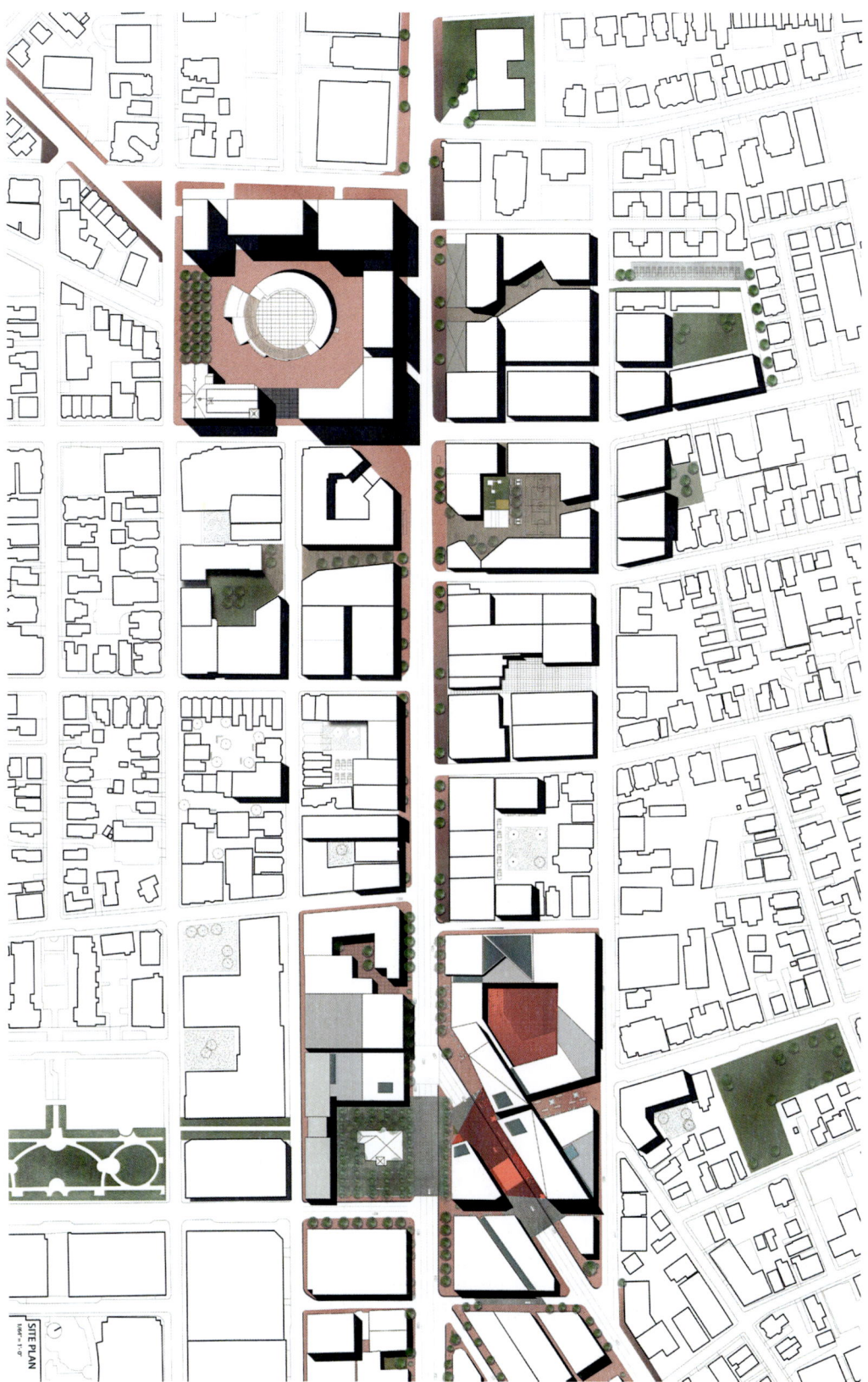

SITE PLAN

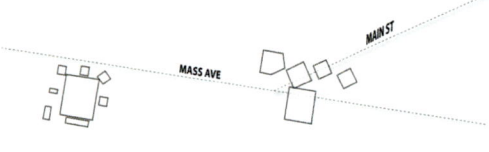

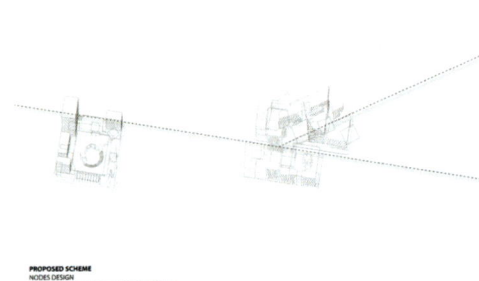

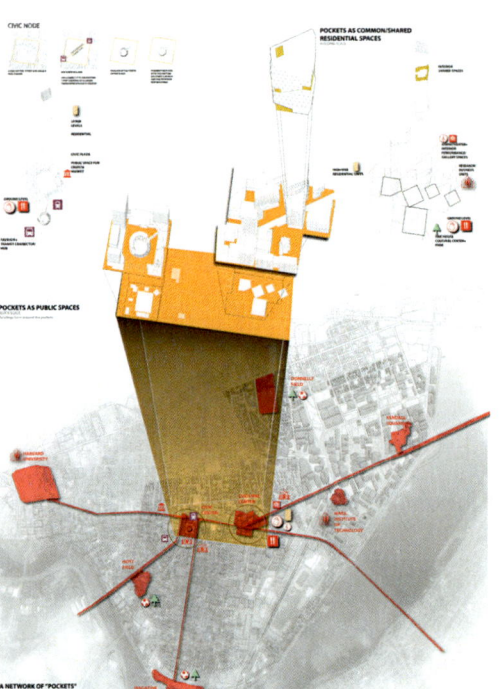

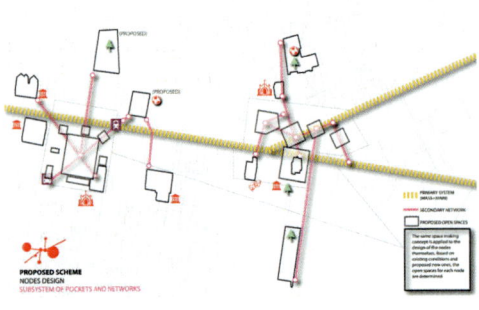

TOP Diagram of forces acting on Central Square site.
MIDDLE Diagrams of initial massing arrangement on the main
street intersections.
BOTTOM Diagrams of programmatic nodes.

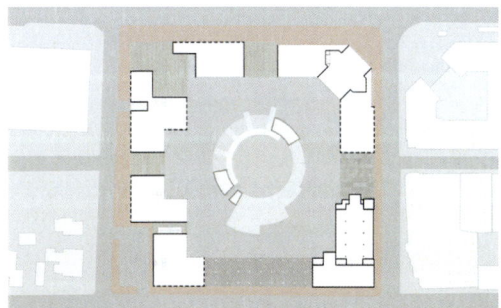
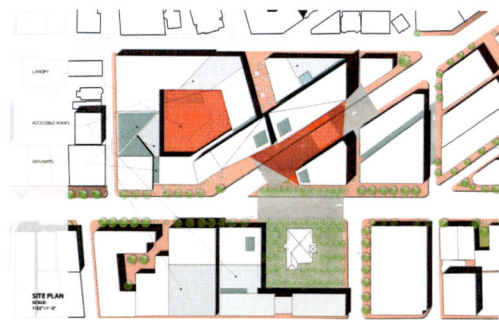

TOP Plans of civic (left) and cultural (right) nodes.
MIDDLE Site model.
BOTTOM Views of civic (left) and cultural (right) nodes.

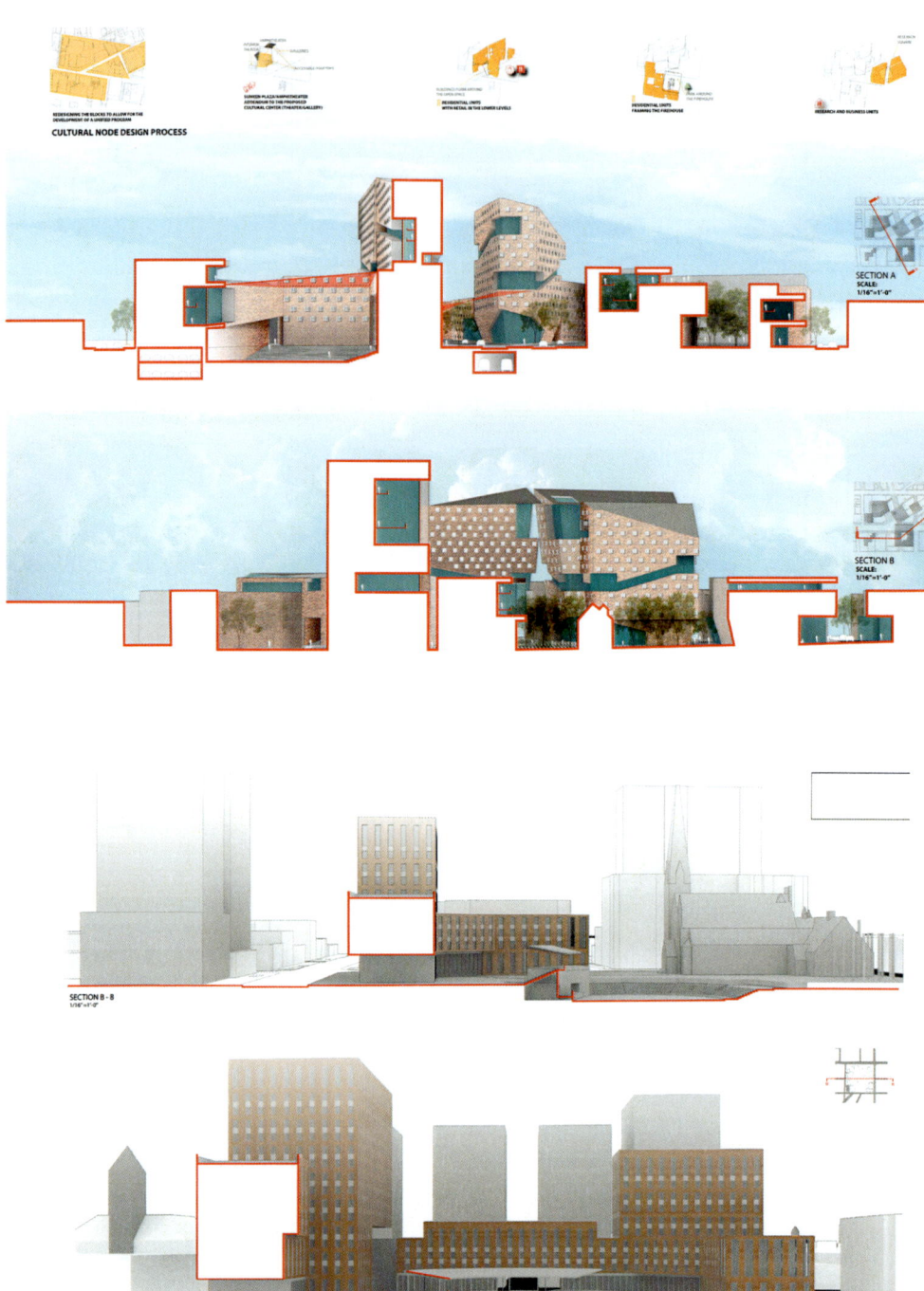

ABOVE Sections through cultural (top) and civic (bottom) nodes.
OPPOSITE Model photographs.

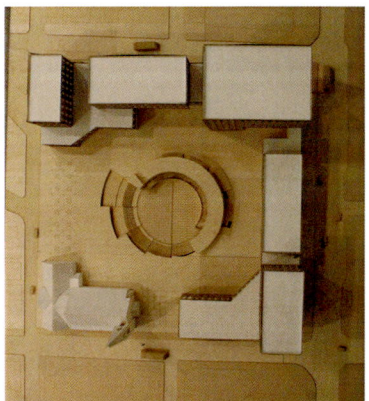

Central Square Bazaar

Central Square

Karolina Czeczek + Kate Lisi

As a place where "the 99-cent Big Mac and a $6.99 carrot-beet juice with wheatgrass boosters can co-exist," Central Square is diverse, vibrant, and scruffy. It is a complex collection of architectures and demographics. The current street-block-building organization of the area, however, overpowers the elaborate network of murals, parking lots, and benches that make up this area, limiting public space along the street wall of Mass Ave.

This project plays up the messy urbanism of the area in order to eradicate hierarchy of public space in future development. By amplifying the intricate and downplaying the big, a new urban order is created—one in which a building is just as important as a street, a bench, or a tree; where edges are dissolved; and the linearity of Mass Ave is abandoned for a nonhierarchical porosity of space. Anchored by a large parking garage underground, the space above is free to be residential, commercial, or institutional, but always emphatically public. The arrangement of buildings and urban street furniture is carefully orchestrated to relate to the fractured urban fabric while still identifying and developing more intimate public spaces and casual place-making efforts reminiscent of a bazaar within an eclectic urban fabric.

TOP Rendered perspective of the main public plaza.
OPPOSITE Site plan of illuminated pathways.

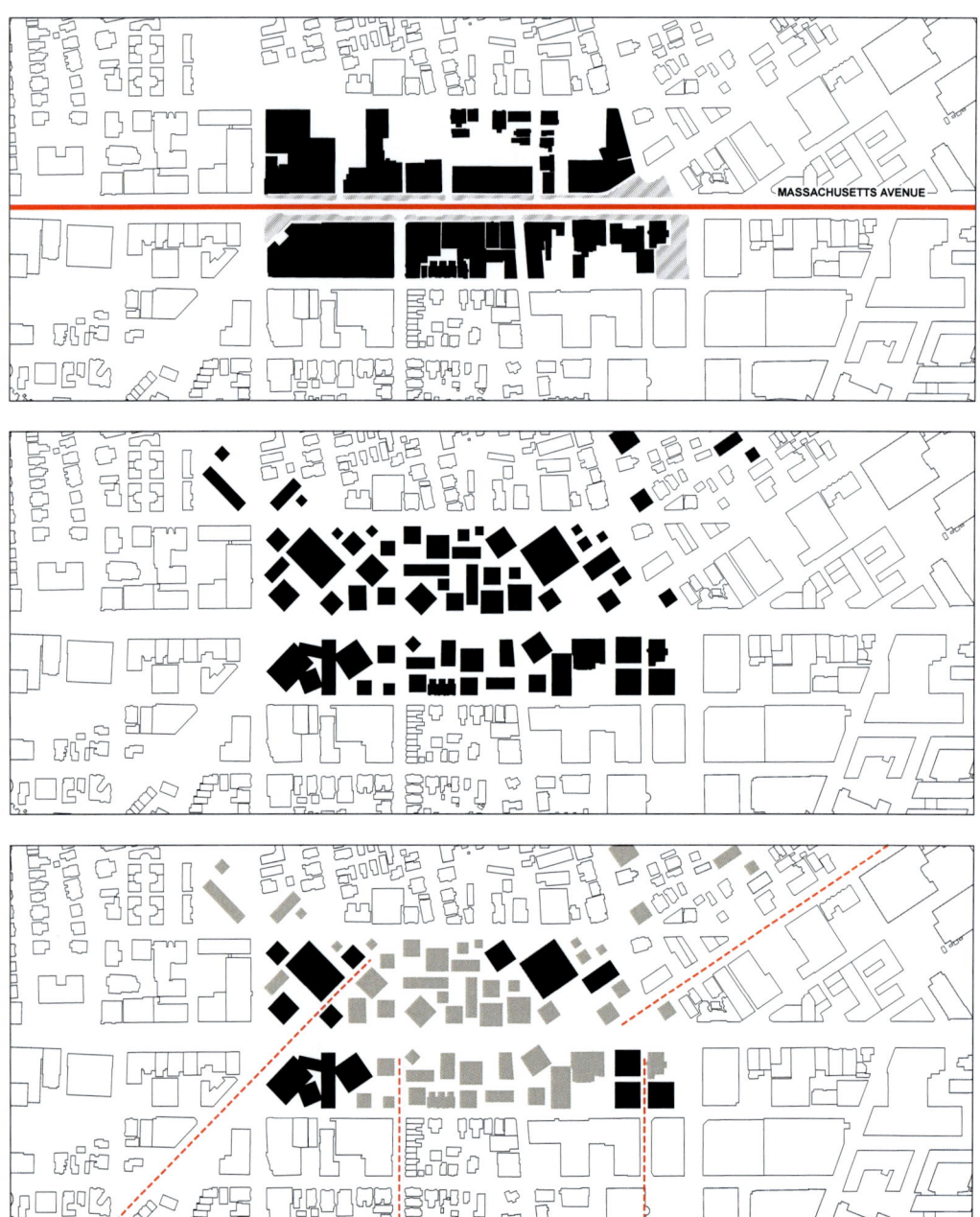

TOP Diagram of existing site datum.
MIDDLE Massing diagram of proposal.
BOTTOM Diagram of the four anchors in the proposal.
OPPOSITE TOP Axonometric series depicting massing organization relative to ground plane and subgrade parking.
OPPOSITE BOTTOM Taxonomy of organizational elements.

ground lights

loose seating

dining areas

exhibition spaces

street lights

trees

cores

buildings

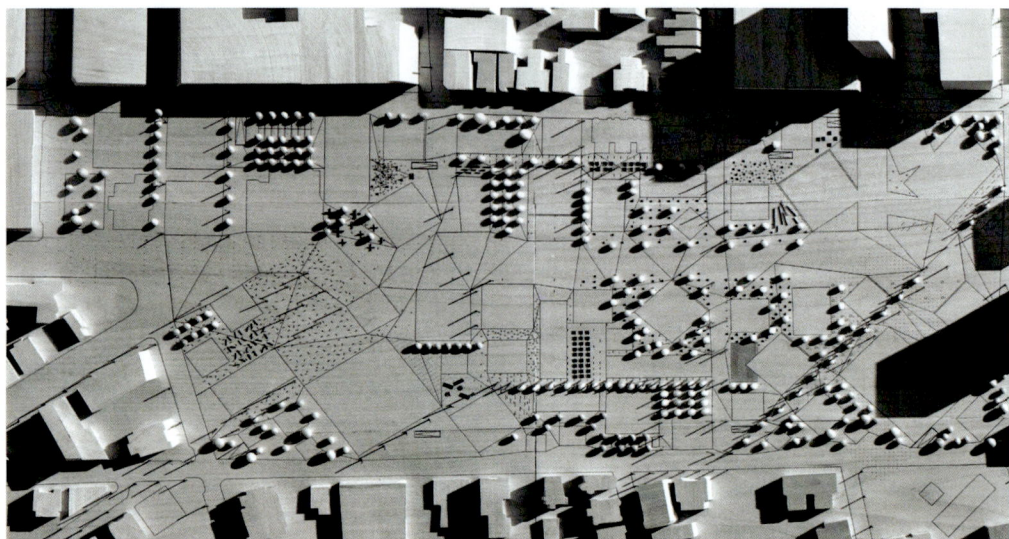

TOP Plan view of the model.
BOTTOM Scenario rendering at the T stop entry.

TOP Aerialview of the site showing lighting scheme.
BOTTOM Scenario rendering.

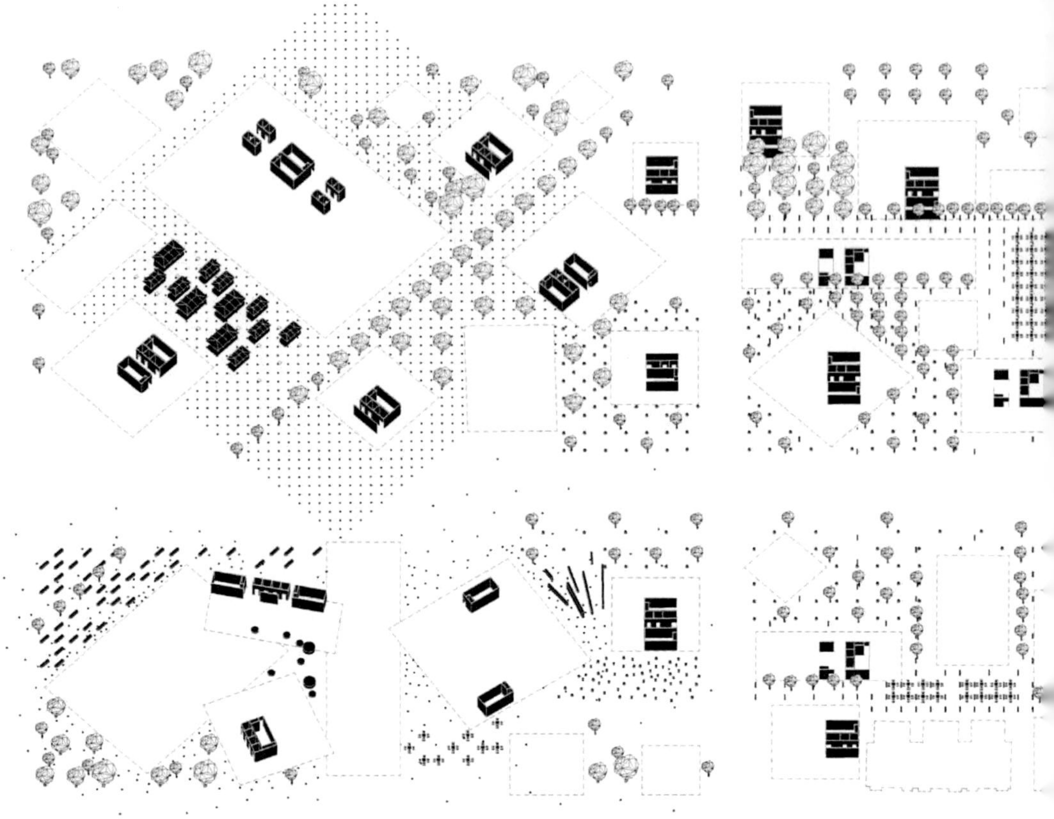

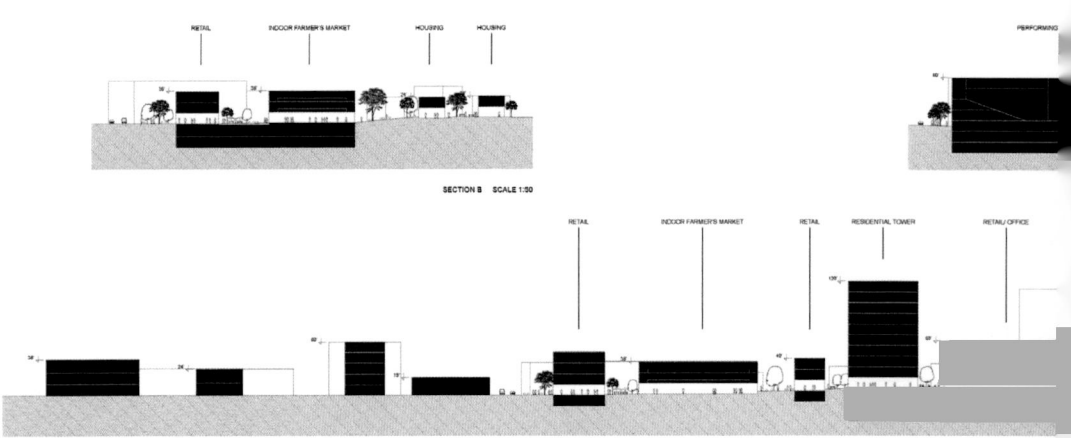

TOP Ground floor plan with highlighted cores.
BOTTOM Longitudinal and transverse sections.

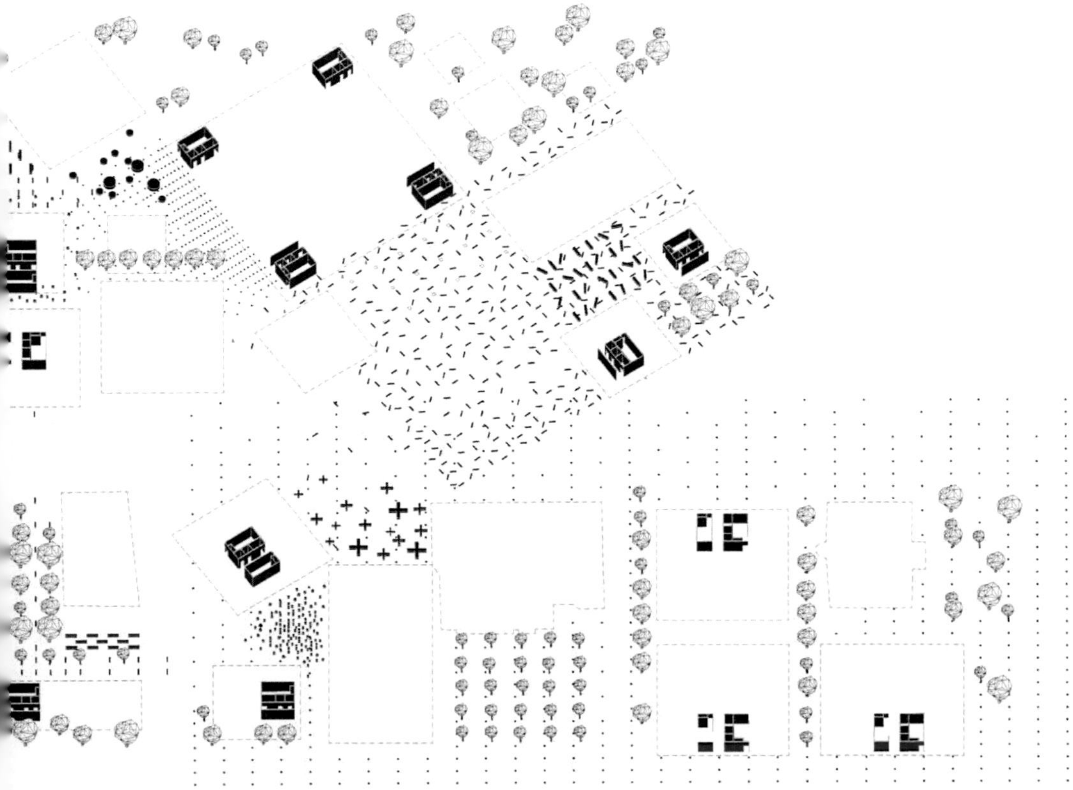

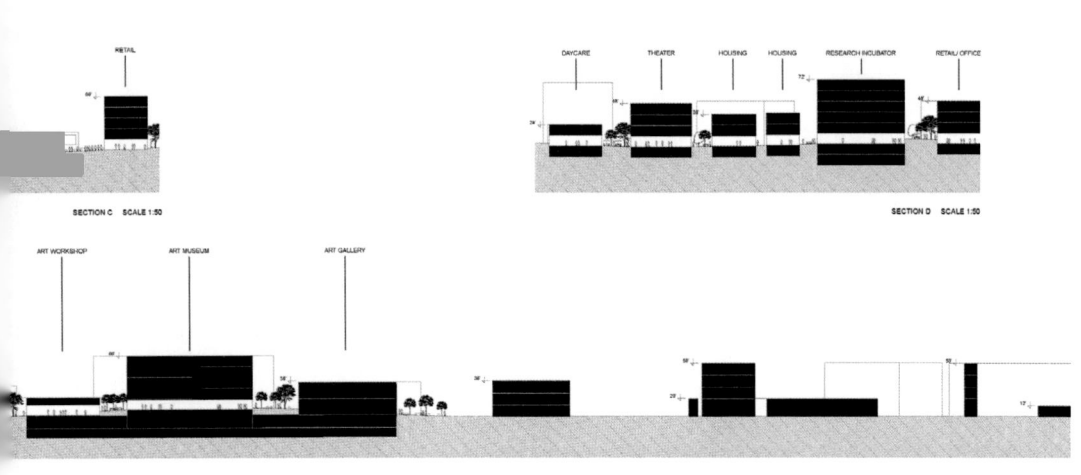

RETAIL

DAYCARE   THEATER   HOUSING   HOUSING   RESEARCH INCUBATOR   RETAIL OFFICE

SECTION C   SCALE 1:50

SECTION D   SCALE 1:50

ART WORKSHOP   ART MUSEUM   ART GALLERY

Urban Flotilla
Central Square

Read Langworthy + Julcsi Futo

ABOVE Rendering of new Massachusetts Avenue elevation.

Cambridge is a city of diverse cultures and ethnicities. This project proposes that heterogeneity and difference are the products of built form. This guides the decisions to preserve all the existing buildings, introduce incremental units of housing, and provide small courtyards for both public and private uses throughout the vertical section of the project. Despite the relative contextualism of these guidelines, the project also gives Central Square a strong new physical identity. A new, dense mass of housing hovers above the buildings on Mass Ave. The project elaborates a development strategy that ensures variety in materials, fenestration, spatial configuration, and program. The ground-floor public squares—used as ad hoc market spaces, cafes, and for other public gatherings—transition upward into a series of shared terraces that form semi-public spaces for the apartments above. This provides residents with spaces that visually participate in the ground-floor public realm without compromising the private domain. The complex massing requires a clearly organized circulation system. The glass-covered green atriums in the interior corridors are both social and wayfinding areas within the plan. Each apartment unit then has a complex relationship to its neighbors. Each affiliates to at least two distinct groupings of units, providing a complexity indicative of lively urban fabrics.

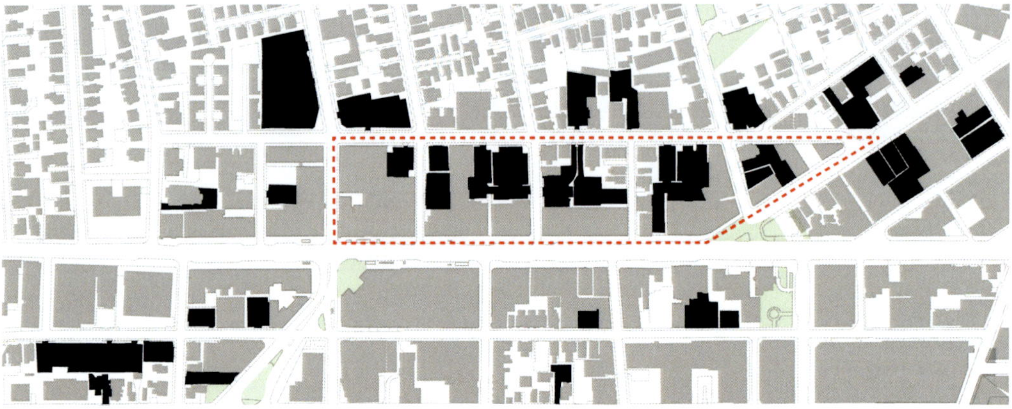

TOP Diagram of abundant surface parking in Central Square.
MIDDLE Diagram of relatively taut streetfront of Massachusetts
Avenue.
BOTTOM Rendering of new Massachusetts Avenue streetfront.

OPPOSITE TOP (COLUMNS LEFT TO RIGHT) Process diagrams
of carve and stack operations on each unit; subtraction of voids and
courtyards; and propagation of these operations across site.
OPPOSITE BOTTOM Model photo of final scheme.

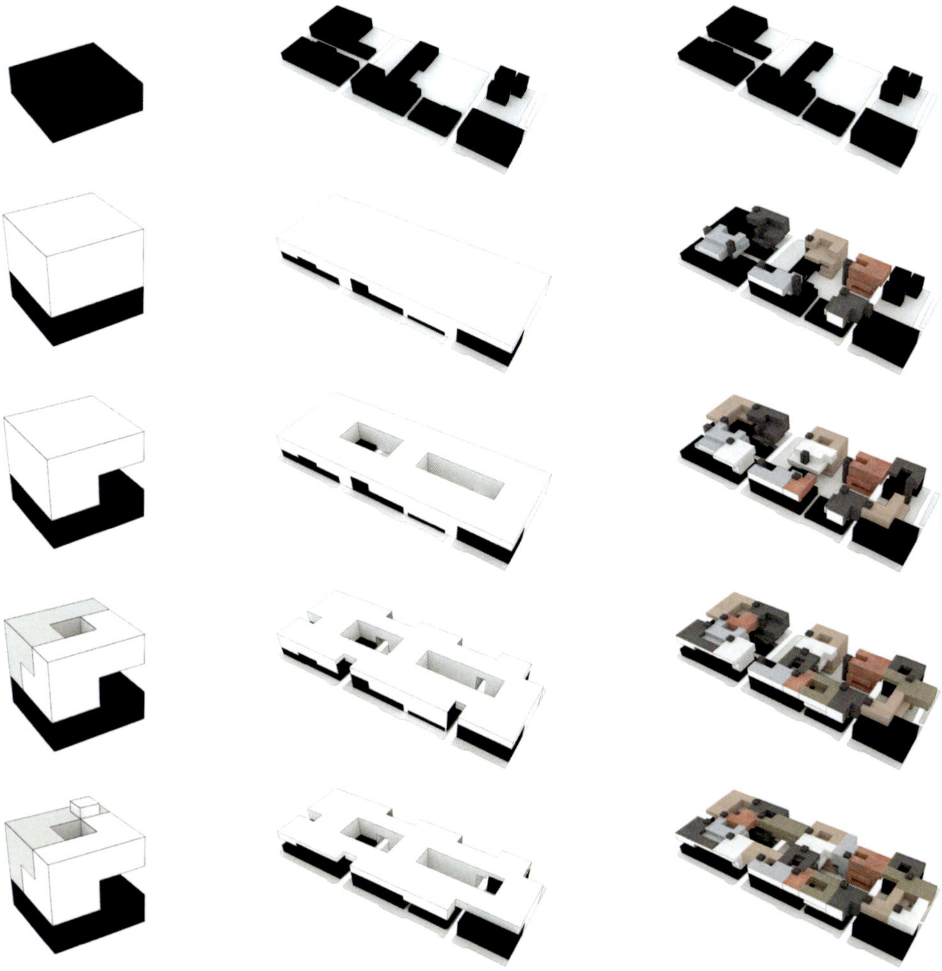

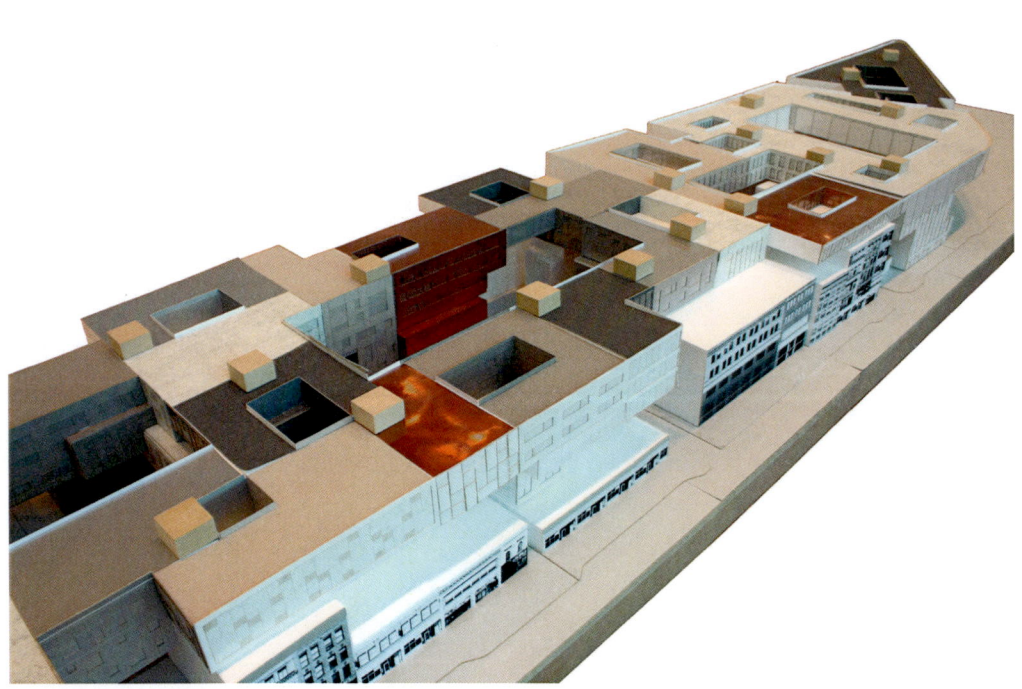

GROUND FLOOR PLAN   1/32"=1'-0"

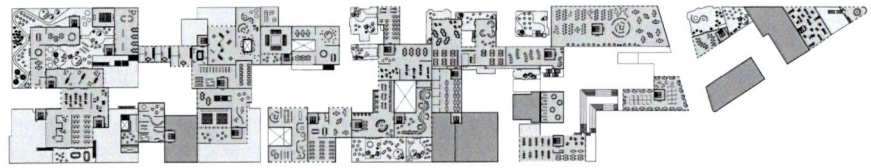

4TH FLOOR PLAN   1/32"=1'-0"

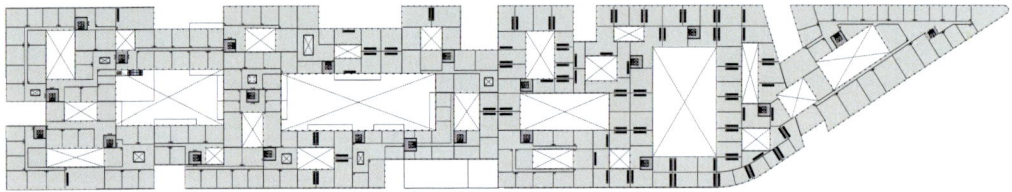

4TH FLOOR PLAN   1/32"=1'-0"

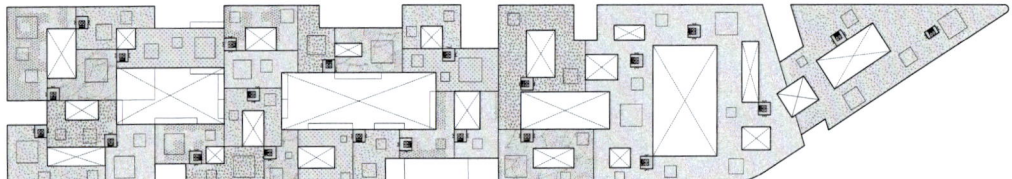

ROOF PLAN   1/32"=1'-0"

ABOVE (TOP TO BOTTOM) Ground, fourth floor, sixth floor, and roof
plans; model photo of final elevation.

TOP Transverse sections of selected courtyards.
MIDDLE Transverse sections of selected courtyards.
BOTTOM Rendering of courtyard.

Central Square Circuitry
Central Square

Peter McInish + Laurence Lumley

Unlike the grand public spaces of Boston,
Cambridge is a collection of small, intimate, and
contained open spaces. This project proposes to
intensify this network by structuring new development around new and existing alleys and hidden
squares. By incorporating a series of fixed small-
scale interventions such as a new paving system,
in conjunction with temporary and mobile devices
like metal barricades, lighting, and folding chairs, a
system is provided for intensifying and managing
the public life of the city. New building interventions which increase density do so in accordance
with the picturesque and happenstance massing of
the current fabric. Buildings are tucked into inner
blocks, small courtyards are formed by additions
and new types, and a sequence of wayfinding for
public spaces become clues towards entering the
neighborhood from Mass Ave. While conforming to
new targets for urban density, the scheme retains
the more intimate and circumstantial qualities of
Central Square.

ABOVE Site plan.

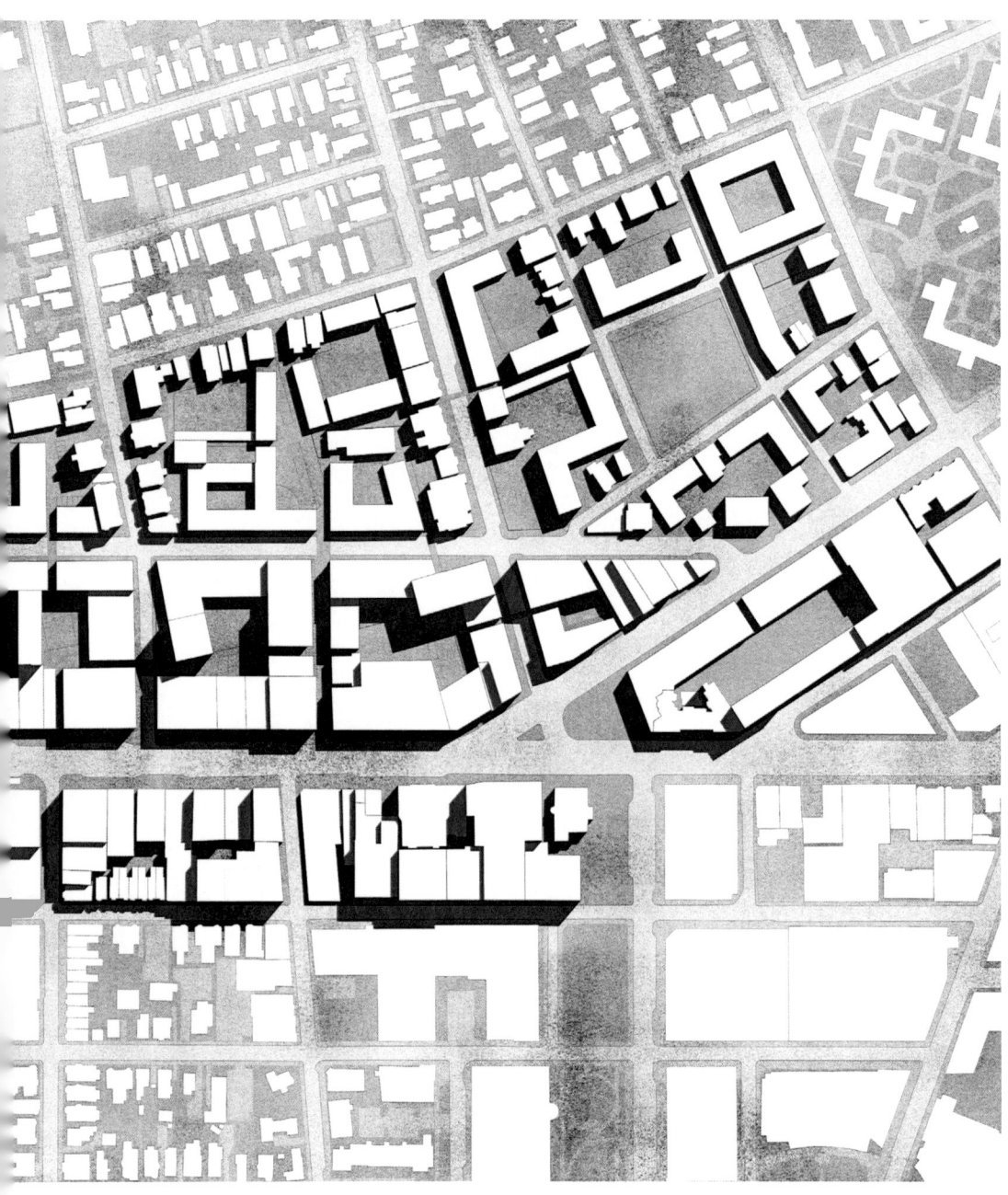

Cambridge

Boston

CONTAINED   **INTIMATE**   **SEQUENTIAL**   **OPEN**   **GRANDIOSE**   **SCENOGRAPHIC**

Existing

Proposed

TOP View of Central Square and Massachusetts Avenue
promenade from adjacent building.
BOTTOM Diagrams of public spaces showing the major scale of
Boston against the finer grain of Cambridge.
OPPOSITE TOP Site plan.
OPPOSITE MIDDLE Before and after photo collage.
OPPOSITE BOTTOM Vignettes of alleyways, existing and proposed.

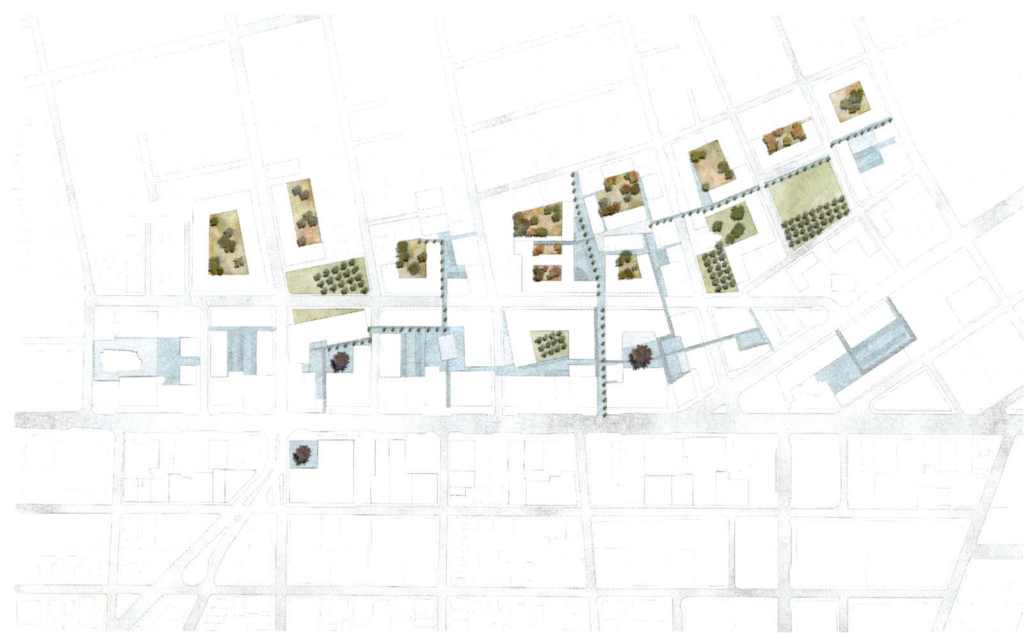

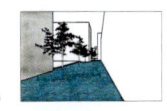

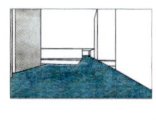
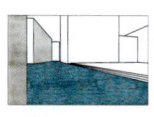
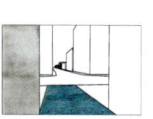

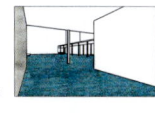
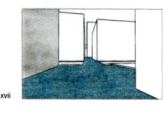
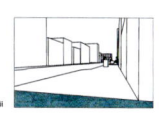

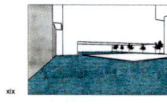
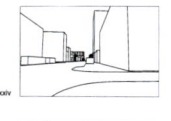

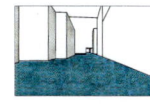

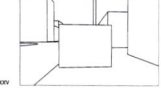

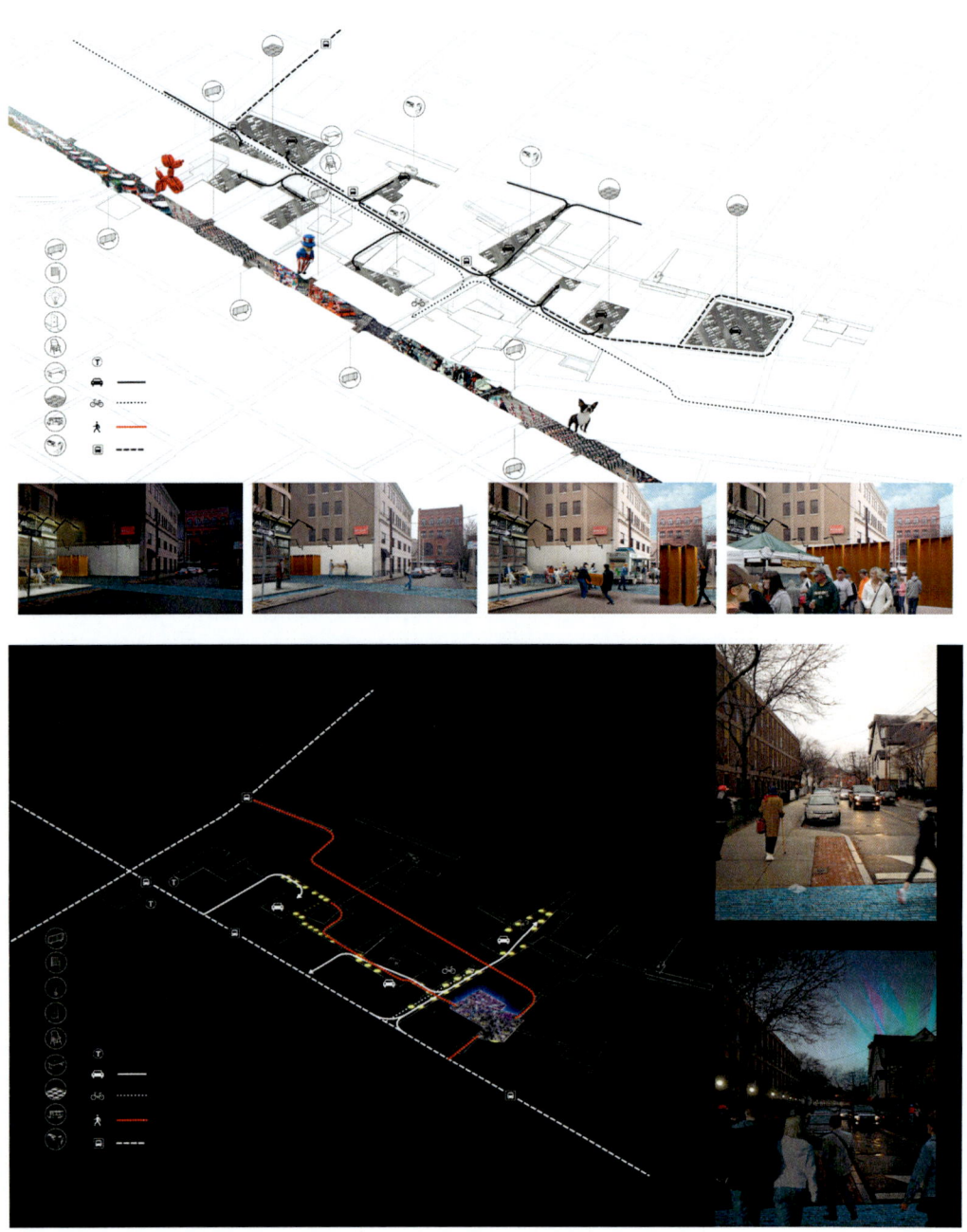

TOP   Axonometric of public event structure for the arts, daytime.
BOTTOM Axonometric of public event structure, nighttime.

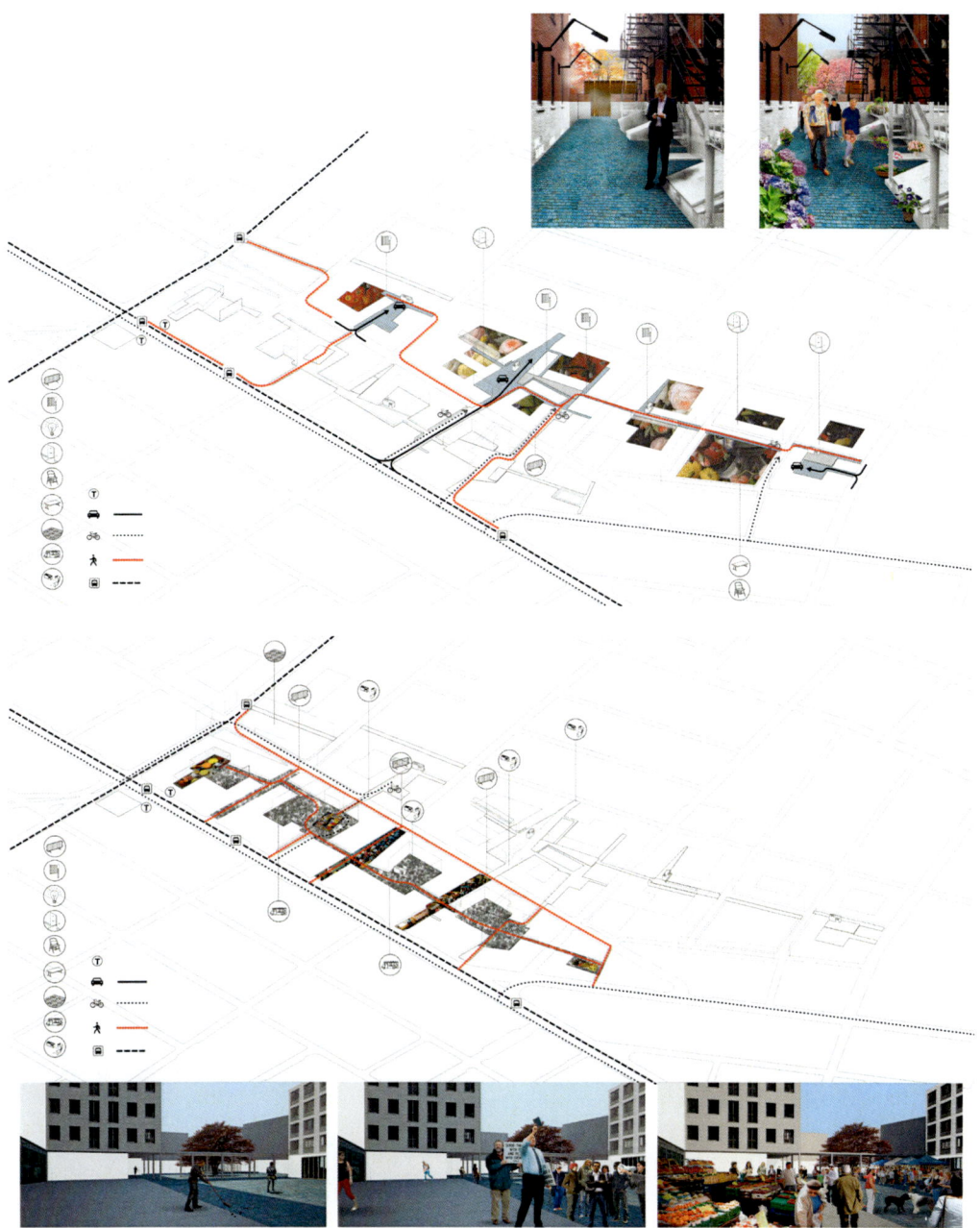

TOP Axonometric of public event structure for the market, daytime.
BOTTOM Axonometric of public event structure through the
courtyards off Mass Ave.

PIT - Public Infrastructure Terminal
Central Square

Katarzyna Pozniak + Raphael de la Fontaine

Parking, as everyone in greater Boston knows, is a major problem. Though dense development and modifications to zoning may alleviate the need for the car, one cannot easily dismiss its use in the future of the city. In the tradition of Boston's vast landfill enterprises, this project proposes a sixty-foot-deep excavation in the underdeveloped superblock on the north side of Mass Ave. The sectional shift enables eight full stories of housing on the block interior without disrupting the relatively low-rise typologies that make up many of Boston's existing streets. This seemingly sensitive approach to the existing urban context belies the radical nature of the "big dig" behind the street wall. An underground train station, parking garage, residential lobbies, and a large grocery store produce a dynamic new public space, blurring the lines between urban and suburban motifs, commercial and public spaces. The programs anticipated in this design also reflect the needs and desires of many of Boston/Cambridge's well-heeled neighborhoods and accommodate larger building footprints for the hybrid of boutique grocery stores and large entertainment complexes that populate the new downtowns of our cities.

ABOVE View of newly excavated public promenade.

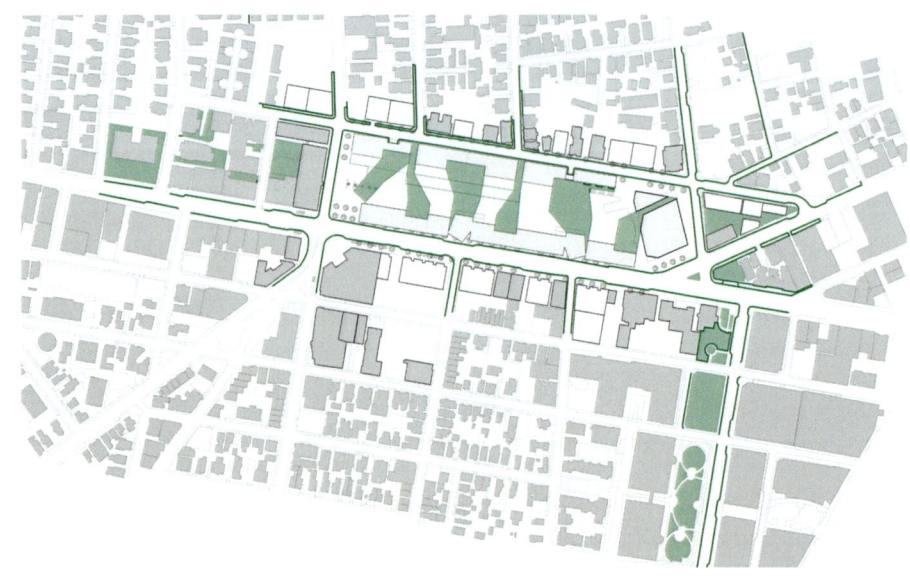

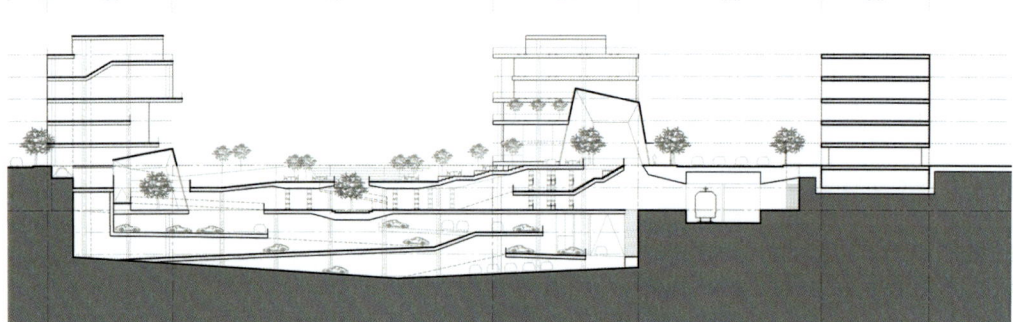

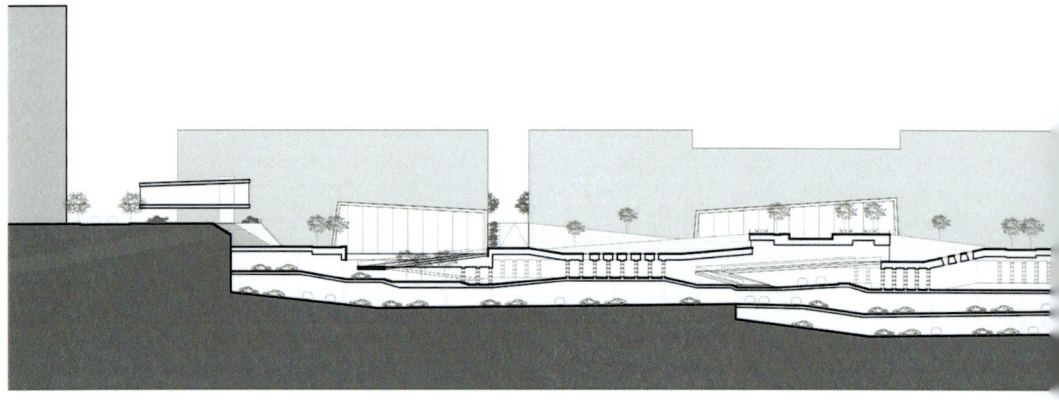

ABOVE (TOP TO BOTTOM) Master plan; longitudinal section
looking north; transverse section looking towards City Hall.

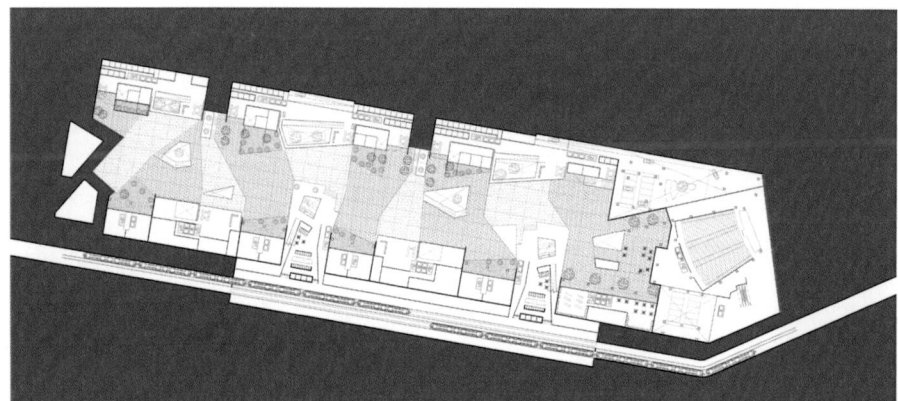

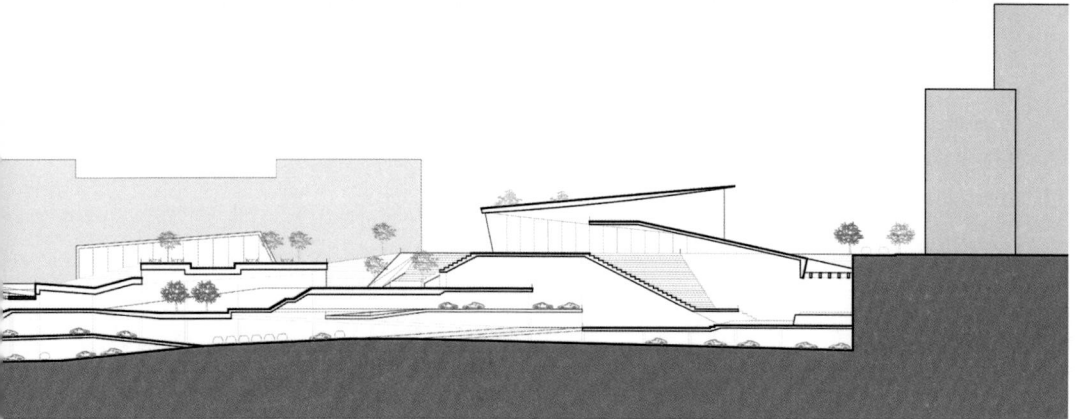

ABOVE (TOP TO BOTTOM) Grade level plan; T stop level plan.

**7:00 AM
MORNING COFFEE ON THE BALCONY**

**8:00 AM
HOPPING ON THE SUBWAY**

ALL IMAGES Scenario vignettes of residential balcony, new T Stop,
public park, and grocery store.

**12:30 PM
LUNCH BREAK**

**6:15 PM
AFTER WORK GROCERY SHOPPING**

**6:45 PM
UNWINDING IN THE PRIVATE GARDEN**

**WEEKEND
BACK FROM ERRANDS, LEAVING THE CAR**

ALL IMAGES Scenario vignettes of private gardens, approach into public park, experience of new promenade, and new cultural center.

**WEEKEND
STROLLING IN THE NEIGHBORHOOD**

**WEEKEND
GOING OUT TO SEE A SHOW**

Cambridge Common
Central Square

Daniel Luster + Olen Milholland

Boston's Emerald Necklace —The Commons, The
Gardens, and The Fens—is in an evolving relationship to the city. The Commons, once a place for
everything from cow grazing to public hangings
is now more of an exceptional space in daily life.
Though its relationship to the city has changed, its
importance in supporting an idea of the "Public"
has not.

This project posits that Cambridge, which lacks
any sort of central public square, needs to create
and support its own notion of "Public." By splitting
Mass Ave into two one-way streets, space is freed
for a new park. The complex section of the project
weaves pedestrian paths into the green, separate
from the busy automobile traffic on Mass Ave. To
achieve greater overall density, development is
postulated in the form of linear towers that hover
over the park and both define the edge and activate
the center, seamlessly integrating people, cars,
nature, shopping, and social gathering into the
regular routines of the city. More importantly, this
project gives Cambridge something that currently
is desperately lacking: a Commons in the lineage of
the great public spaces across the river.

TOP LEFT View of Central Square and Massachusetts Avenue
promenade from adjacent building.
BOTTOM LEFT Commerical terrace view.
OPPOSITE TOP View of Central Square.
OPPOSITE BOTTOM Public theater as seen from Central Square
common.

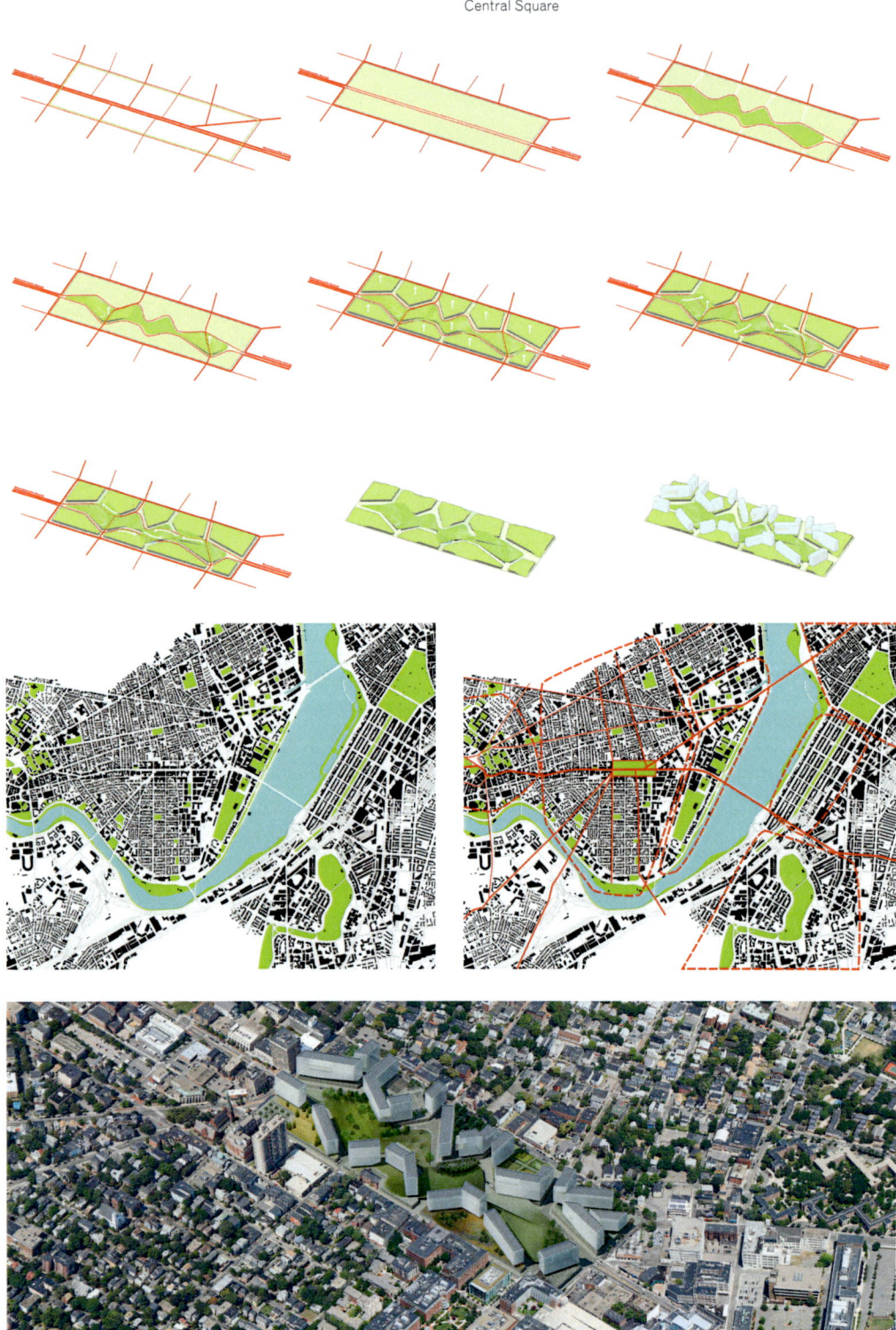

TOP Axonometrics showing the generation of the park section.
MIDDLE Existing urban plan showing public spaces and the new
Central Square common with major road connections.
BOTTOM Aerial rendering.
OPPOSITE TOP Site plan showing the ground floor.
OPPOSITE BOTTOM Site plan showing upper floors of the new
buildings.

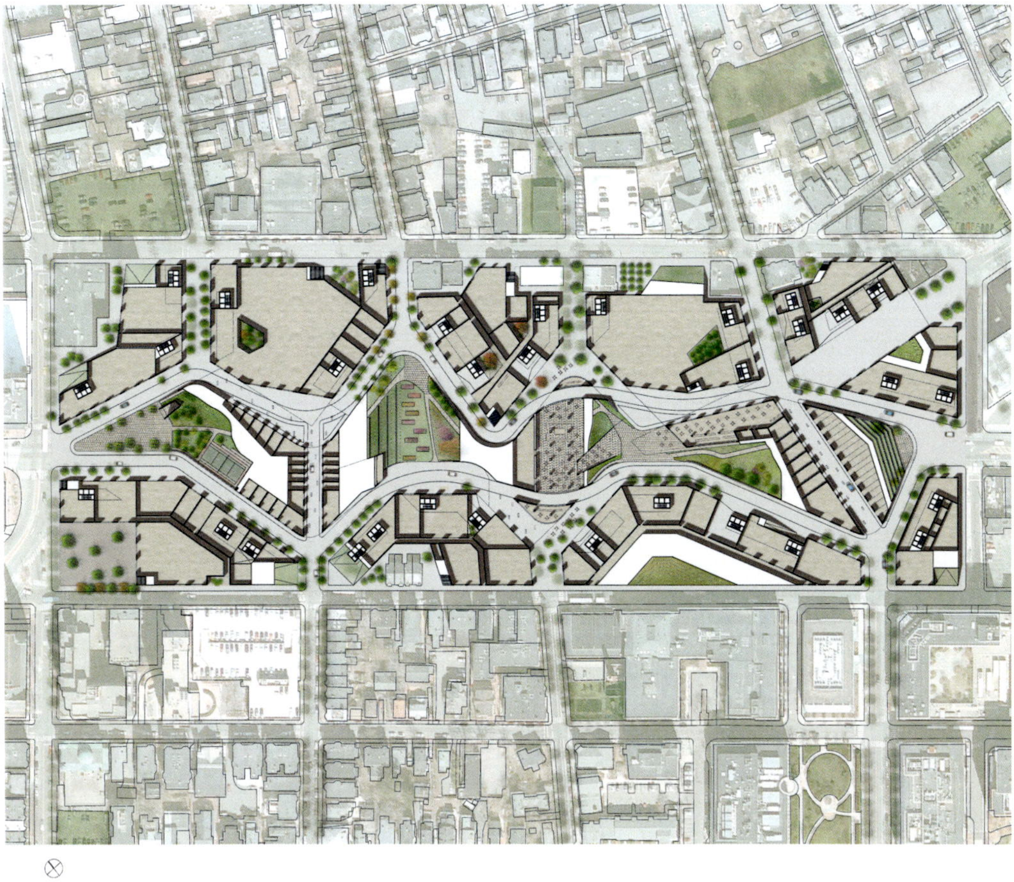

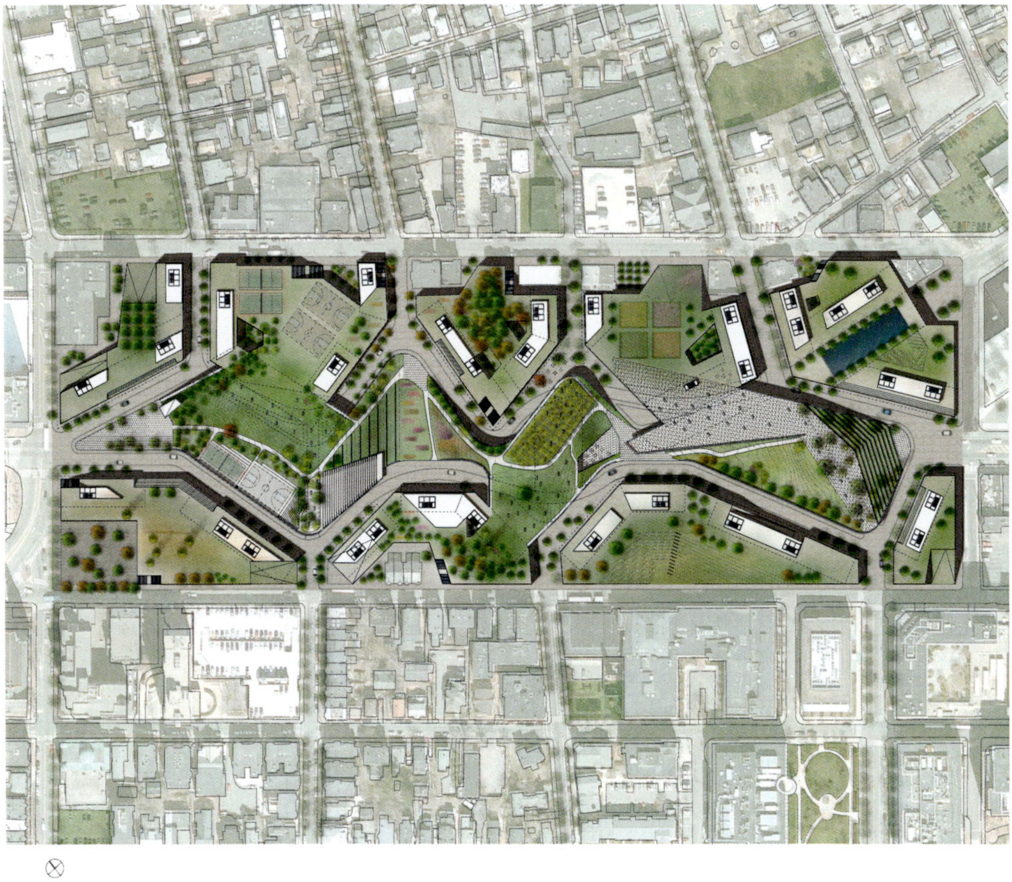

TOP Section through the site.
MIDDLE Detailed section.
BOTTOM Site model.

ABOVE Site model.

ABOVE Model photographs.
OPPOSITE TOP View from interior terrace to the common.
OPPOSITE BOTTOM View from private exterior terrace to the common.

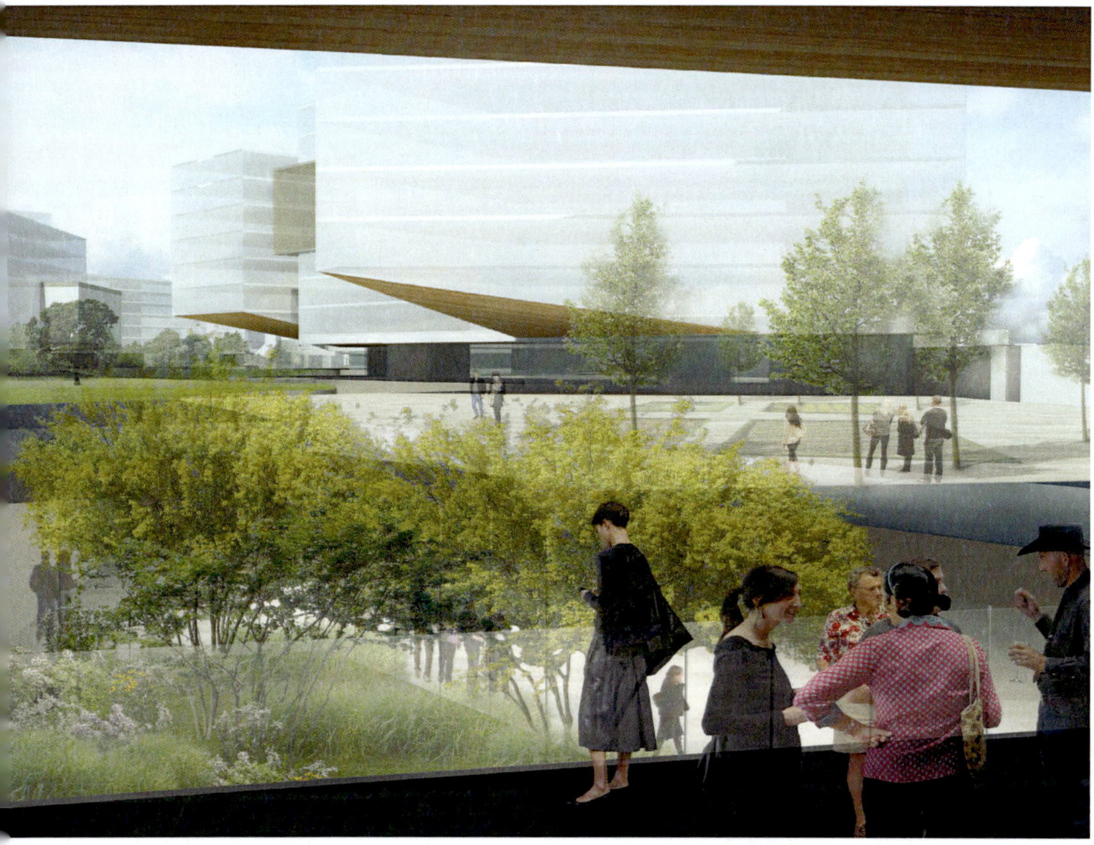

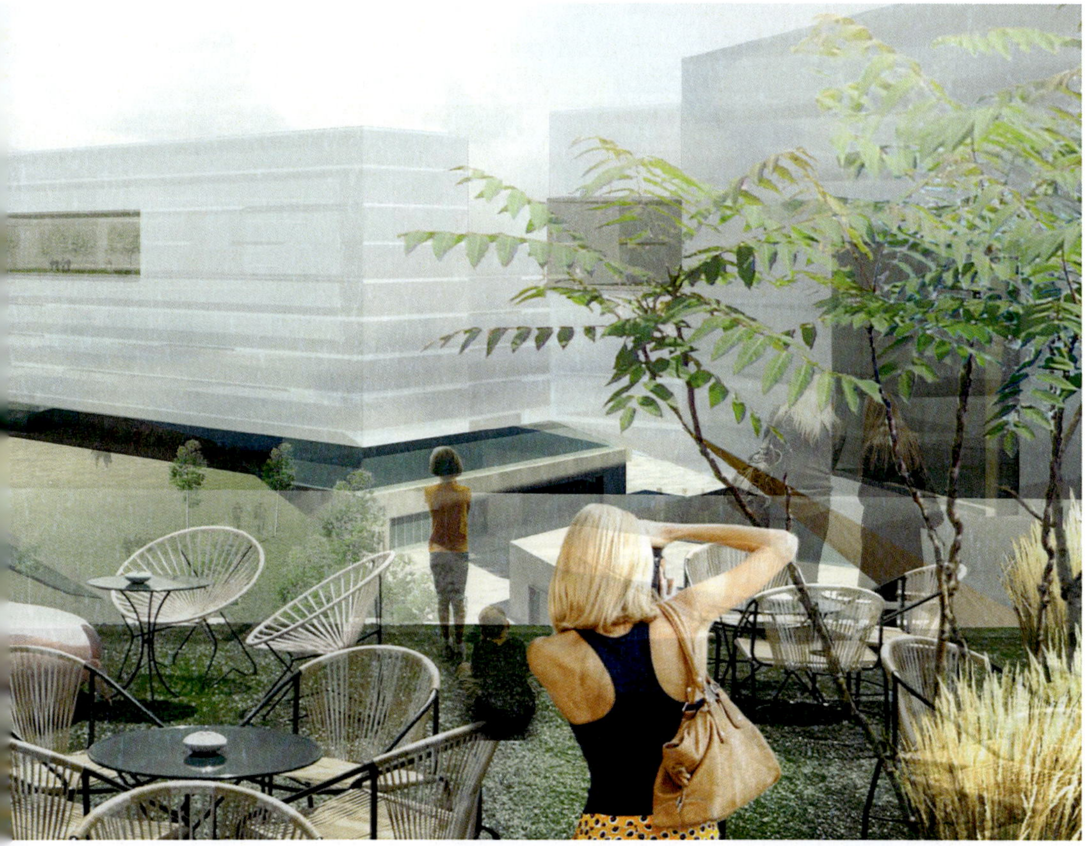

City Hall

Edward Mitchell

During the era of Urban Renewal, inevitable changes modernized the city infrastructure, but the general consensus is that those changes to the city—most notably the demolition of the North End neighborhood and the fragmentation of the city by the highway—had, at best, mixed results with short-term gains. Interventions geared to the automobile tore apart the historic fabric, and the large-scale buildings and roadways of that campaign often negatively impacted Boston's residential neighborhoods. Urban renewal and flight to the outlying suburbs were blamed for the demise of the city in the 1960s and '70s.

The architectural centerpiece of the Urban Renewal campaign run by the Boston Redevelopment Authority (BRA) under the direction of Ed Logue was the construction of City Hall. I. M. Pei did the master plan for the government center and the BRA held an international competition for the building. The brief, used by our studio, is a document of its time. The program is an encyclopedia of detailed bureaucratic hierarchy, each office space carefully calibrated for both its specific use and for internal workplace politics. Though the symbolism of the building is emphasized in the brief, the details of the program itself are symptomatic of the shift of the democratic systems of American government, whose foundations were in Boston, towards a less intimate, more civic bureaucracy. One must recall that John F. Kennedy's victory in the presidential election meant that the new City Hall would be more than a provincial exercise. As the new president's home city, Boston had an opportunity through federal funding to create a new vital image of itself.

The 1962 competition was won by the then young firm of Kallmann McKinnell & Knowles. The project took more than seven years to complete, but remained very close to the original design. The building's Brutalist style was deemed by the architects to break away from the polished Miesian corporate modernism of its time, evident in the entry by Gertrude Kerbis, Yau Chun Wong, T. C. Chang, Otto G. Stark, Sam Sit, and C. F. Murphy Associates. The building's Brutalist style was seen as a return to integrating formal expression with structure. The second-place entry by Ehrman B. Mitchell, Jr., Romaldo Giurgola, and Thomas R. Vreeland is also in some ways a Brutalist project, its raked profiles and articulation of served and service spaces reminiscent of Kahn. The Dallas City Hall by Pei appears to owe a debt to the runner-up entry.

OPPOSITE City Hall site plan.

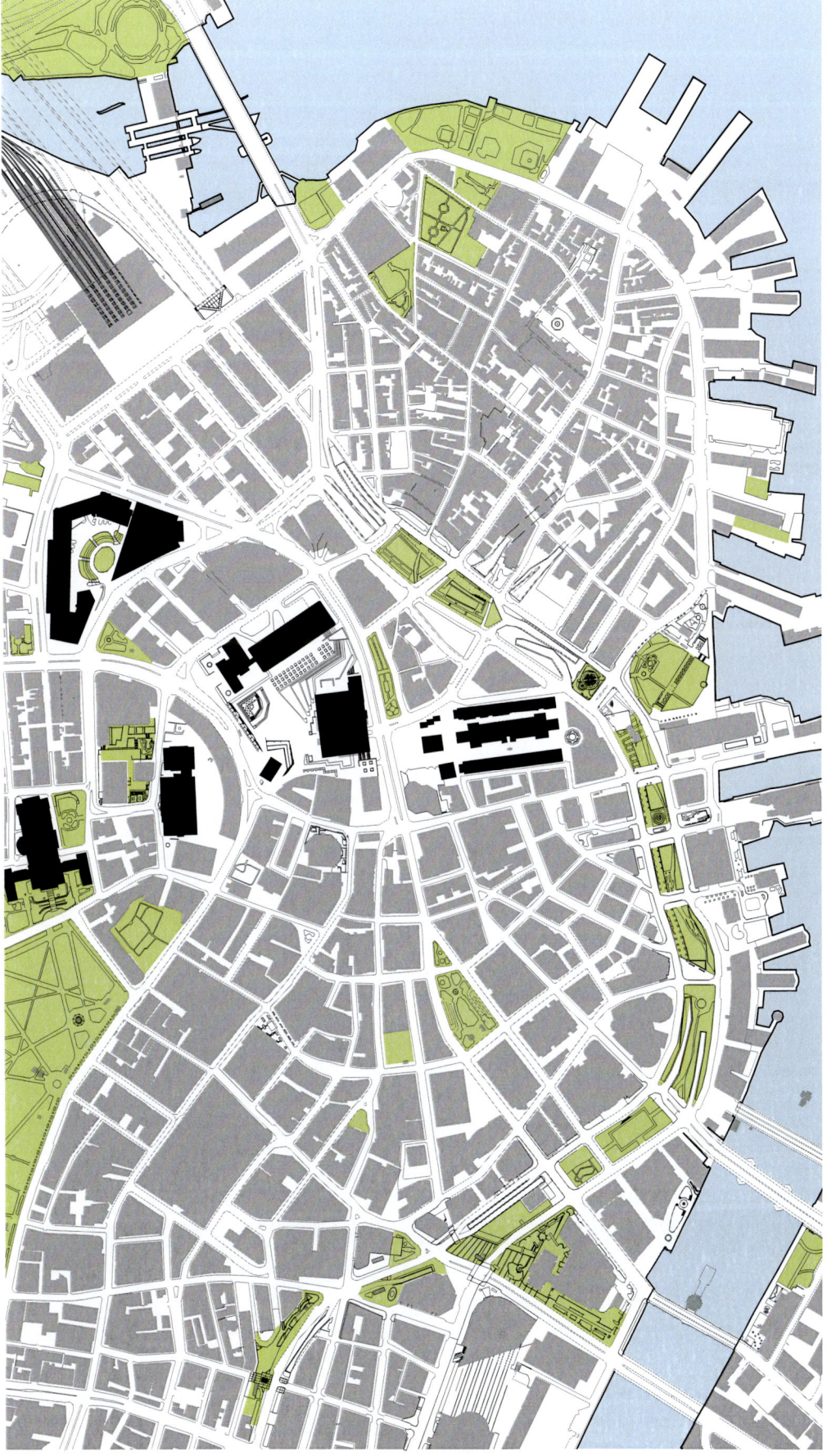

Brutalism had two distinct manifestations. One was grandiose, exemplified by Le Corbusier's work of the 1950s which coupled the use of *béton brut* with heroic and monumental form. Indeed, if the Dallas City Hall by Pei is part of a family of Brutalist civic buildings, its public reception too has been intrepid. In the 1987 apocalyptic film, *RoboCop*, the Dallas City Hall forms the base of a bureaucratic complex that has grown into a sublime and terrifying monument. But the second definition, as sketched by Reyner Banham, saw Brutalism as an open framework which would allow for events to unfold, governing circumstances but open to change—an answer to the problem of architecture's limited ability to change.

When introducing the studio project, we told the students that the Boston City Hall was an example of the first definition of Brutalism. Boston City Hall's heroic massing, its command of the plaza, and the highly articulated structure, which recalled Le Corbusier's La Tourette, all clearly identified it with the more conservative definition. However, when we met Michael McKinnell in Boston and he shared the concept sketches with us, he clearly intended Banham's more progressive definition. The concept sketch for the building, a floating block of office spaces that hovered over the site, was intended to free the ground plane so that, according to McKinnell, street protests and demonstration might move across the open public space. Like our own Rudolph Hall—which McKinnell confessed he had seen in sketch and had influenced his design— the City Hall design was a complex spatial system of programmatic overlays to inspire and solicit collaboration and open dialogue. Furthermore, he thought that the building's concrete frame would be added to over time, receiving marble cladding when desired and affordable; it's scaffold a device for public displays of art; and its fluid section, a complex spatial system of programmatic overlays to inspire and solicit collaboration and open dialogue.

In 1969, the Boston City Hall received a national Honor Award from the American Institute of Architects, and *Interiors* magazine declared that it was "the best public building of our time." In 1970, the Boston Society of Architects presented City Hall's architects with the prestigious Harleston Parker Medal for the best new building in Boston. But, during the intervening seven years, architectural discourse began to shift too. Robert Venturi attacked "architectural ducks" and called for a more complex, contradictory, and "ordinary," if still "ugly," semantic system. Aldo Rossi in *The Architecture of the City* advocated for the study of typology. His plans for city halls in Italy were examples of his use of ur-types and the critical "silence" of mute types skewered and connected. And of course, Colin Rowe and Fred Koetter promoted the dense textures of the city against the singular articulation of an architectural icon. The belated architectural sensibility of the Boston City Hall, in many ways, seemed anachronistic on completion, a last gasp of Modernist heroics. It came to symbolize the gathering negative public reaction to the concerns of the architectural profession. This schism between architects and the public, and within the discipline itself, is captured in this anecdote told by McKinnell:

> "After we won the City Hall competition, we were walking along Madison Avenue, and we spied [Philip] Johnson coming towards us, waving his arms in typical Johnsonian fashion. 'Ah! I'm so happy for you two young boys who have won this competition. Absolutely marvelous. I think it's wonderful. And it's so ugly!' We thought that was the greatest praise we could get."

ABOVE Sketches by Kallmann McKinnell & Knowles for City Hall
competition. Courtesy of the New England Historical Society.

Shortly after its completion, the companion project to the urban design proposal—the renovation and restoration of Faneuil Hall—was completed in time for the country's Bicentennial. That piece of the downtown urban puzzle was widely praised by the profession and the public and may have boosted an appreciation for the wonderful older fabric of the city. City Hall's legacy fared more poorly. The large public spaces surrounding the building are often lifeless, windblown wastelands, and the building has suffered from changes to its interior, and flaws in its design, poor access, environmental problems, and an unpopular aesthetic. In June of 2012, *The Huffington Post* ran an item that put the building as number one in the "25 Buildings to be Demolished Right Now," and the website Spike, among many others, listed it as the number one "Ugliest Building in America" (slightly ahead of another frequent target, Frank Gehry's Experience Music Project). The architects seemed to achieve their intentions to provoke just about everyone.

Many small competitions have been run to renovate or reconsider the building. Generally speaking, the building's space requirements are still viable for the purpose for which it was originally intended, but on December 12, 2006, Boston Mayor Thomas Menino proposed selling the current City Hall and adjacent plaza to private developers, and moving the city government to a site in South Boston. His proclamation spoke to several issues, including the schism between the profession's admiration and the public's animosity for the building, and, perhaps, the pressure that development puts on desirable sites such as these. Moving the City Hall to South Boston would displace it from its central and symbolic urban situation. Friends of the building tried to get it landmark status, noting that, in contrast to Paul Rudolph's A & A Building, which was restored to its original grandeur, the City Hall has not been well treated. The 2008

recession halted Menino's plans and the building remains, significant yet largely unloved.

Our problem, fully supported in concept by McKinnell, was to design a new City Hall. We did not entertain projects that renovated Kallman McKinnell and Knowles's masterpiece. This would have been mildly distracting, revealing an atrophied engagement with the architectural issues that the building initially addressed. To date, most proposals to renovate or modify the existing building simply "green it up" or make its public space into a tepid, user-friendly playscape. Nor were we interested in turning the clock back so as to preserve the pre-urban renewal urban fabric and promote a simplistic return to historic origins. We asked for a truly new urbanism and a new idea of government.

We were concerned with revisiting the disciplinary moment in which the competition was launched, one that marked the end of High Modernism at the date of the building's conception. The studio investigation was an opportunity to engage the subsequent debate about the role of the building in the city, the idea of a "public architecture," and the concept of the "public" as it might be currently constructed. Today we might imagine the clichés of what the brief for a similar competition might engage—sustainable architecture, public access, and a more friendly and accommodating series of spaces and uses. The characteristic responses of today, which also characterize some smaller competitions to "fix" City Hall, would likely feature decorative patterns or plant material wrapped indifferently around building envelopes. At best, such responses might be symptomatic of an awkward and somewhat ambiguous response to Venturi's critique of iconicity and symbol, and testify to the temporal and eclectic nature of the contemporary city. At the very least, they exemplify the continuing and complicated problem of fashion and taste in architecture to which the original building—and perhaps no building—is immune.

As stated, the program for the project and the site was taken directly from the 1961 brief, with some modifications of the neighboring districts to acknowledge existing buildings constructed since the competition. In other words, the site was as found minus the City Hall, the program was as it was given in 1961, but we did not restrict building across the plaza and the context was the physical and conceptual problems of the contemporary city in general and Boston in particular. Over the course of the first few weeks we examined the brief, trying to analyze its subtext and possible reconsiderations of that brief given contemporary concerns. We also looked at several precedents for city halls and significant works of architecture during the time of the competition and their possible impact on the different entries for the original competition.

In the final count, the projects varied as much as the precedents. Highly monumentalized efforts, like Eunil Cho's and Roberto Jenkins' project, see the future of City Hall as a doubled effort between conventional political services and a commercial addition of shops and conference center; in contrast, the more fragmented and surprisingly human scale of Charlotte Algie's playful menagerie of offices arranged in a loose circle is less officious, though exhibiting no less gravitas. Others, like Alicia Pozniak, discovered hidden connections into the rest of the public buildings of the city. She concocted a convincing idea of a forum leading from the State House up Beacon Hill through the City Hall plaza and ending in Faneuil Hall. Others were suspect of the continuous need of a single central location for an increasingly franchised institution that does much of its public work online. Abdulgader Naseer,

Adil Mansure, and Karl Karam virtually buried the building, using the newfound open space of the plaza as an information park and gathering spot at the heart of the city.

Whether one shares that group's mild pessimism about the future of our oldest institutions, or the user-friendly, accessible, and less monumental visions of some of the other projects, is, as it should be, open for debate.

In Praise of Ducks

Ila Berman

If Academicism can be defined as yesterday's answers to today's problems, then obviously the objectives and aesthetic techniques of a real architecture (or a real art) must be in constant change. In the immediate postwar period it seemed important to show that architecture was still possible, and we determined to set against loose planning and form—abdication, a compact disciplined, architecture. . . .

From individual buildings, disciplined on the whole by classical aesthetic techniques, we moved on to an examination of the whole problem of human associations and the relationship that building and community has to them. From this study has grown a completely new attitude and a nonclassical aesthetic.

Any discussion of Brutalism will miss the point if it does not take into account Brutalism's attempt to be objective about "reality"— the cultural objectives of society, its urges, its techniques, and so on. Brutalism tries to face up to a mass-produced society, and drag a rough poetry out of the confused and powerful forces which are at work.

Up to now Brutalism has been discussed stylistically, whereas its essence is ethical.

Alison and Peter Smithson, *The New Brutalism*

If the introduction of the Boston City Hall building through the lens of Brutalism is appropriate, it is perhaps because of both the enormous praise this building has received from the architectural community and the intense animosity it has elicited from the general populace. For over a half-century, its reception has been rooted in its relationship to the larger ideological positions and the histories that have surrounded it. Although thoroughly modern in form, materiality, and functionalist rhetoric, Brutalism's empirical stance was intended to operate as a counter to an international style. Brutalism desired to be abstract, neutral, and universal, and therefore disengaged from the specificity of its historical and material context—thus, the so-called "brute" reality from which it was born. This first trajectory of Brutalism was most clearly presented through the postwar monumental work of Le Corbusier that emerged, in part, from a wide-spread disillusionment with the values of a utopic industrialism, given the evidence of its destructive power during World War II and the ruins that it left in its wake. Mass-housing prototypes like the Unite d'Habitation in Marseille (1947–1952) simultaneously met a need to house the postwar population and rebuild the metropolis at a much larger scale. In this work, and in concurrent projects like the capital of Chandigarh in India (1951) and the Dominican monastery of La Tourette (1960), the gridded facades referencing Modernism's social ideology were maintained. Yet, the material indexes of the realities of construction, evidenced through exposed concrete ("béton brut") and the traces of timber formwork left embedded in its surfaces, replaced the clean white surfaces of Modernism's earlier abstractions, just as the thick sectional profiles, deep recesses, textured forms, and sculptural volumes supplanted the taut, lightweight skins

signifying the machine tectonic of the previous era. The body of architecture returned, and with it the desire to embed itself in material and cultural history. Although operating quite distinctly in each context, the notion of the monumental embodied in the heavy and substantial forms and rough materiality of each of these projects referred not to the authority of an absolute governing state, but rather to the power and material presence of a grounded, collective ideal, something to which the Boston City Hall also clearly aspired.

The second lineage of Brutalism traced through the writings of Reyner Banham, and the work and writings of the Smithsons follows a parallel yet divergent trajectory, operating as a counter to both the monumental architecture that had secured the British Empire's imperialist identity on the one hand, and the architectural mediocrity and anti-

architectural stance of the emerging welfare-state ideology on the other. The latter—a form of British socialist realism which manifested itself as a "people's architecture"—aspired to little more than a cottage-scaled, vernacular realized through the uninspired utilitarianism of London's government officials and its equally utilitarian and bureaucratic architects. In his 1955 essay on the New Brutalism, Banham refers to this as a quasi-historical form of "New Humanism," which signified a brick, pitched-roof architecture, with small windows and picturesque detailing recalling a stripped-down version of the English Arts and Crafts movement, nostalgically harkening back to the mid-nineteenth century, a period reminiscent of "Marxism's Golden Age." The reining-in of aspirations in Europe following the war was a less-than-optimistic attitude towards the capacity of modern architecture to realize its projected utopia and a more modest desire to at-

ABOVE Perspective of City Hall by Kallmann McKinnell & Knowles. Courtesy of the New England Historical Society.

tend to the everyday needs of the people in a way that would still reflect Britain's Labour Government and its social ideals. For the Smithsons, Brutalism offered an alternative to the routine functionalism of utilitarianism, the empty banality of vernacular populisms, and the superficiality of academic pseudo-historicisms with their humanist sentimentalist rhetoric. It offered a "real" architecture for the people, grounded in the political, social, and material realities of the postwar era and the tough conditions of a working-class existence. In architectural terms, this notion of the real focused on programs such as housing and educational facilities organized through formal clarity, and demanded an exposure of structure, construction, and materiality achieved by shedding the simulated surfaces used to cloak architecture's true physical nature. The resurrection of the form-function-construction triad was given a new power under the banner of Brutalism. Rather than a building's material and structure operating as a symbol of industrial production (as is found in the articulated mullions of Mies's Crown Hall building at IIT, for example), it would directly reflect the found matter inherent in the very process of its construction, just as a splatter of paint in a Jackson Pollock painting indexes the material facts of its making—the viscosity of the paint in combination with the force and trajectory of the throw.

As Banham had noted in his essay, there was certainly no lack of critics of this movement for precisely its overtly stated architectural values—its sublimation of found brute material reality to (what Banham would define as) a "conceptual image"—perhaps the same reasons that the Boston City Hall was subjected to the same critique. Yet, for the latter, the desire to draw upon a Brutalist aesthetic emerges within the context of the "new world," one which was searching for a monumental-

ity with which to more thoroughly instantiate and concretize an image of modern democracy while offering a more complex and material sculptural language to resist the ease with which capitalism was able to co-opt the logic of Modernism's thin tectonic skins and infinitely repeatable floor plates and structures—industrialism turning space into profit. Following the European Brutalists, Kallmann, McKinnell & Knowles drew upon an architectural language that would therefore resist the abstraction, neutrality, and insubstantiality of an earlier Modernism in order to situate the building within the urban specificity of its site and its concrete social reality. The monumentality of the City Hall became a clear indicator of its civic ambitions, assured not only by its scale, heavy materiality, and prismatic form, but also by its inverted section that tapers outward as one moves towards the top of the building. In its tripartite sectional configuration, the building reveals the double-sided nature of democracy, where top-down and bottom-up—the governing body and the public—might meet. Unlike the hierarchies and axial symmetries governing classical state structures, here governance, representing the needs and desires of the multitude, rather than the singularity of a centralized authority, is underscored by the extreme repetition of elements defining the building's entablature, simultaneously signifying the standardized pool of government workers that comprise the bureaucratic machine housed within.

The building is raised up to expose its underbelly, allowing the exterior plaza to continue uninterrupted into the interior of the building. As the top of the building steps down, the ground steps up, rising substantially toward the building's vertical midpoint. This artificial brick terrain—a reference to Boston's architectural and material history, its collective pedestrian underpinnings, and the earthen topography from which the city emerged—not only reflects the public ground which both conceptually and physically supports the civic structure, but also provides a rambling occupiable landscape that brings the public into the building's interior, rendering the governing body transparent and accessible, and allowing the public to directly engage with its civic leaders. Positioned at the vertical center of the facade—suspended below the building's monolithic perimeter ring of offices at the upper levels and floating above the open public terrain—are the most articulated elements of the building. These singular sculptural components suspended at the center of the structure form the true public heart of City Hall. These protrude from and activate the facade, breaking down the monotony of repetitive elements above while demarcating the communal civic and ceremonial spaces where city government and populace might meet.

The desire to combine abstract ideals with empirical concrete realities, and monumentally scaled civic aspirations with an informality in support of the public realm, reveals both the inherent contradictions at the core of the City Hall's architecture and also the strong affiliations that it had to both its American contemporaries and European predecessors. Yet, in the span of a decade and a half past the completion of Le Corbusier's housing project in Marseille, when the City Hall was finally completed, the tide had certainly turned in both Europe and America, bringing back into the forefront the very arguments, albeit in different form—for an easily legible, ordinary, and vernacular "peoples architecture," on the one hand, and a nostalgic return to historicist typologies, on the other—that the Smithsons had so vehemently critiqued. Indeed, the return of the repressed of Modernism flooded back with a vengeance, attempting to undermine, as Venturi did with a single child-like drawing of

a duck, the social attitude, monumental aspirations, and overt material and concrete constructive realities integral to the Brutalist agenda that were intended to guarantee both its architectural value and permanence. Yet, unlike the banality that Venturi championed, and the Disneyfied historicism that followed, the Boston City Hall remains as a substantial architectural artifact in the core of the city, to be reckoned with for decades to come. If Bernard Tschumi is correct in his statement that "Architecture only survives where it negates the form that society expects of it," then perhaps the Boston City Hall will go down in the annals of history as an architecture that survived precisely because its sculptural form and social, spatial, and material agenda overtly negated society's expectations of what a civic institution should be. One should always hope, as the Smithsons did, that despite the dominant set of cultural myths that define, and most often mask, our present social reality, that architecture would still be possible.

Instant City Hall

Edward Mitchell

"Instant City Hall," is a variation on the "Instant City" exercise. Precedents included I. M. Pei's Dallas City Hall, Paul Rudolph's Orange County Civic Center in Goshen, New York; Viljo Revell and Bruce Kuwabara's Toronto City Hall; BIG's Tallinn City Hall in Estonia; Antoine Predock's Austin City Hall; Kenzō Tange's Imabari City Hall Complex and Kurashiki City Hall; OMA's Rotterdam City Hall; Edward Jones's Mississauga City Hall; Alvar Aalto's Säynätsalo Town Hall; Frank Lloyd Wright's Marin County Center; Giuseppe Terragni's building in Como; Willem Dudok's Hilversum, Netherlands; Aldo Rossi's competition entries for Scandicci and Perugia; Charles Eames' unrealized City Hall project; James Sterling's Derby Civic Center; Philip Johnson's building for Celebration, Florida; Louis Kahn's Philadelphia Civic Center proposal; Rafael Moneo's civic building in Murcia, Spain; and the Philadelphia City Hall by John McArthur, Jr., among others. Each of these city halls was a clear reflection of the political and architectural aspirations of its time. Students were asked to articulate the conceptual link between the buildings' programs and their physical arrangements and make a simple collage drop into the site of the Boston City Hall to see what the scale and impact of the precedent might do to the site.

In the second part of the exercise, the students hybridized two of the precedents in order to come up with a new model. Those hybrids revealed potential relationships between the intentions of the architects. The hybrids were more synthetic when the architectural pairs held common compositional and tectonic values, as in the case between Frank Lloyd Wright and Paul Rudolph. But the pairing could also be humorous, as when the seriousness of Raphael Moneo's work was matched with the often simplistic diagrammatic flips that characterize the work of BIG.

ABOVE Paul Rudolph and Frank Lloyd Wright hybrid by Daphne Binder and Jared Abraham. The link between Wright and Rudolph was exposed by the close fit between the two precedents, making this scheme architecturally plausible and perhaps even more relevant in the site when the two models were combined.

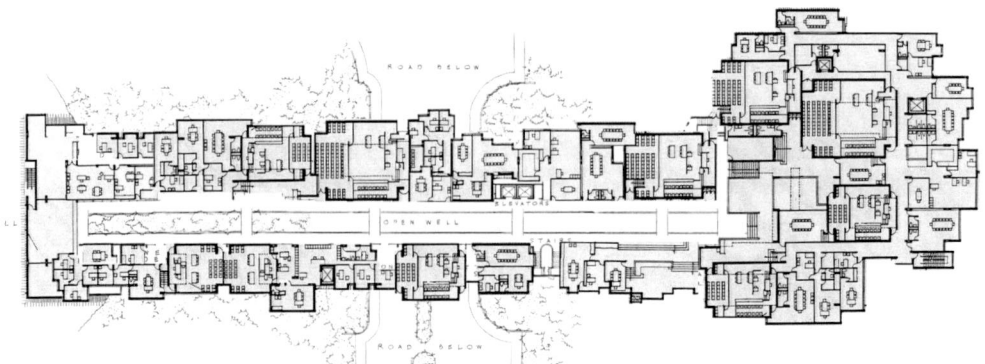

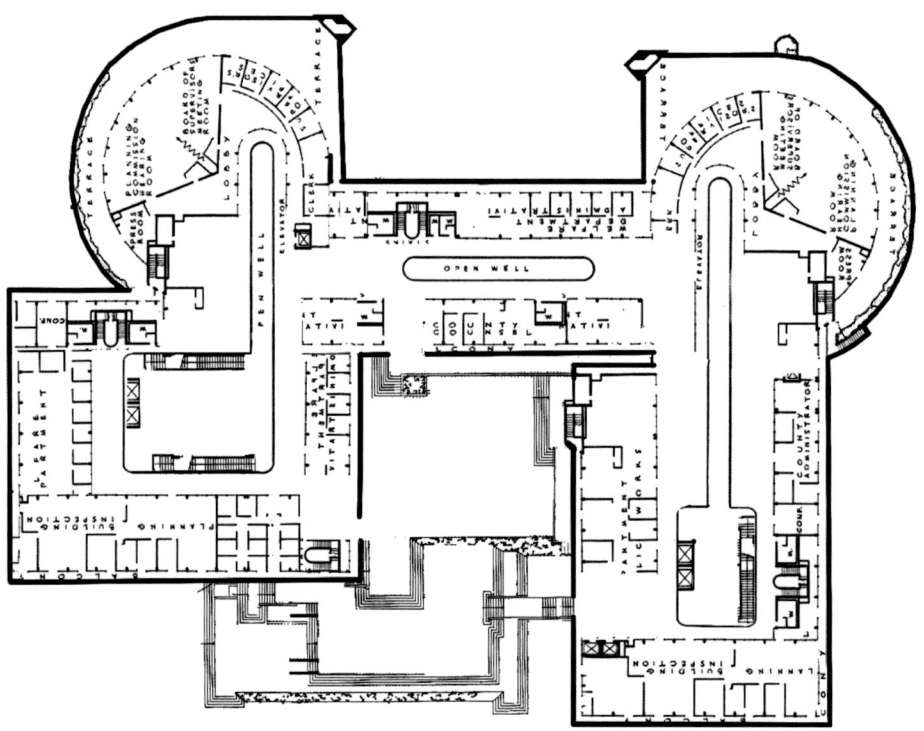

TOP Paul Rudolph and Frank Lloyd Wright hybrid by Daphne Binder and Jared Abraham. Goshen is redeployed as a head and tail scheme similar in organization to Marin.
BOTTOM Paul Rudolph and Frank Lloyd Wright hybrid by Daphne Binder and Jared Abraham. Marin is turned in on itself as a courtyard scheme.

OPPOSITE TOP City Hall Hybrid of Alvar Aalto's Säynätsalo Town Hall and Gottfried Böhm's Bensberg Town Hall by Sofia Singler and Apoorva Khanolkar.
OPPOSITE BOTTOM Instant City Hall an Open Forum by Sofia Singler and Apoorva Khanolkar.

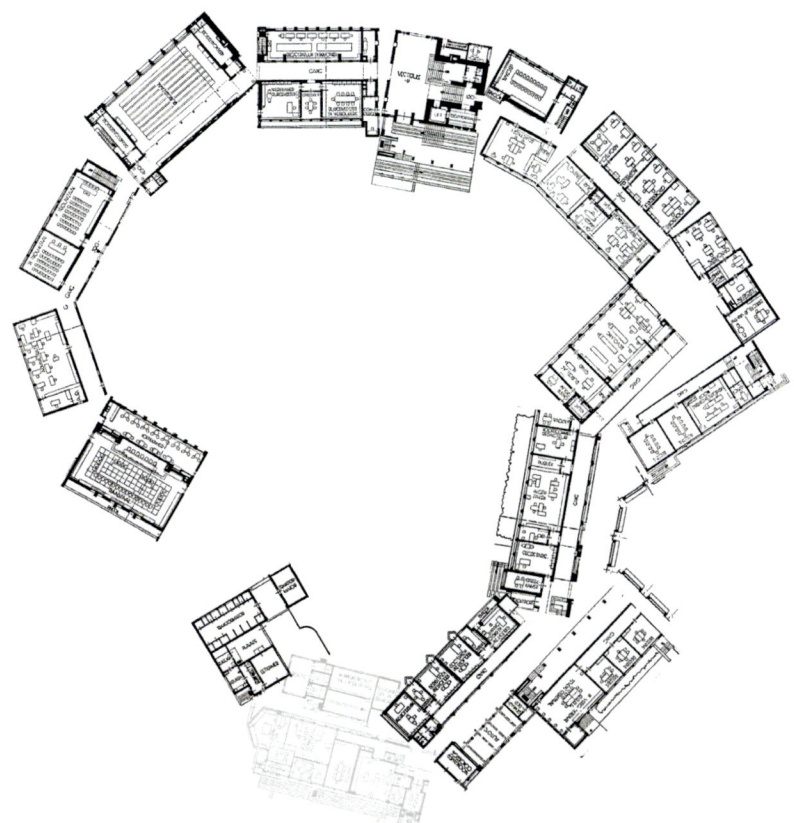

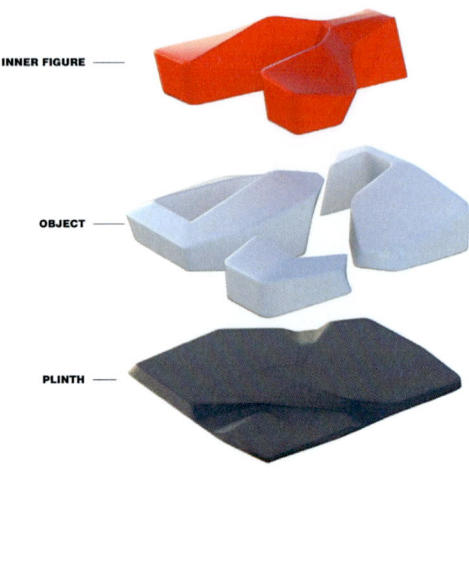

TOP LEFT City Hall as Information Source, "Instant City Hall" by
Mengshi Sun and Shuangjing Hu.
TOP RIGHT City Hall as a Hybrid Icon by Isaac Southard and
Roberto Jenkins.
BOTTOM Instant City Hall Hybrid of Rafael Moneo and BIG by
Mengshi Sun and Shuangjing Hu.

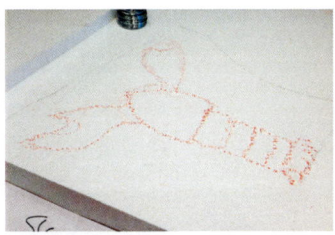 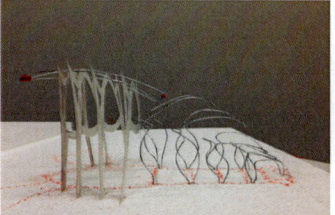 

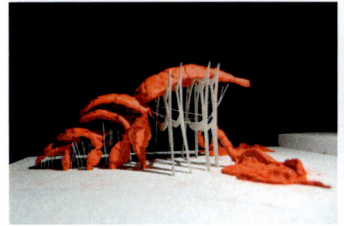 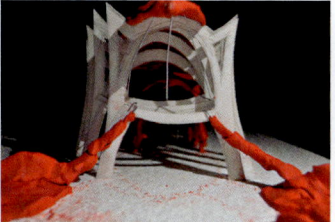 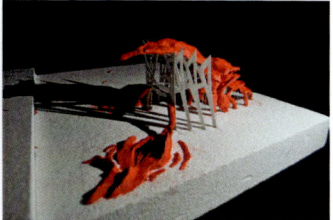

ABOVE "Instant City Hall" by Mengshi Sun and Shuangjing Hu.
Early studies for an iconic structure for the main hall.

City Hall Campus
City Hall

Karl Karam + Abgdulgader Naseer + Adil Mansure

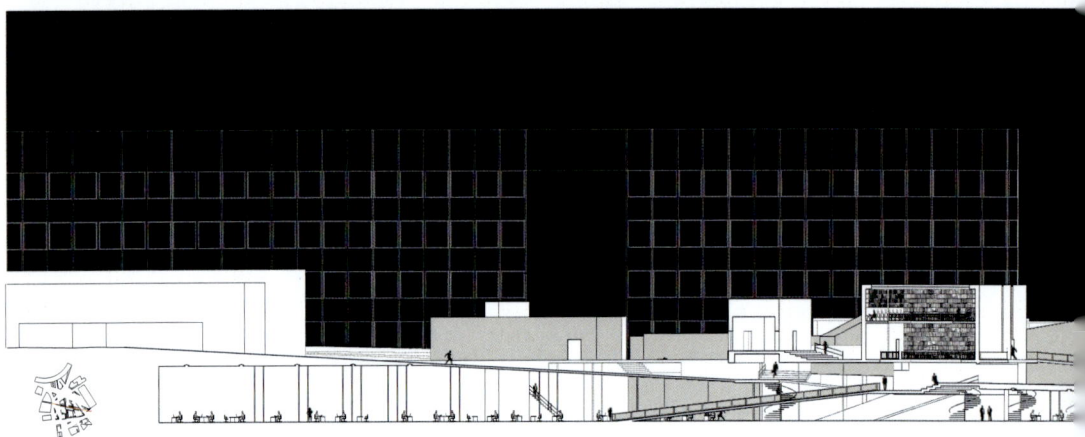

TOP View in the great hall.
BOTTOM Site section.

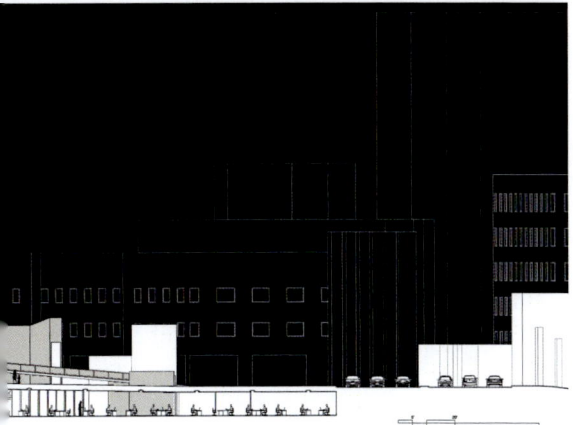

Today, social interactions, business, and politics increasingly cross traditional hierarchical boundaries. We believe City Hall should reflect this change and that its singular symbolic, vertical expression is no longer valid.

Instead, while retaining some of its key bureaucratic functions, City Hall should provide a seamless, continuous platform between the activities of government and the city at large. The scheme features a multi-accessed platform punctuated by a series of equally dynamic spaces, which would suppress the symbolic role of the complex, provide a horizontal operational logic, and attempt to celebrate both traditional and progressive urban performances. To achieve that, the City Hall Campus proposal spreads the program across the site in a series of spaces agglomerating around an oversized, abundant working space: the "great hall."

The hall is marked by a point grid of columns and differentiated by groupings of furniture. It is characterized by a large sunken space marked by two types of columns and three different types of furniture that inflect passage through the large room and seamlessly accommodate different functions between city and City Hall. Above, the light wells, flooding the space with natural light, mark various vantage points into the hall while the complaints office, the Boston library, conference rooms, and a series of shops occupy the aboveground spaces and are composed to offer a variety of outdoor moments, intimate plazas, or larger gathering areas.

The project, in its totality, sets a new model for the state in the urban real, one that is symptomatic of the fluid, less hierarchical nature of contemporary urban life.

ABOVE Ground plan.

ABOVE Underground plan showing the great hall and connections to Congress Street.

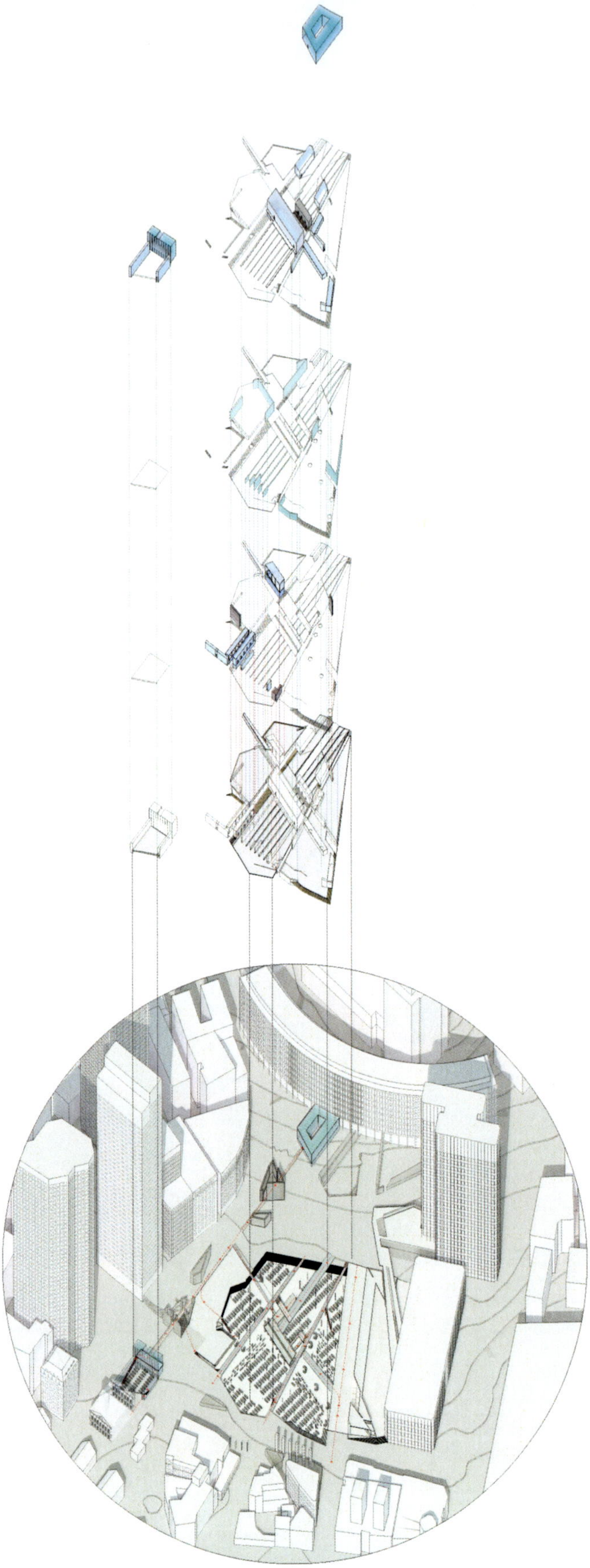

OPPOSITE Exploded axonometric of the site.
TOP An entrance in the plaza to the great hall below.
BOTTOM Great hall.

Common Place

City Hall

Sofia Singler + Apoorva Khanolkar

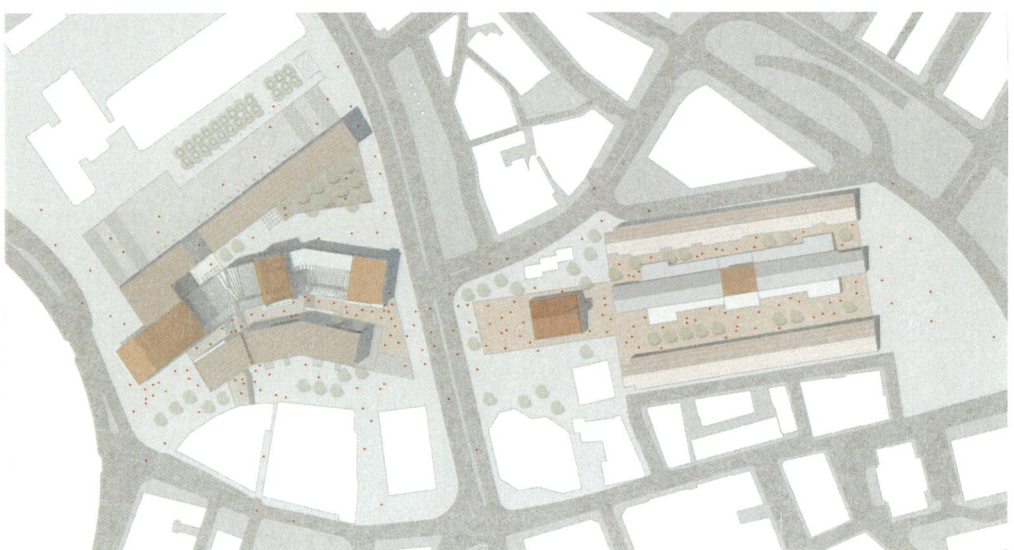

The proposal explores the notion and relevance of Government within the context of contemporary Boston and fast-changing global attitudes. In an age of social media and public relations, where attention spans are limited to 140 characters, there is an increasing need for Government to be public, accessible, and integrated with the everyday life of citizens. The notion of a transparent and approachable ruling body becomes the locus of the project, where the city's administrative aspects are fully integrated with day-to-day activities. The City Hall, therefore, becomes an intrinsic part of the city fabric in both a literal and metaphorical sense.

This three-bar scheme comprises a porous central spine that weaves in the City Council chamber and the Mayor's office with a market thoroughfare. At the heart of the project is a "public living room," a freely programmable space that the Mayor would walk through on his way to a Council meeting, potentially stopping by for a quick cup of coffee with his citizens. This gesture allows for a mixing chamber for the citizens and their leadership, an informal public forum charged with the fundamentals of democracy. The T station below opens up into an atrium with the Council chamber suspended overhead, enabling the citizens to be part of the decision-making process on their way to work.

This carefully calibrated mediation of scales, from the monumental at one end to the scattered towards the other, harkens to the multiplicity of experiences that are such an integral aspect of the urban experience. The symbolism of Faneuil Hall and Quincy Market in their role as Boston's original Government-meets-people endeavor becomes an extension of the new City Hall.

OPPOSITE TOP View of central spine and Mayor's office from Faneuil Hall.
OPPOSITE BOTTOM Public space strategy.
TOP City Hall as a physical and metaphorical extension of Faneuil Hall.
BOTTOM View of Council chamber from subway exit.

TOP Longitudinal section through central spine.
MIDDLE Longitudinal elevation as a rhythmic composition of concrete fins.
BOTTOM Cross section through public living room.

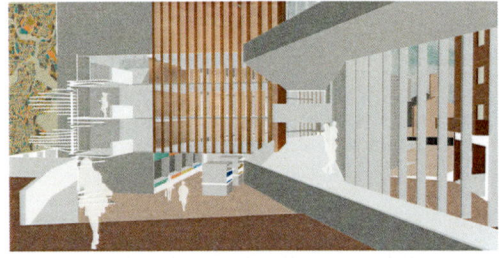

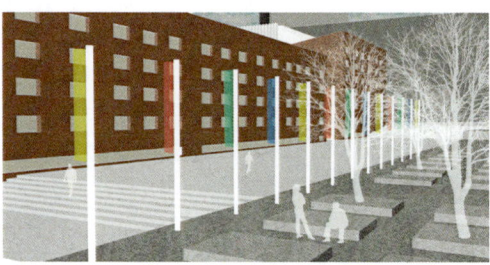

THIRD ROW LEFT View from Council chamber into central atrium.
THIRD ROW RIGHT Public avenue.
BOTTOM Exterior and interior of permeable central spine.

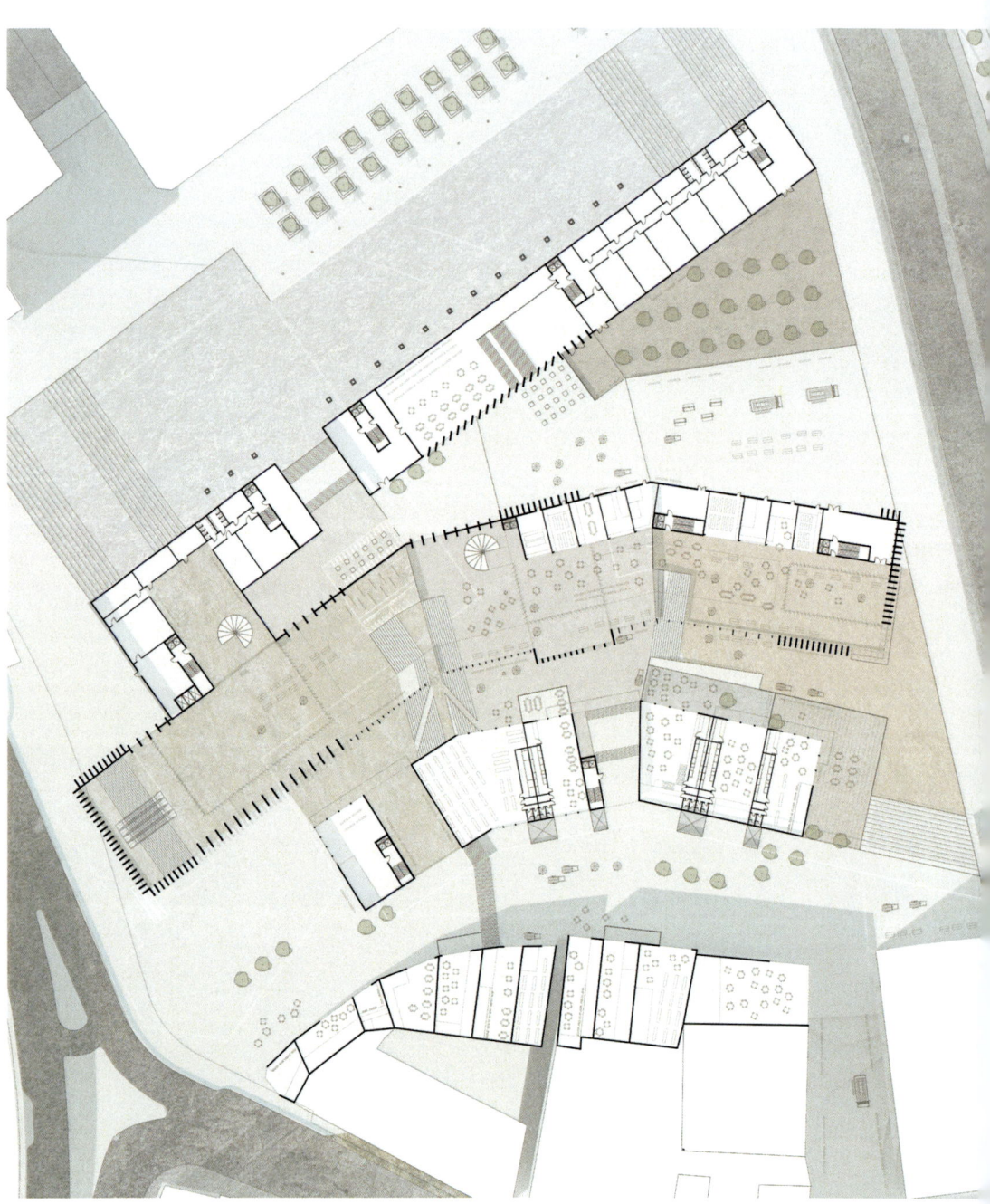

ABOVE First floor plan. The porous tectonic of the central volume is symbolic of Government
as public, transparent, and accessible.
OPPOSITE Composition of central public spine.

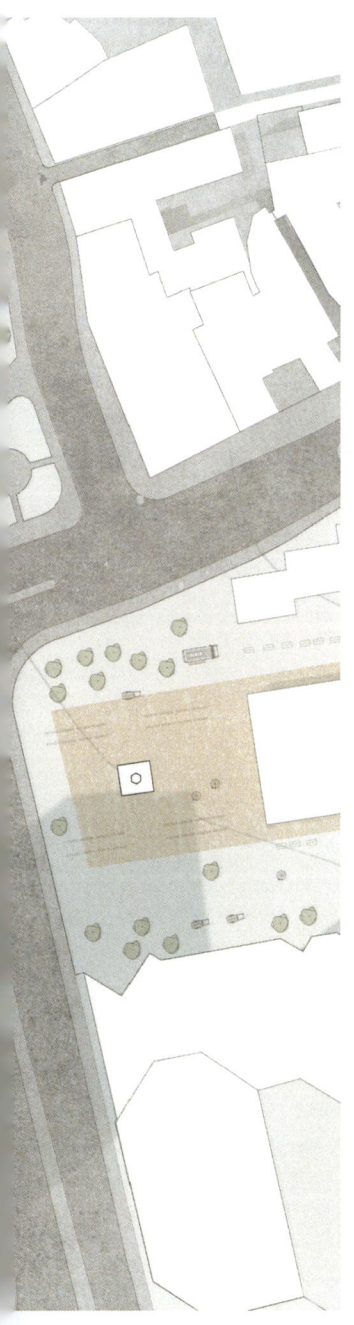

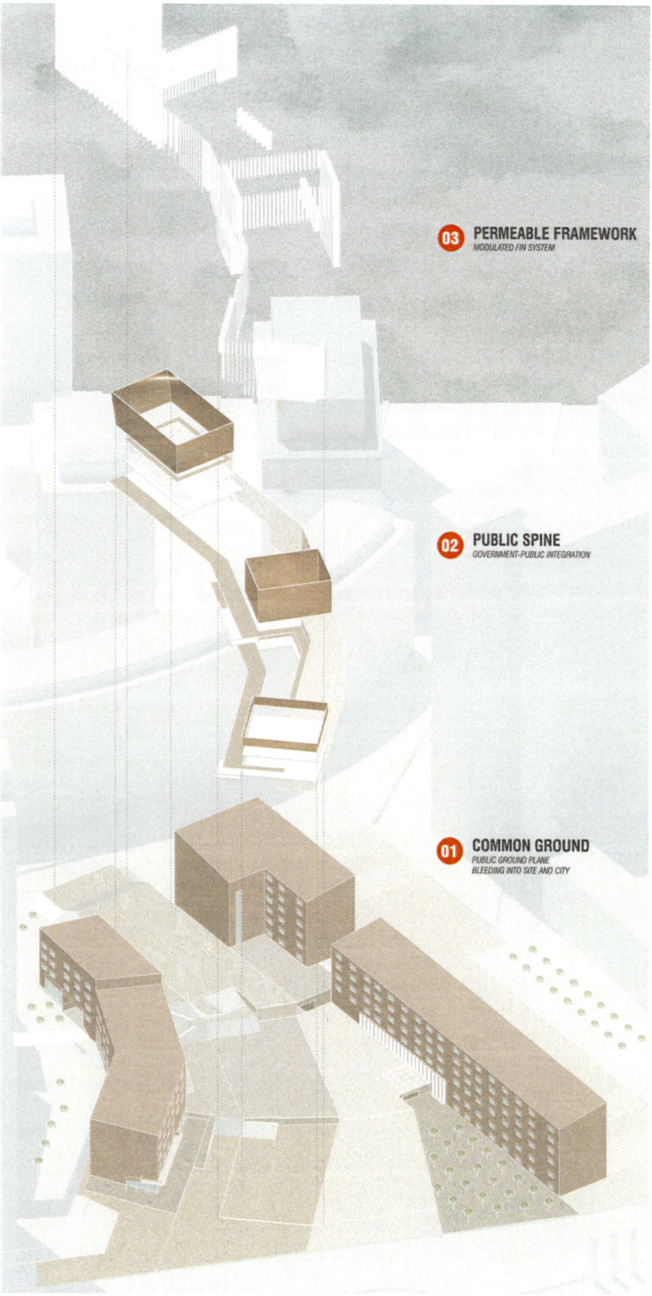

03 PERMEABLE FRAMEWORK
MODULATED FIN SYSTEM

02 PUBLIC SPINE
GOVERNMENT-PUBLIC INTEGRATION

01 COMMON GROUND
PUBLIC GROUND PLANE
BLEEDING INTO SITE AND CITY

Boston Forum
City Hall

Alicia Pozniak

A city hall is a forum, a place for exchange and interchange of ideas about the city. The site for Boston City Hall, located at the heart of Government Center, marks a central convergence of Boston's neighborhoods and central business district. Yet, the vast site remains spatially isolated from its urban context. This proposal creates a new forum for Boston to position City Hall as part of a larger urban composition that incorporates key existing civic structures. The Boston Forum redefines the east-west axis connecting Massachusetts State House and Faneuil Hall through the John Adams Courthouse and Government Center Station. The City Hall complex terminates Washington Street around an upper landscaped plaza spilling out onto the Forum via a grand public stair.

Two public halls ("basilicas") entered from either end of the Forum provide access to local and global services relating to the neighborhood and commercial proximities of central Boston. These are conjoined by a central administrative segment crowned by the Mayor's offices which, in turn, act as a bridge. The City Council takes its place at the head of the Forum, overhanging the principal entry.

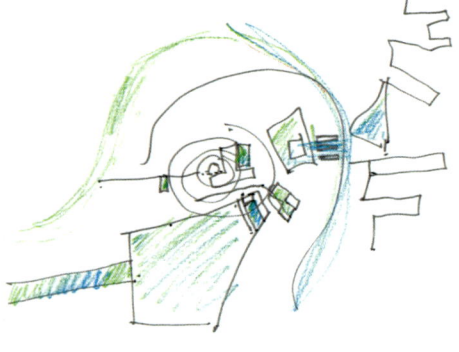

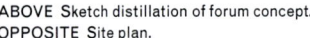

ABOVE Sketch distillation of forum concept.
OPPOSITE Site plan.

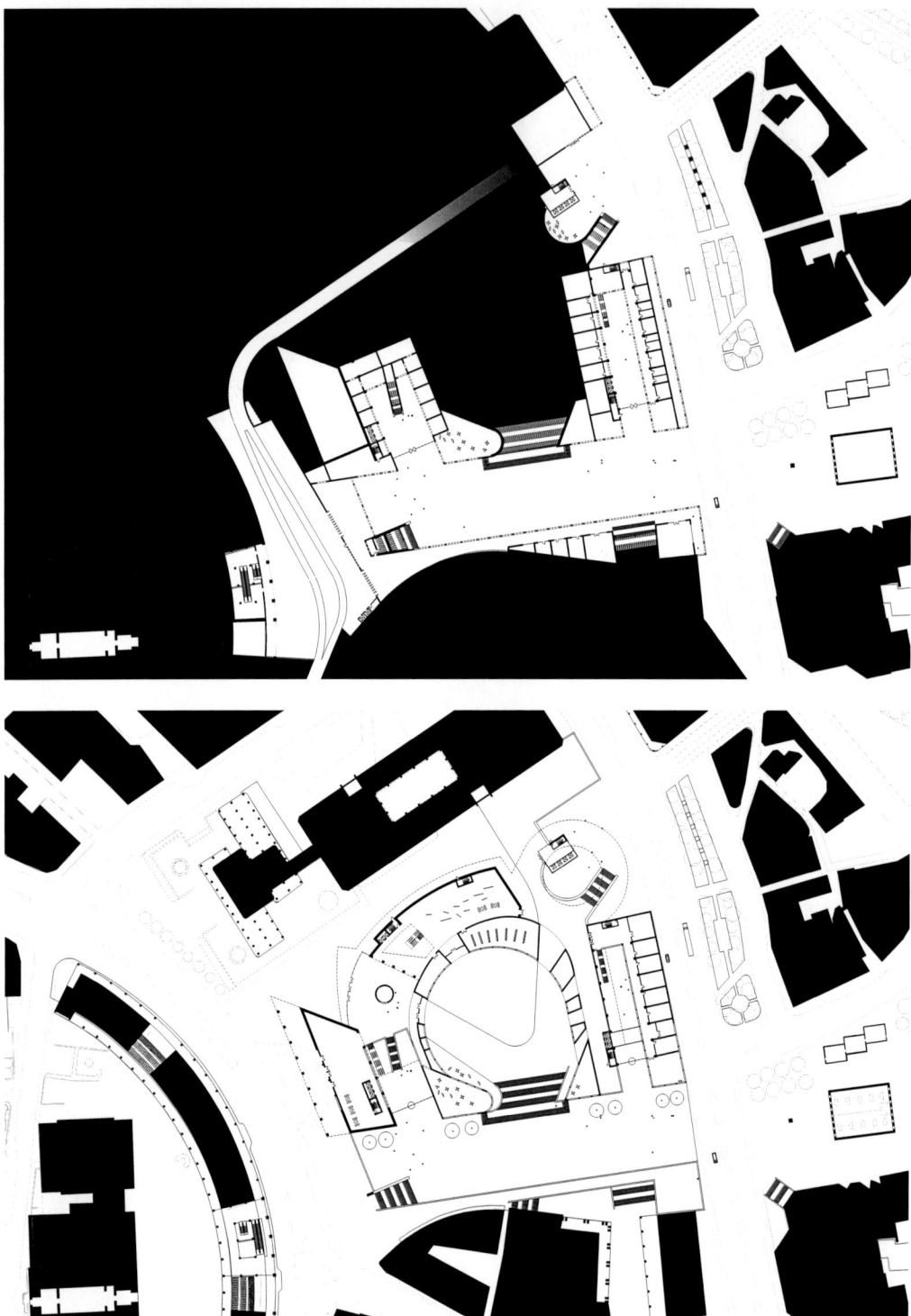

TOP Forum plan at Faneuil Hall level.
BOTTOM Forum plan at Cambridge Street level.

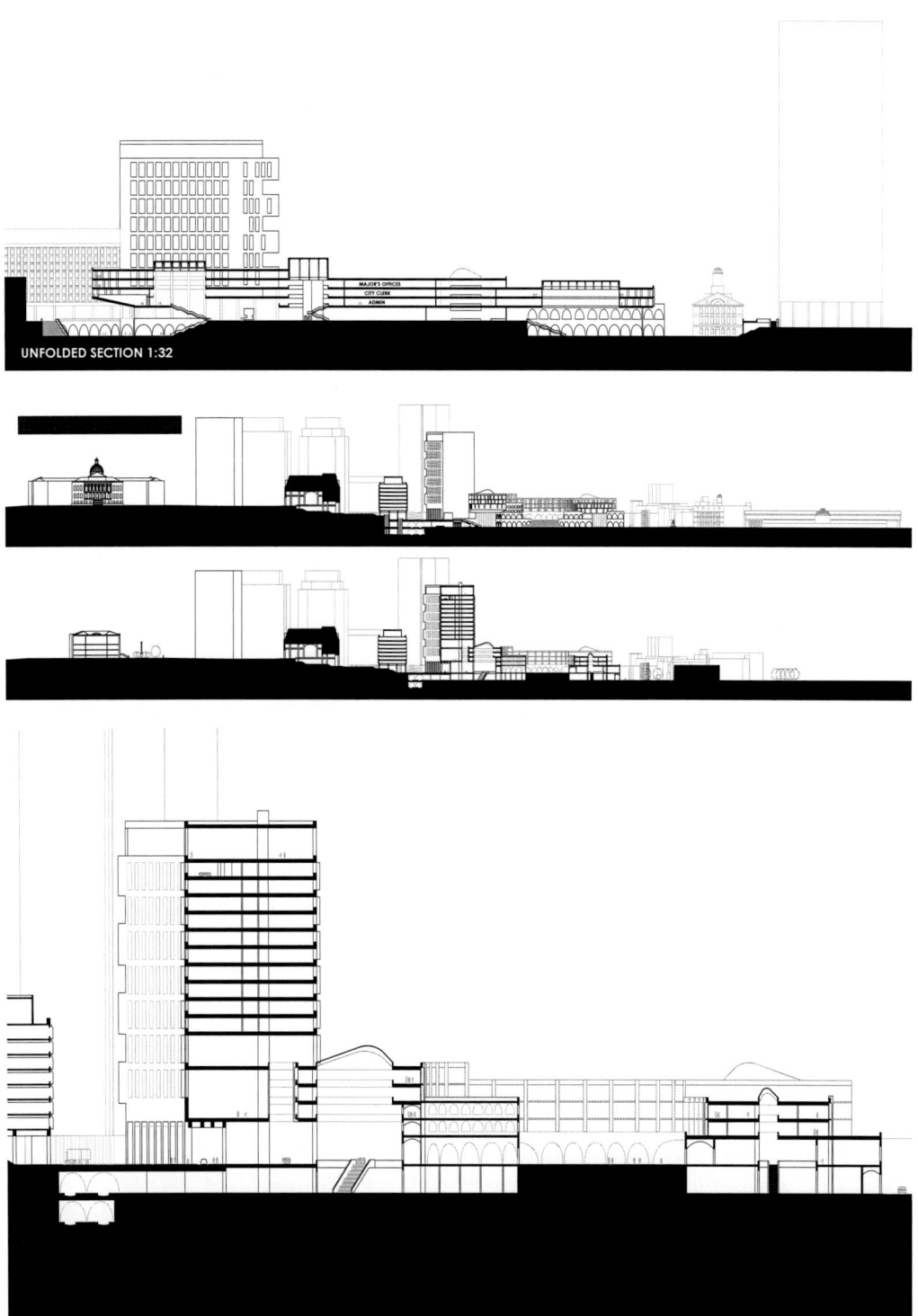

UNFOLDED SECTION 1:32

MAJOR'S OFFICES
CITY CLERK
ADMIN

TOP Site sections.
BOTTOM Building sections showing T line to the left and cutting
through the new City Hall plaza to Congress Street.

 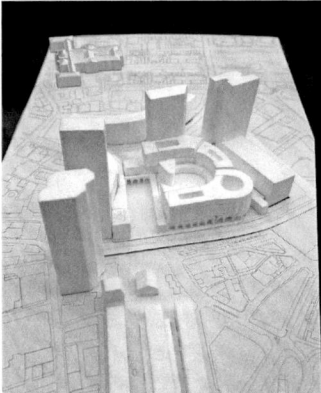 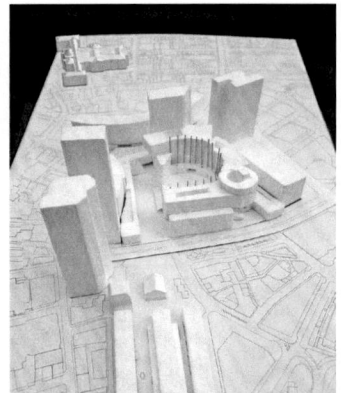

TOP Massing studies.
BOTTOM Aerial view of Boston Forum.

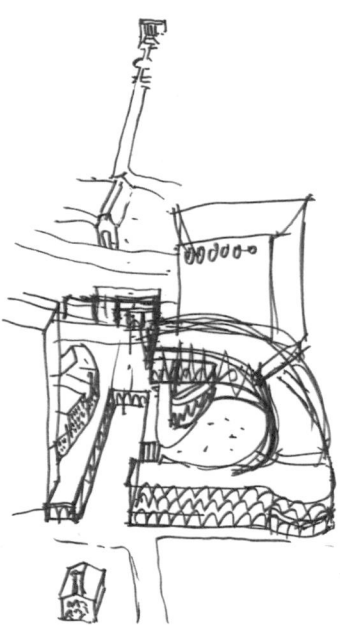

TOP Model.
BOTTOM LEFT View of Forum from Sears Crescent side.
BOTTOM RIGHT Sketch studies of scale and massing.

Assembly
City Hall

Jared Abraham + Daphne Binder

TOP Central Hall interior.
BOTTOM Longitudinal section through Central Hall.

The new Boston City Hall is a space for individual and communal assembly and demonstration. From paying your parking ticket to protesting the Mayor, we believe that a new City Hall should promote interaction between citizens and their leaders while still providing space for the private deliberations of government officials.

Itself an assemblage, the building's identity is concentrated around a series of overlapping urban rooms constituting a large Central Hall. The hall acts as a double-negative, at once voiding City Hall's assemblage while framing its chambers. Designed to foster new forms of public demonstration and interaction, the hall combines the various City departments, a flexible gathering space, and site circulation. Key program adjacencies within it—the Council chamber, the reference library, and the Mayor's office—provide the crucial visual connection between visitors and their elected officials. Finally, a series of transverse ramps connecting Cambridge and Congress Streets and Market Square encourage circulation through and meandering within the Central Hall.

Departments which necessitate heavy public interaction are positioned on the ground floor, thereby facilitating access and transforming the hall into a communal waiting area. Large public cores within it transport visitors to upper-level offices. Office bridges above enable interdepartmental circulation and spaces for collaboration.

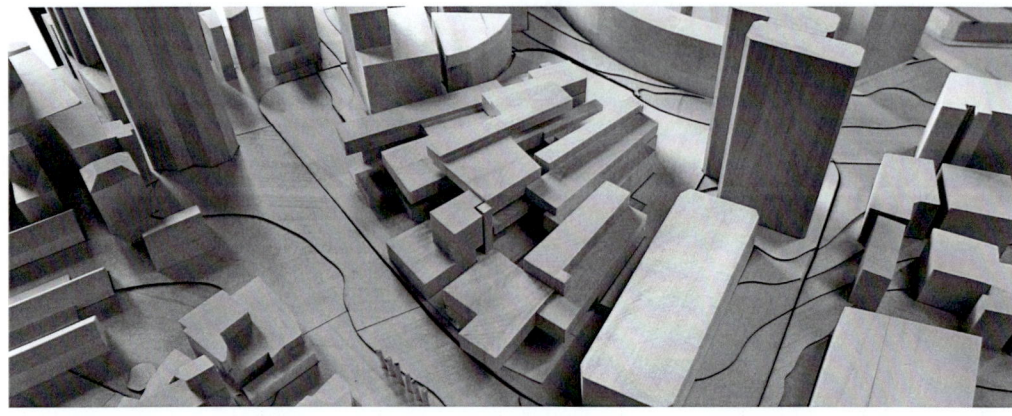

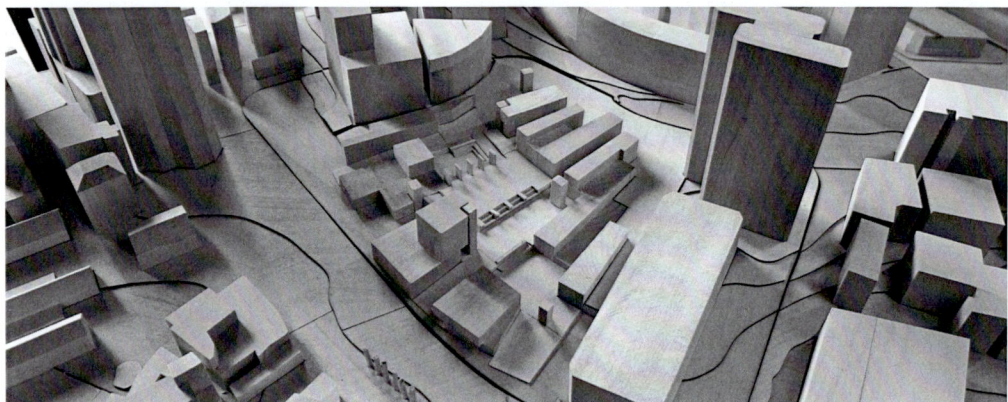

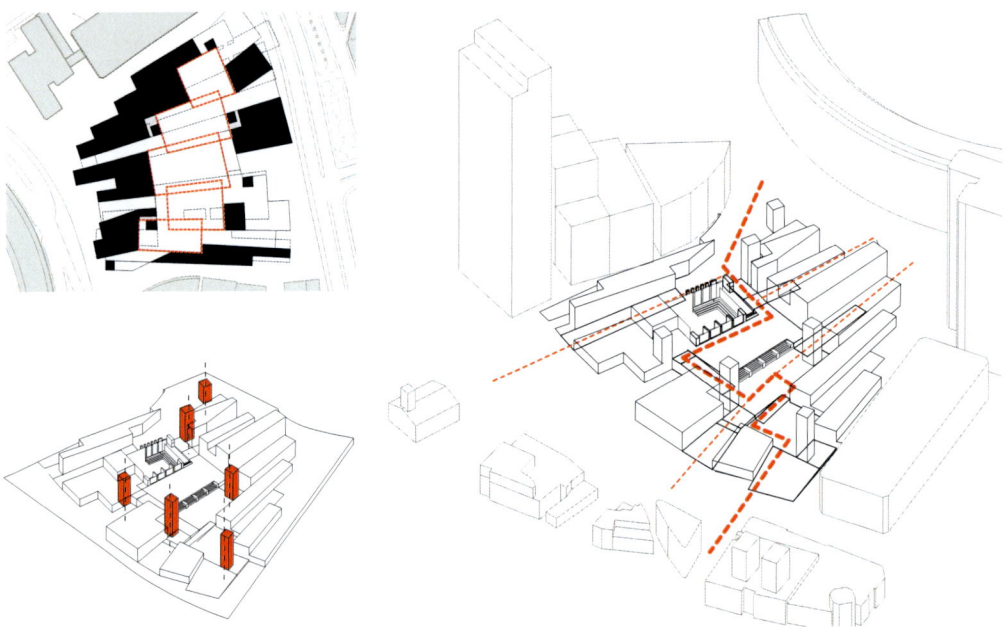

TOP Model photograph.
MIDDLE LEFT Diagram of City Hall urban rooms and public circulation cores.
BELOW LEFT Diagram of City Hall urban rooms and public circulation cores.
BELOW RIGHT Diagram of site connections and circulation.

ABOVE Ground floor plan, Central Hall.
BELOW View of City Hall from Faneuil Hall.

TOP View of Council chamber in session.
BOTTOM LEFT View of office interior.
BOTTOM RIGHT Diagrams of assembly and movement.

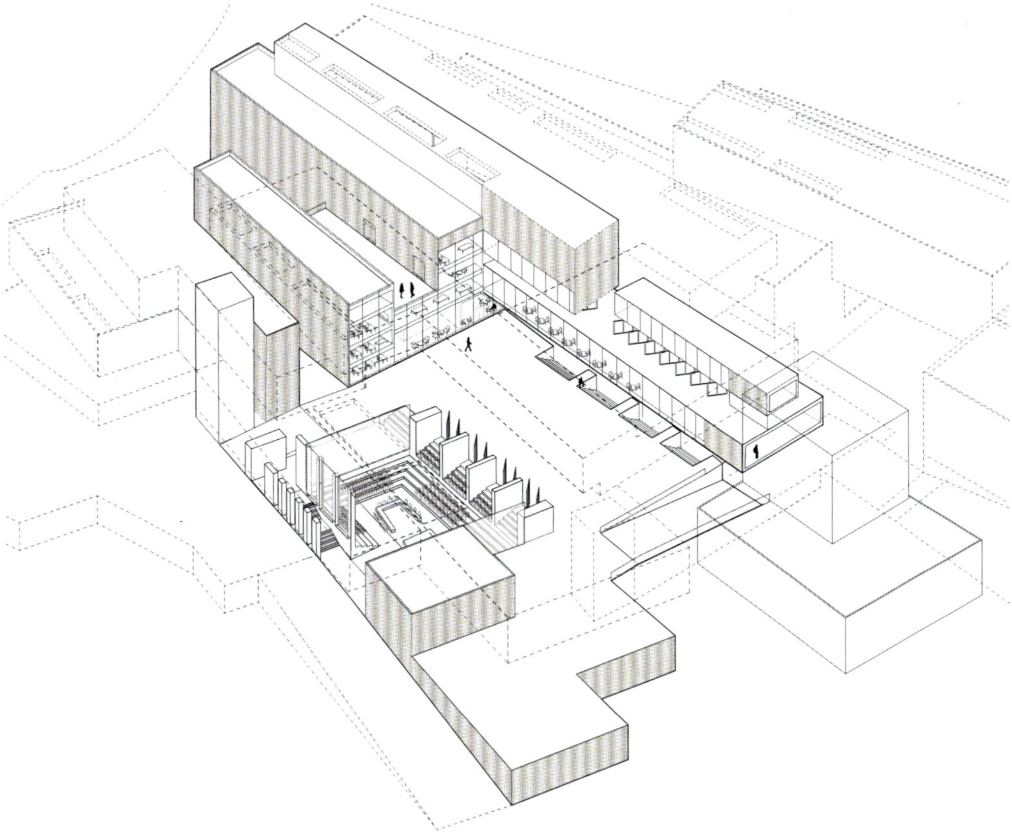

ABOVE View of procession through the Central Hall.
BELOW Axonometric of Central Hall.

Ceremonial City
City Hall

Mengshi Sun + Shuangjing Hu

There is an old Chinese saying that people only take a shower three times during their lifetime: when they are born, when they get married, and when they die. In our project, the place where people get licenses and hold ceremonies for births, weddings, and deaths are just as important as other government functions such as council meetings. For us, City Hall is a place shared by both those who govern and the people who are governed.

The entire site is calibrated into several terraces, making use of the existing twenty-five-foot height difference. Enclosed in the middle is the central courtyard, an oasis within the city that can be accessed by the public. Apart from connecting the courtyard with its city surroundings, the pavilions, which are embedded in the terraces, also work as multi-functional rooms. They could be used as quiet conference rooms for government meetings, or ceremonial space for weddings, even divorces. The intimate nature of these spaces is rendered as a series of small gardens compatible with the intimacy of private relations acted out as, and performed as, part of a larger dignified and symbolic public ritual.

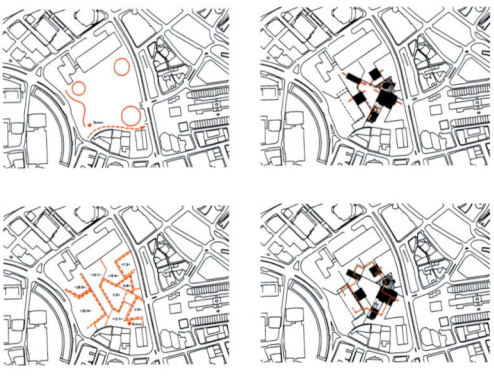

ABOVE Diagrams of site massing.
OPPOSITE Aerial of City Hall Ceremonial City.

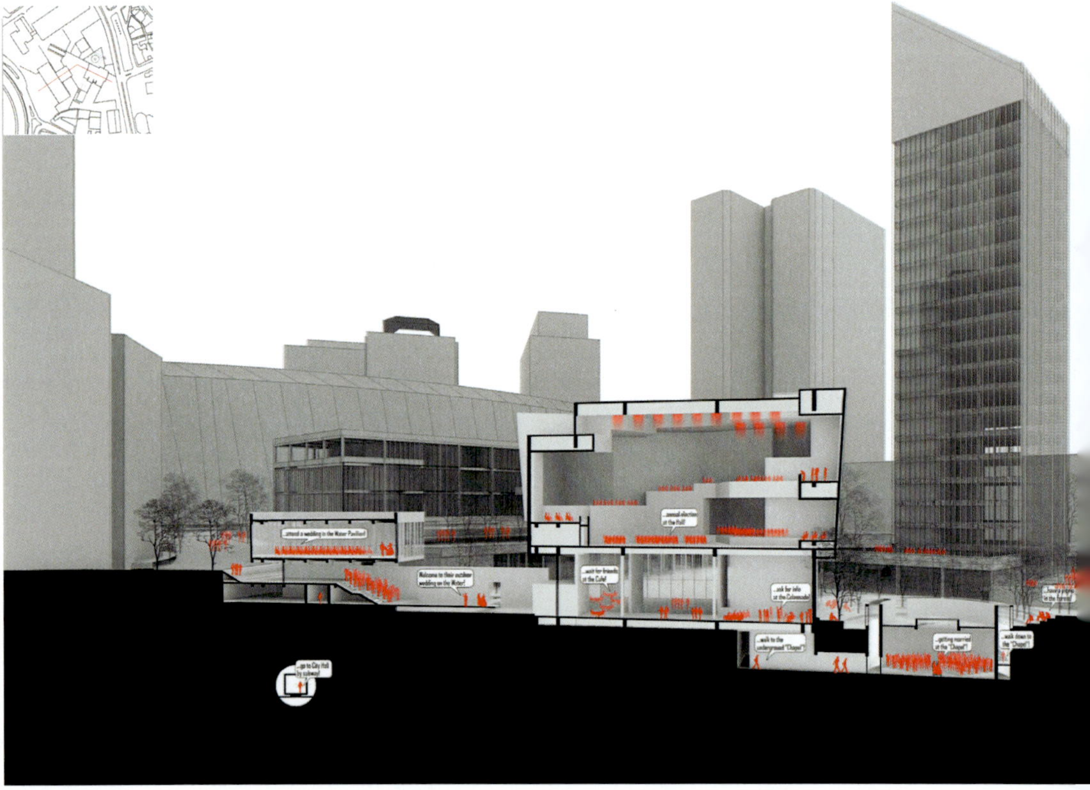

ABOVE Site sections.

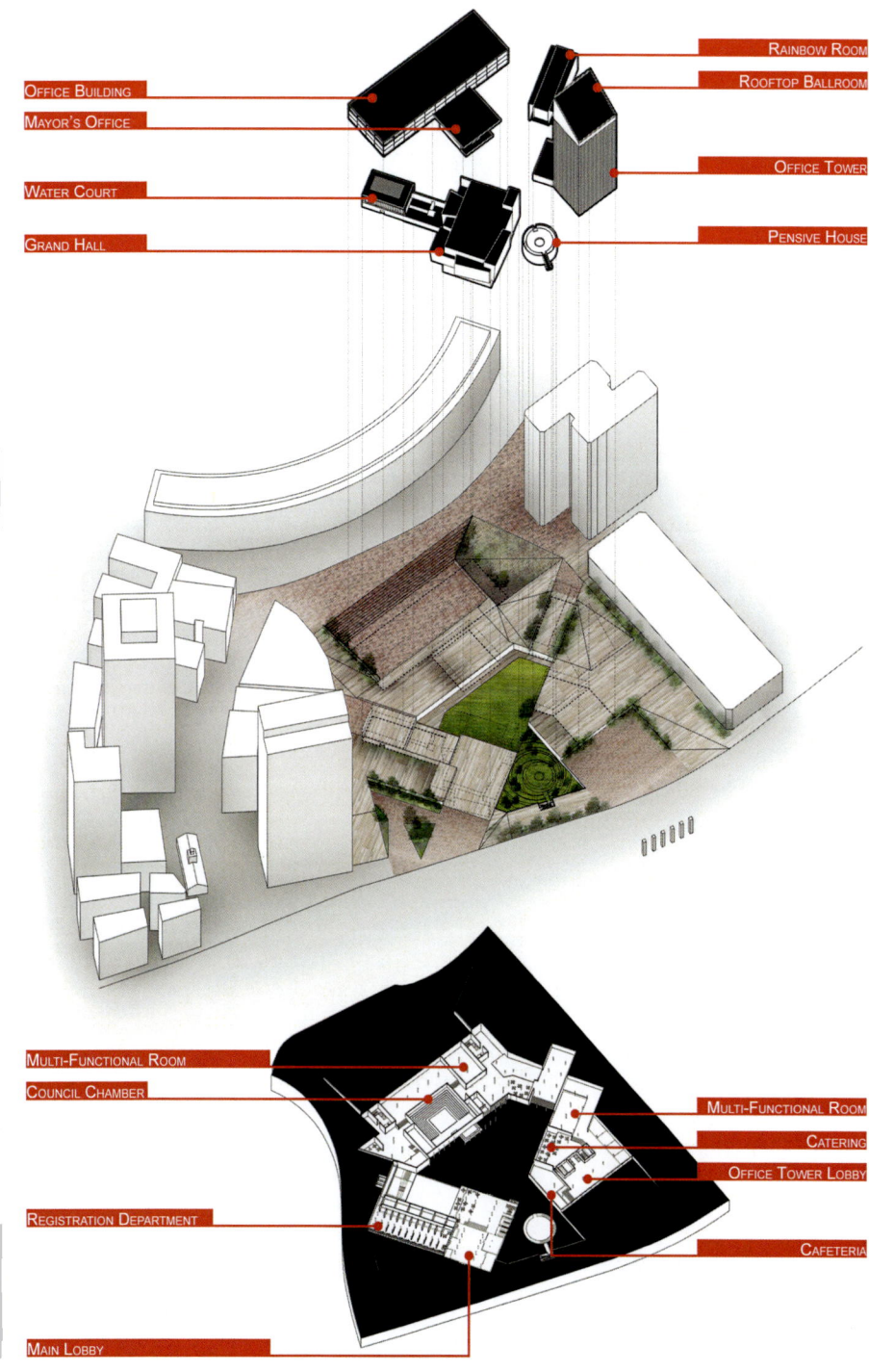

OFFICE BUILDING

MAYOR'S OFFICE

WATER COURT

GRAND HALL

RAINBOW ROOM

ROOFTOP BALLROOM

OFFICE TOWER

PENSIVE HOUSE

MULTI-FUNCTIONAL ROOM

COUNCIL CHAMBER

REGISTRATION DEPARTMENT

MAIN LOBBY

MULTI-FUNCTIONAL ROOM

CATERING

OFFICE TOWER LOBBY

CAFETERIA

ABOVE Exploded axonometric of site and program elements.

TOP View from the Ceremonial Chamber.
BOTTOM Council Chamber and press balcony.

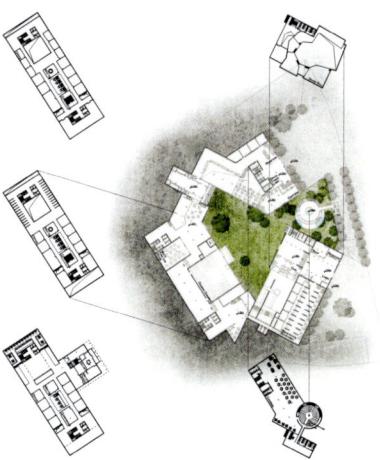

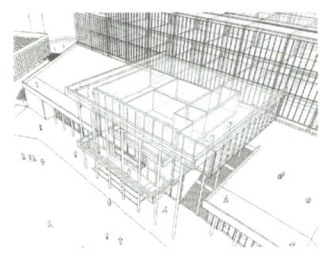

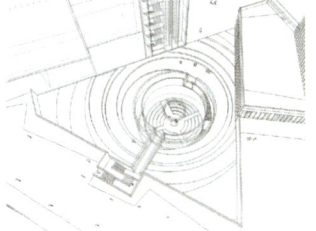

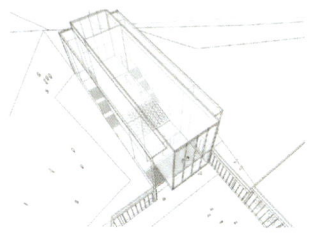

TOP View in central garden space.
MIDDLE Site plans.
BOTTOM Sketch of public halls.

Black Rock Island
City Hall

Eunil Cho + Roberto Jenkins

Our vision for Boston City Hall is greater than an individual government building. We propose a mixing chamber that encourages interaction through shared public programs. In other words, our project becomes a gathering hub for urban life; a microcosm of the city that brings in a multitude of public amenities. The project engages with the existing site by creating a "ground" figure that organizes access into our site. It links the three nearby existing subway stations into a dynamic urban plaza with a centralized location in the city and connects to existing infrastructure leading to the airport and other major landmarks. Pedestrian flow from the neighboring Faneuil Hall Marketplace and the public transit nodes gather at a central courtyard adjacent to each of the four lobbies created for the added programs.

The aggregation of program stems from a couple of issues we've identified in the existing scheme. Mostly, the existing building doesn't engage successfully with the plaza so as to encourage movement throughout the site. Having a singular governmental program leads to a singular mass with a centralized entry point and a limited number of visitors. By adding a hotel, commercial offices, a subway hub, and a series of urban amenities, we aim to create more interaction between urban life and the traditional functions of City Hall while also acknowledging that the practices of governing are as often transacted in hotel lobbies, back rooms, and board rooms as they are in the hallowed spaces of official government.

ABOVE: View of public plaza looking towards Faneuil Hall.

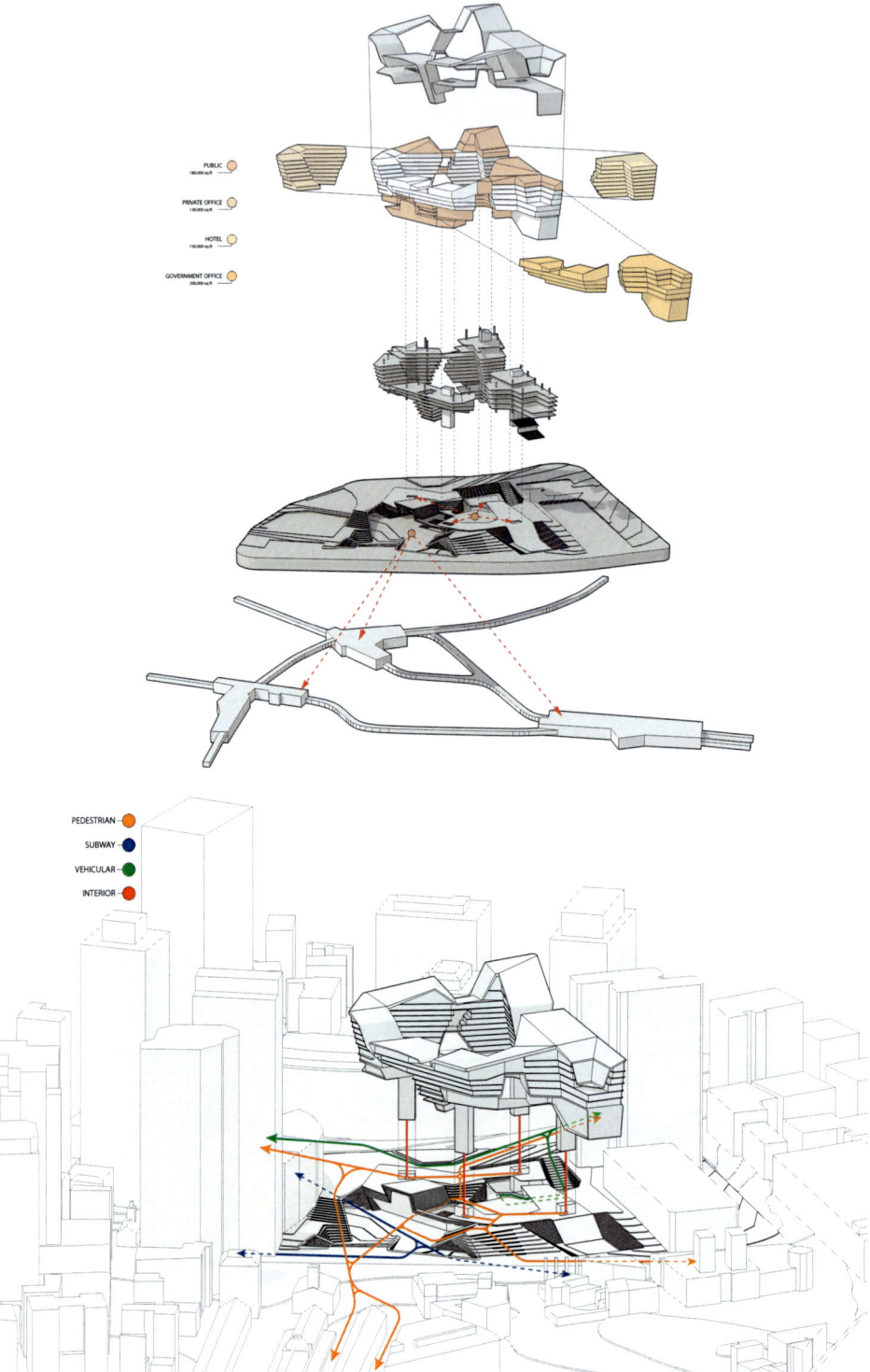

PUBLIC
140,000 sq ft

PRIVATE OFFICE
130,000 sq ft

HOTEL
150,000 sq ft

GOVERNMENT OFFICE
200,000 sq ft

PEDESTRIAN
SUBWAY
VEHICULAR
INTERIOR

TOP Exploded axonometric, top to bottom, of the roof surface, program elements, components of City Hall, ground plane, underground
circulation, and T lines.
BOTTOM Main circulation systems.

TOP Model study.
BOTTOM Ground floor plan.

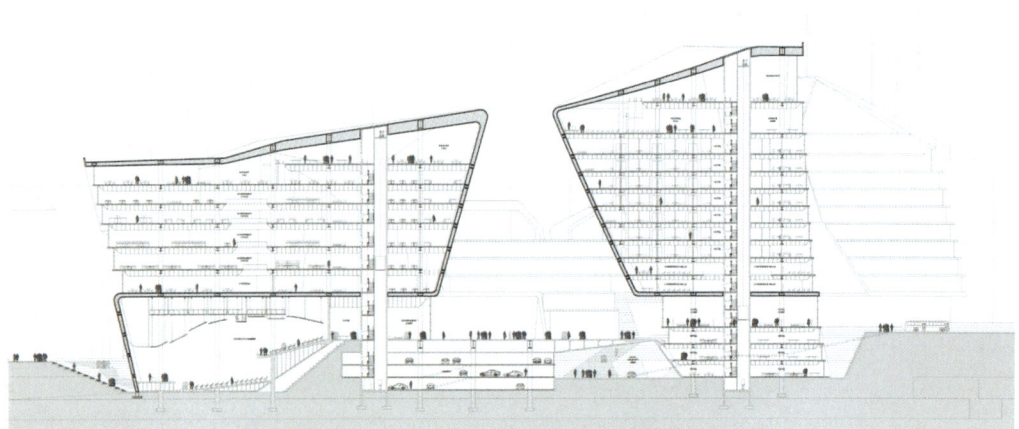

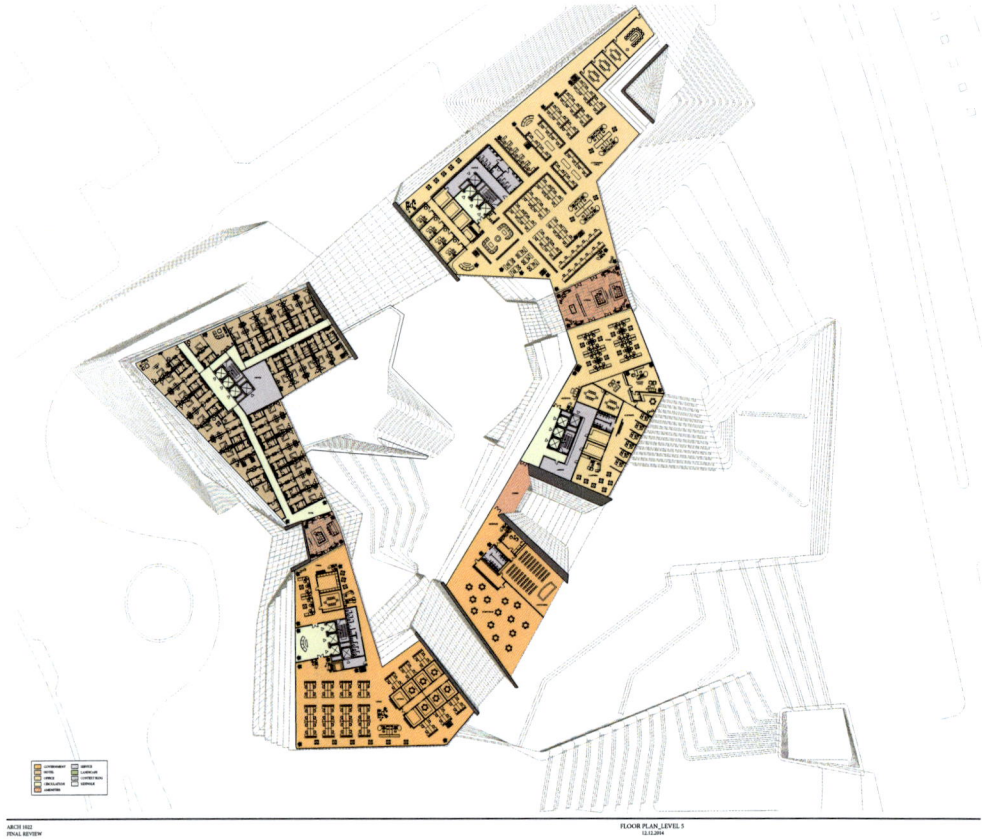

TOP   Section through the City Hall Council chamber and the hotel.
BOTTOM Typical upper floor plan.

TOP View from the interior of office floor across the inner courtyard.
BOTTOM City Hall lobby view.

Exclusive + Inclusive Figure
City Hall

Jingwen Li + Jizhou Liu

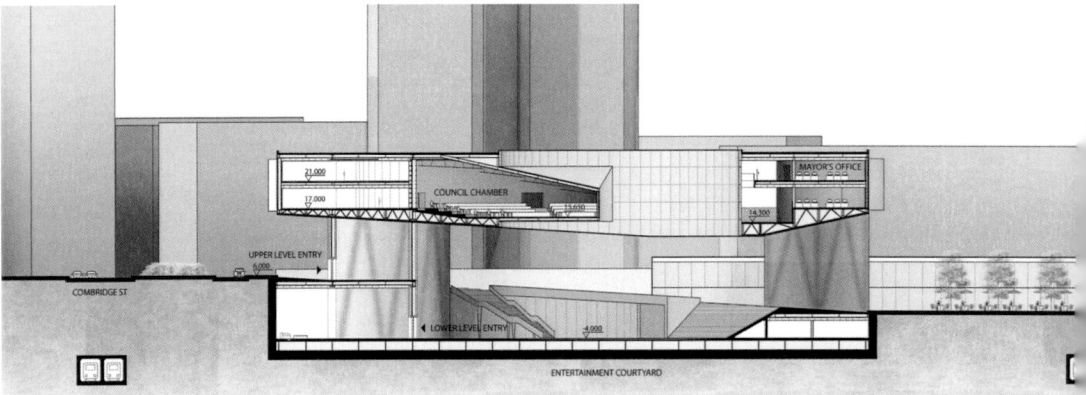

TOP Model photograph.
BOTTOM Site section.

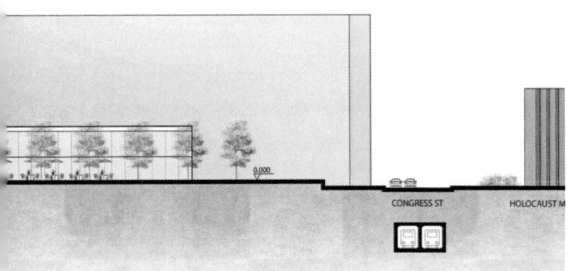

The project started from the fundamental question of this studio: what is a city hall? We propose that a city hall is an engaging, urban figure. There are two distinct features of a city hall. On the one hand, it symbolizes the government, so it should be a clearly legible icon in the urban context. On the other hand, it is a place for congregation where people deal with their daily affairs. This requires that the city hall be attractive and that it encourage civic participation. Hence, city hall is iconic and engaging.

The programs are separated into three large geometric solids: the major figure is for governmental use, including the Mayor's office and Council chamber; the smaller south square is for ceremonial programs; and the rectangular bar to the north is for daily affairs. The major figure is divided vertically into two parts: the ceremonial governmental block is lifted up in the air to make it more exclusive, leaving the public open space continuous on the ground level; the lower southern square is sunken one level down. Its inclined roof serves as a sloping plaza for the citizens and sectionally connects Congress Street and Cambridge Street. The northern block re-establishes the edge of Hanover Street.

Each figure has a courtyard, and these are connected together in series to generate a secondary network of public spaces. The geometrical courtyards echo the three main figural building volumes. The location of each courtyard and connective pathways respond to the surrounding city building context and its roads, attracting and welcoming the potential visitors to the city hall complex.

ABOVE Site plan.

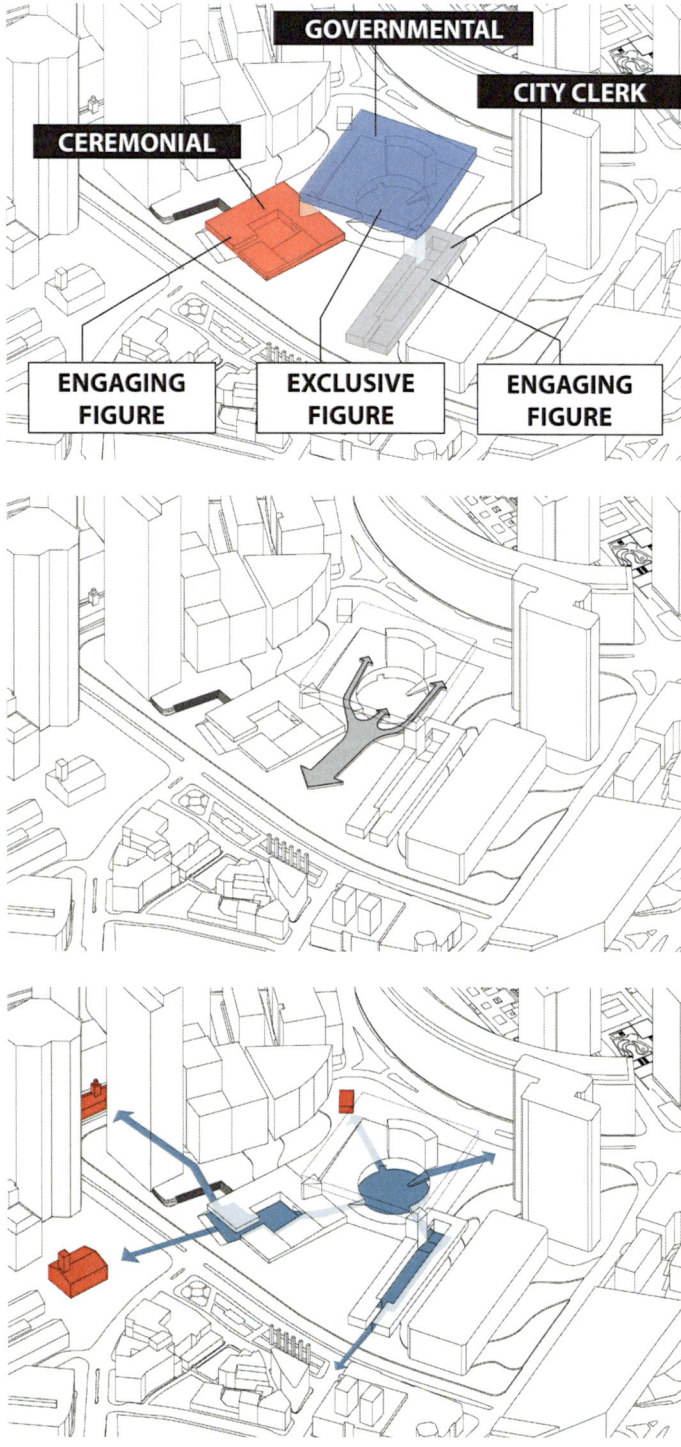

ABOVE Site diagrams showing the main buildings, public access through the main lower public space to the T stop and Congress Street, and the public circulation through the building to key urban sites.

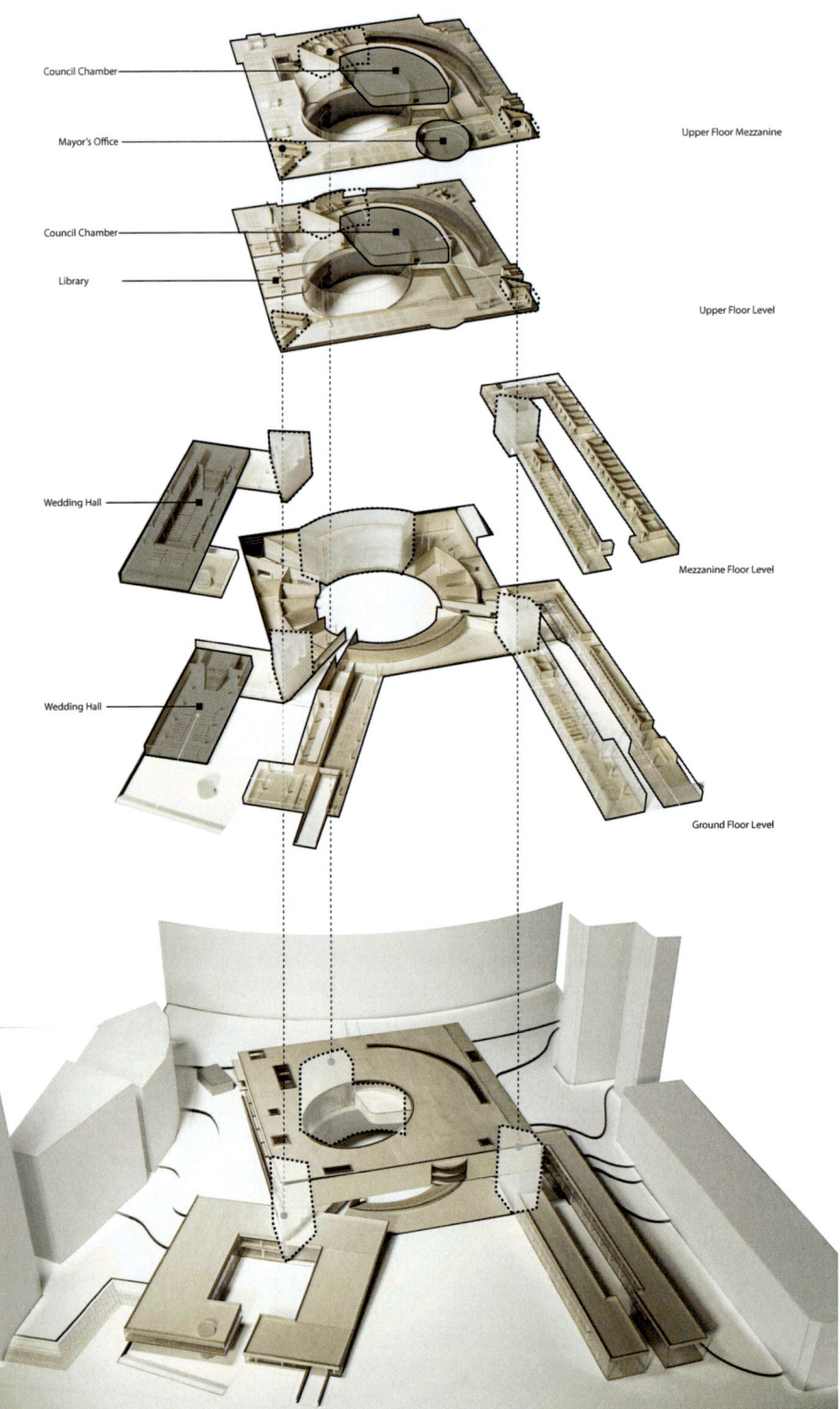

Council Chamber

Mayor's Office

Upper Floor Mezzanine

Council Chamber

Library

Upper Floor Level

Wedding Hall

Mezzanine Floor Level

Wedding Hall

Ground Floor Level

ABOVE Exploded axonometric.

TOP   Perspective through the central public space.
MIDDLE   Perspective through the central public space in winter.
BOTTOM View looking towards City Hall from Congress Street.

Redux
City Hall

Charlotte Algie

TOP View of City Hall.
BOTTOM Site section.

City Hall is the the smallest scale of official public representation. It embodies democracy at a community level, so its architecture must likewise be scaled to one-on-one human interaction. The original brief called for a more bureaucratic form of governance; this proposal seeks to bring back a more immediate and intimate scale to civic architecture. The smallest possible dimensions of interior control including the doorway, the desk, and the conference table are crucial to the project.

In online videos Boston's mayor is most often seen floating through the city, visiting school gymnasiums, local businesses, and attending charity functions. These eclectic, informal spaces are crucial sites of city governance. For this reprised Boston City Hall, meeting rooms are given priority and expressed on the exterior as unique, connected pavilions. In keeping with the mayor's itinerant movement between coffee shops, cafeterias, school playgrounds, and the homes of his constituents, this project argues that a successful city hall should reflect such intimacy back to where the mayor works. In the City Hall, the mayor does not sit aloof behind his desk; instead, he drifts from room to room, pursued in the building's main corridor by the press and his public.

That space is a single level, linear public hall that unites the disparate City Hall departments and creates an active public street for any citizen to connect with governmental and administrative teams. This public lobby evokes Boston's winding Georgian laneways and encourages casual encounters with government officials. Visitors perambulate across bridges and linkages, pause at small public squares, and look across to the offices of their City Hall representatives. From the exterior, the public lobby forms a necklace that wraps the plaza and defines the eastern edge of the site. A tower for bureaucrats who have no interaction with the public marks the site to the south, while the plaza is carved into the topography and allows those with no business inside to pass freely through and under City Hall to alternate destinations.

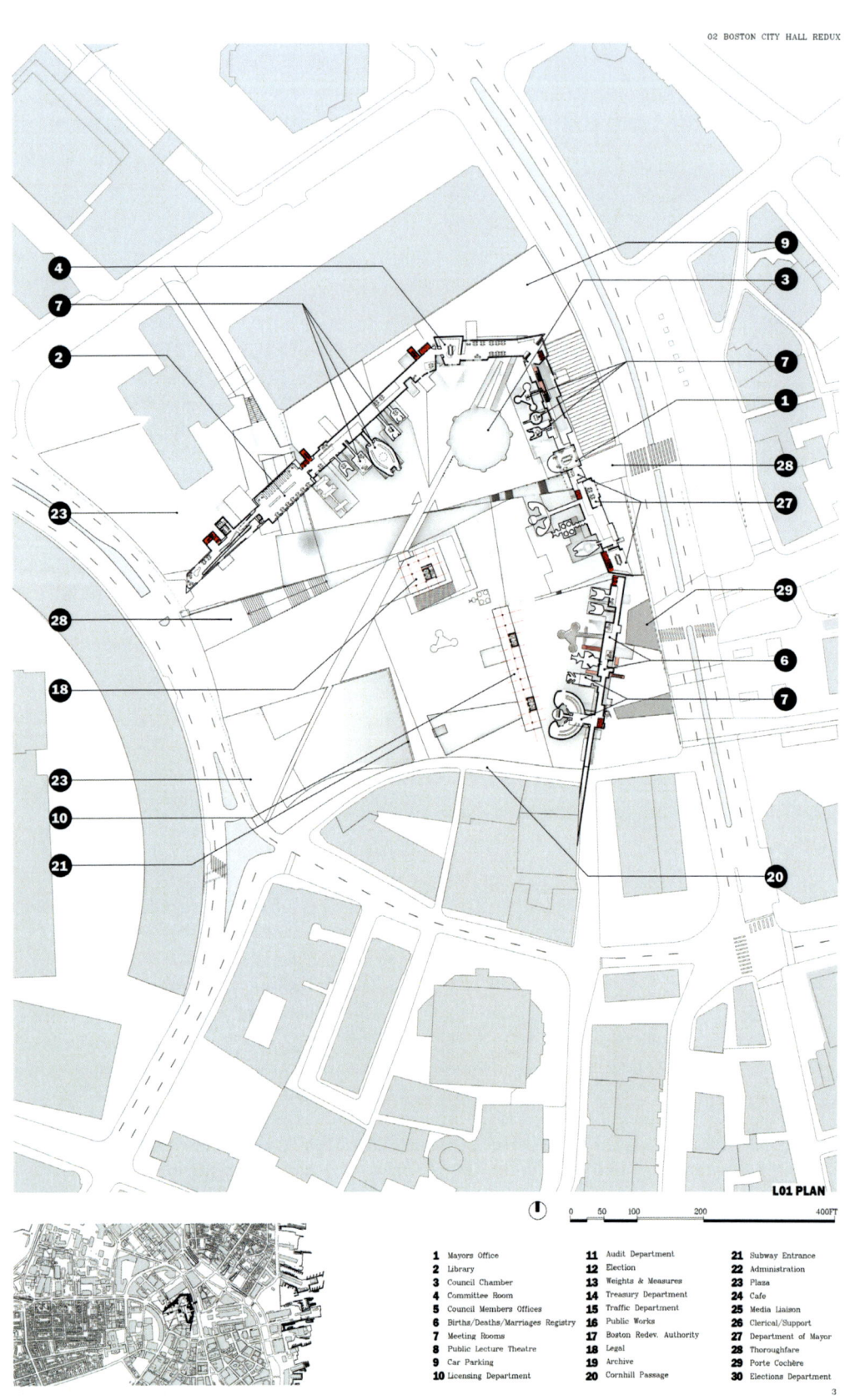

L01 PLAN

0   50   100   200   400FT

1 Mayors Office	**11** Audit Department	**21** Subway Entrance
2 Library	**12** Election	**22** Administration
3 Council Chamber	**13** Weights & Measures	**23** Plaza
4 Committee Room	**14** Treasury Department	**24** Cafe
5 Council Members Offices	**15** Traffic Department	**25** Media Liaison
6 Births/Deaths/Marriages Registry	**16** Public Works	**26** Clerical/Support
7 Meeting Rooms	**17** Boston Redev. Authority	**27** Department of Mayor
8 Public Lecture Theatre	**18** Legal	**28** Thoroughfare
9 Car Parking	**19** Archive	**29** Porte Cochère
10 Licensing Department	**20** Cornhill Passage	**30** Elections Department

3

Cannibalizing the quality of corporate lobby space, the ground level of linear semi-public realm functions both to unite disparate City Hall departments as network of access between the mayor, governmental and administrative teams, and as vector for visitor interface to the activities of these teams.

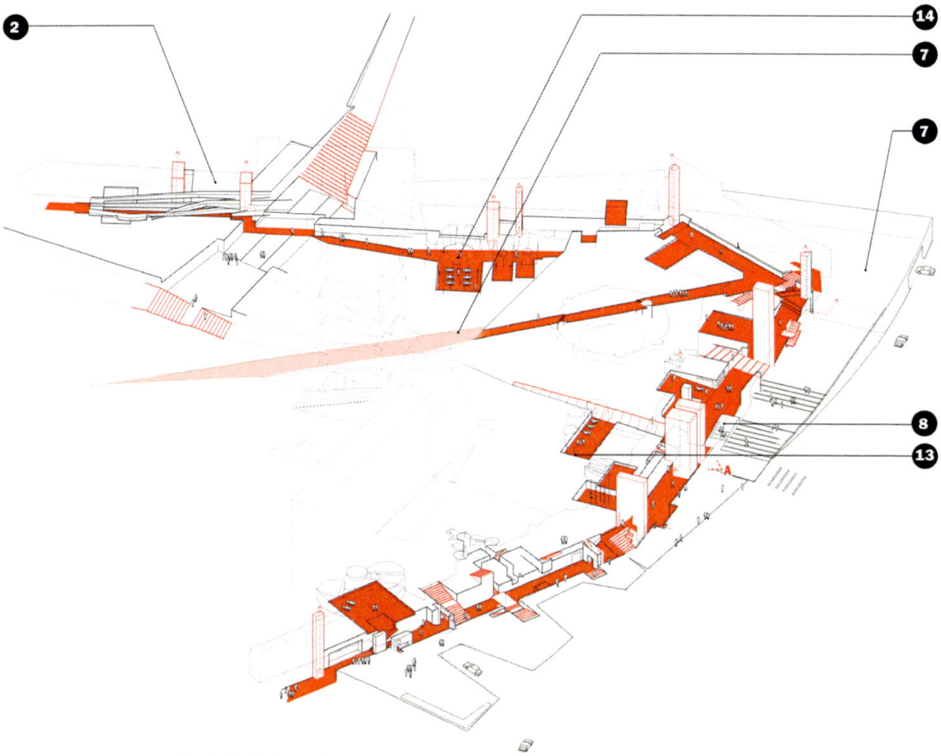

1	Mayors Office	**11**	Audit Department	**21**	Subway Entrance
2	Library	**12**	Election	**22**	Administration
3	Council Chamber	**13**	Weights & Measures	**23**	Plaza
4	Committee Room	**14**	Treasury Department	**24**	Cafe
5	Council Members Offices	**15**	Traffic Department	**25**	Media Liaison
6	Births/Deaths/Marriages Registry	**16**	Public Works	**26**	Clerical/Support
7	Meeting Rooms	**17**	Boston Redev. Authority	**27**	Department of Mayor
8	Public Lecture Theatre	**18**	Legal	**28**	Thoroughfare
9	Car Parking	**19**	Archive	**29**	Porte Cochère
10	Licensing Department	**20**	Cornhill Passage	**30**	Elections Department

Groups of visitors perambulate line, bridges and linkages, pausing at small public squares, surveying both through and upwards to offices of their City Hall representatives. Lobby/line space, pushed to the limits of smallness, then suggests a (warm/dry) street - evoking Boston's Georgian laneways thus implicitly informalising visitor encounter with government. Also those with no business inside the building, can pass freely across or through the City Hall as urban threshold, toward their alternate city

A Pinched through east-west corridor

OPPOSITE Plan showing the functions of the indvidual meeting rooms and public spaces.
ABOVE Axonometric highlighting the main connecting hall.

TOP Entry view of the Green Room.
BOTTOM Interior view of the Ochre Lobby.
OPPOSITE Sections.

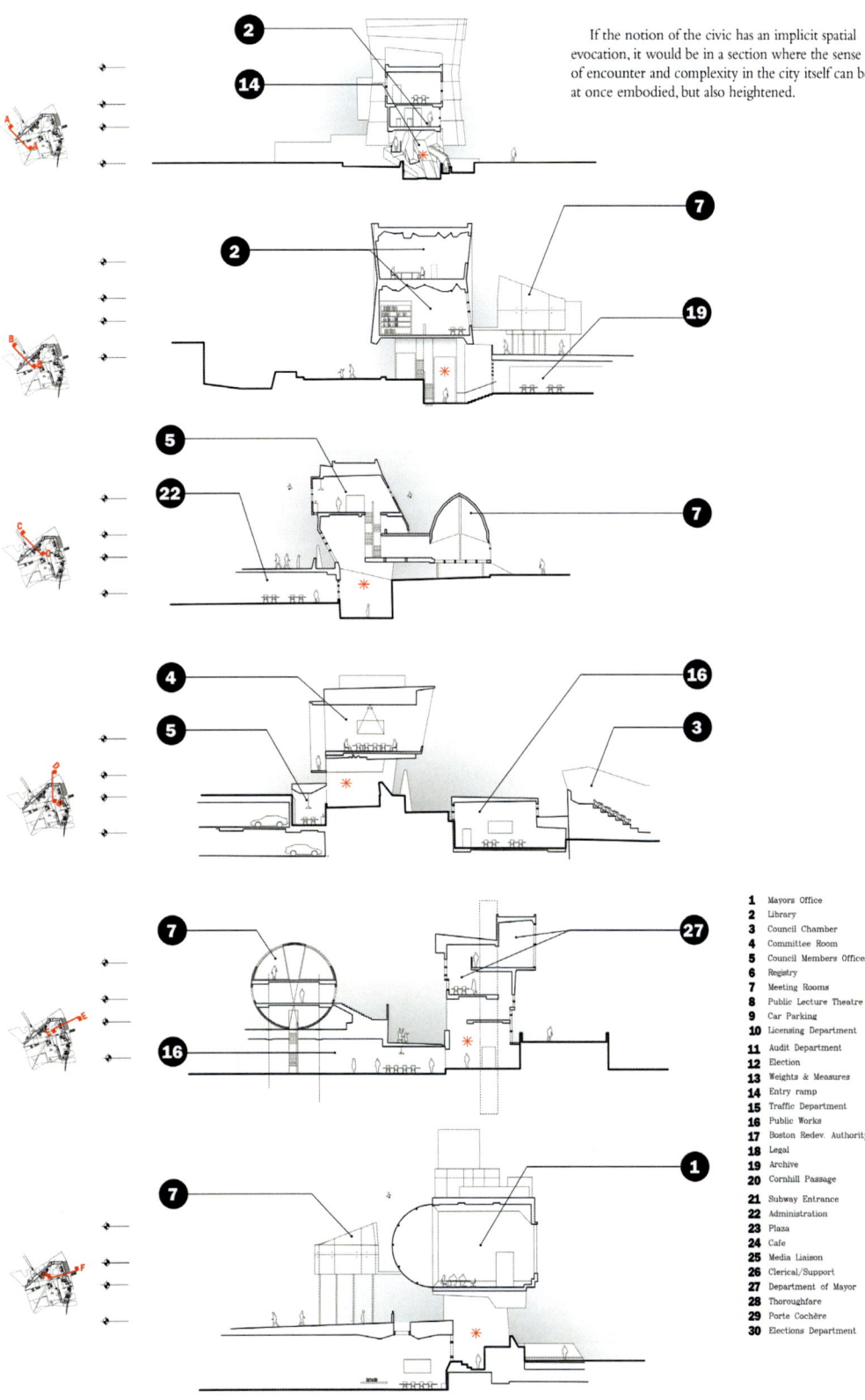

If the notion of the civic has an implicit spatial evocation, it would be in a section where the sense of encounter and complexity in the city itself can be at once embodied, but also heightened.

1	Mayors Office
2	Library
3	Council Chamber
4	Committee Room
5	Council Members Offices
6	Registry
7	Meeting Rooms
8	Public Lecture Theatre
9	Car Parking
10	Licensing Department
11	Audit Department
12	Election
13	Weights & Measures
14	Entry ramp
15	Traffic Department
16	Public Works
17	Boston Redev. Authority
18	Legal
19	Archive
20	Cornhill Passage
21	Subway Entrance
22	Administration
23	Plaza
24	Cafe
25	Media Liaison
26	Clerical/Support
27	Department of Mayor
28	Thoroughfare
29	Porte Cochère
30	Elections Department

0 5 10   20   50ft

TOP Yellow Interior.
BOTTOM Photograph of the model.

TOP Model photograph.
BOTTOM Model photograph looking north.

Resonant Chambers
City Hall

Isaac Southard

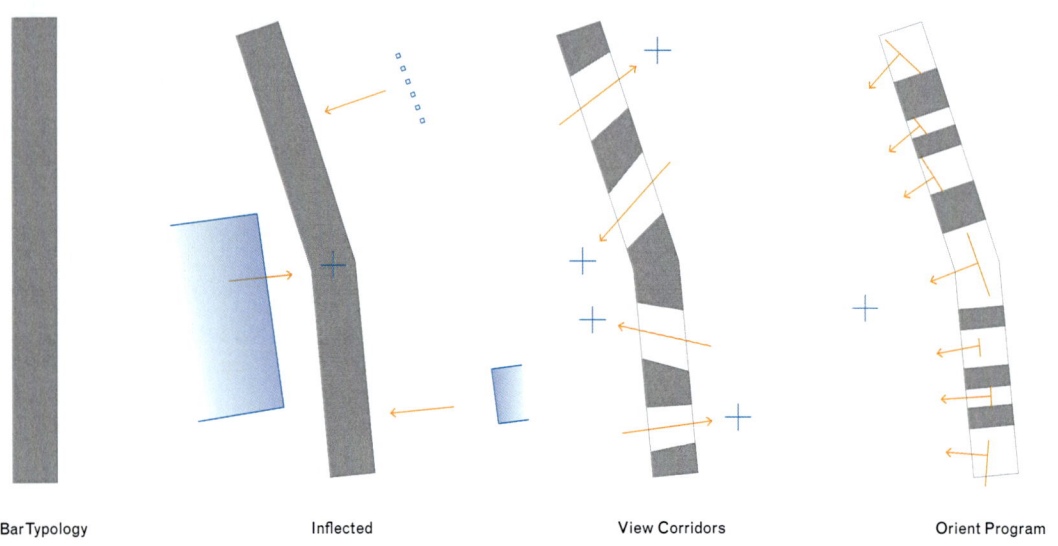

Bar Typology   Inflected   View Corridors   Orient Program

TOP View From Plaza.
BOTTOM Plan Diagrams.

Boston is a city of many neighborhoods. Fenway, Back Bay, Beacon Hill, West End, North End, Chinatown, South End, Bay Village, Roxbury, Dorchester, Allston, Brookline, and Jamaica Plain compose the urban fabric of Boston. Each exhibits a strong sense of place, and a distinct character.

Boston City Hall exists between identifiable neighborhood fabrics of the city and is conceived as a center but with no single character to its own public space. The building is at once a large wall made up of distinct building blocks; the plaza is one large space made up of smaller parterres. Resonant Chambers/A City Hall Between argues for a new form of democratic assembly which embodies the multivalent conditions of the city.

This project inverts the formal, centered, symmetrical, and object-like language of the modern city hall typology. The first move, at the scale of the city, proposes a linear bar building at the eastern edge of the site that shapes a figural space, a square, at the city's center. The second move, at the scale of the street, fragments the building into vertical "neighborhoods" for the alderman. A series of public chambers sit between the programmatic neighborhoods, where negotiations and discussions between constituents might take place. The final move occurs within the building and consists of a linear promenade that connects the chambers, the "neighborhoods," and the square to the city at large.

By limiting the City Hall to an edge condition, the city center emphasizes the pluralistic nature of Boston's neighborhoods and allows for civic functions to occur at the heart of the city. Resonant Chambers, a proposal for a new city hall in Boston, seeks to embody a multivalent and decentered architecture like that of the contemporary city. Resonant Chambers/A City Hall Between transforms the physical framework of the city hall, integrating the bureaucratic and political processes within the public realm.

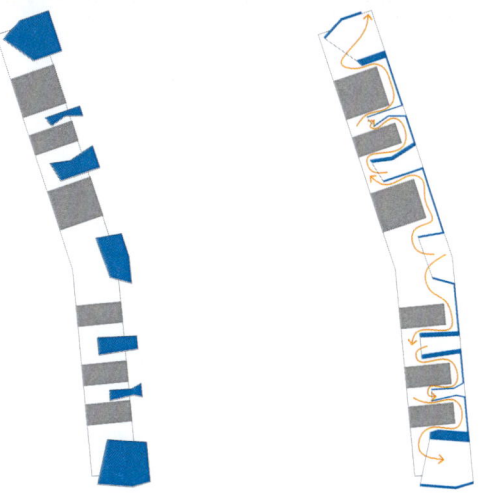

Insert Symbolic Spaces   Promenade

TOP Model studies of building section.
BOTTOM Site model.

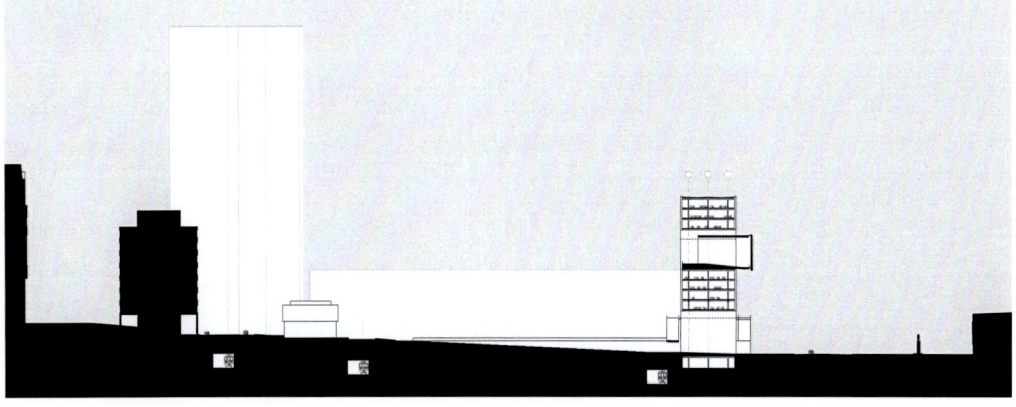

TOP Site plan with an upper-level plan of the connecting lobby and public areas.
BOTTOM Site section.

ABOVE View from City Hall across the plaza.

Biographies

Edward Mitchell is an Associate Professor and Director of the Post-Professional Program at the School of Architecture at Yale University. His practice in New Haven ranges from architecture to urban design. He has shown work in a number of international exhibitions and journals. Recent publications include *A Train of Cities* on the potential impact of commuter rail service in the cities and towns of the South Coast of Massachusetts, *New Constellations/New Ecologies* with focus on emerging trends in architectural practice and urban design, and contributions in the book *Formerly Urban: Projecting Rustbelt Futures*.

Aniket Shahane is a Critic at the Yale School of Architecture, where he has been co-teaching the Post-Professional studio with Edward Mitchell since 2012. He is principal at Office of Architecture, a Brooklyn based architecture practice. Aniket received a B.Arch from the University of Texas at Austin and an M.Arch from Yale University.

Fred Koetter is the former Dean and former Professor at the Yale School of Architecture. He is principal of Koetter Kim & Associates in Boston, a winner of numerous awards including the AIA Academy of Architecture for Justice Merit Award for Architectural Design, the Boston Society of Architects' Willo von Moltke Award for Urban Design, and the City of Dallas Urban Design Award. Fred is co-author with Colin Rowe of *Collage City*.

Ila Berman, Dean and Edward E. Elson Professor of the University of Virginia School of Architecture and principal of Scaleshift design, is an architect, theorist, and curator of architecture and urbanism whose research investigates the relationship between culture and the evolution of contemporary material and spatial practices. Berman's recent projects and publications include URBANbuild local/global, winner of an AIGA award for the top fifty books of 2009, *New Constellations New Ecologies, FLUX: Architecture in a Parametric Landscape,* and her recent book on art and architectural installation, *Expanded Field,* based on her installation at the Wattis Institute for Contemporary Arts.

Brian Healy established his architectural practice in Boston in 1986. Healy has compiled a distinguished record of creative activity, community service, and professional achievement. The architectural projects produced by his office received over fifty national and regional design awards, including seven within the *Progressive Architecture Award* program. For the past twenty years, Brian has also been consistently active in teaching architectural design studios and seminars at universities and colleges across North America.

Tim Love is the founding principal of Utile, a fifty-person architecture and urban design firm in Boston and a tenured associate professor at Northeastern University School or Architecture. Love's focus is the relationship of individual works of architecture to the larger city and the way that speculative market forces shape the built environment.

Kishore Varanasi is an award-winning urban designer, strategist, innovator, teacher, and writer. His influential work in both the public and private sectors has shaped a number of cities and communities locally, nationally and globally. As the principal and Director of Urban Design at CBT Architects in Boston, Varanasi leads a multi-disciplinary team in the design and development of highly sustainable master plans for downtowns, waterfronts, institutions, new cities and communities and innovation clusters.

Photo Credits

New York Public Library, p. v
Koetter Kim Architects, p. 3
Lowery Aerial Photos/West End Museum, p. 13
The Boston Globe Archive, p. 28
Kevin Lynch, p. 30
The Boston Public Library, p. 96
Library of Congress, p. 97
The New England Historical Society and Kallman
McKinnell & Knowles, pp. 166, 170
All other photographs courtesy of the Yale School
of Architecture.

Photo by Daphne Binder